3rd Edition

The Complete Guide to Getting Financial Help Through the U.S. Small Business Administration

The SBA LOAN BOOK

Charles H. Green

A
BUSINESS
Avon, Massachusetts

Published by Adams Media, a division of F+W Media, Inc.
57 Littlefield Street, Avon, MA 02322. U.S.A.
www.adamsmedia.com

ISBN 10: 1-4405-0982-4
ISBN 13: 978-1-4405-0982-7
eISBN 10: 1-4405-1002-4
eISBN 13: 978-1-4405-1002-1

Printed in the United States of America.

10 9 8 7 6 5 4 3 2 1

Library of Congress Cataloging-in-Publication Data
Green, Charles H.
The SBA loan book / Charles H. Green. — 3rd ed.
p. cm.
Includes index.
ISBN-13: 978-1-4405-0982-7
ISBN-10: 1-4405-0982-4
ISBN-13: 978-1-4405-1002-1 (ebk)
ISBN-10: (invalid) 1-4405-1002-4 (ebk)
1. United States. Small Business Administration. 2. Small
business—United States—Finance. 3. Loans—United
States—Government guaranty. I. Title.

HG4027.7.G74 2010
658.15'224—dc22
2010038809

This publication is intended to provide current and prospective business owners with useful information that may assist them in preparing for and obtaining an SBA 7(a) or 504 guaranteed business loan. This information is general in nature and is not intended to provide specific advice for any individual or business entity without qualification. While the information contained herein should be helpful to the reader, appropriate financial, accounting, tax, or legal advice should always be sought from a competent professional engaged for any specific situation.

The U.S. Small Business Administration is an agency of the United States government. Every effort has been made to provide accurate and current information as publicly published by the agency. As with any government agency, many regulations, procedures, and programs are constantly under review and revision, and consequently, depending on when the book is read, some information may have changed or been rendered obsolete. The author regrets any errors that may have subsequently been published herein.

This book is available at quantity discounts for bulk purchases.
For information, call 1-800-289-0963.

Contents

Acknowledgments

There are many people I wish to thank that contributed to the production and revision of this book, the third edition. My longtime friend Gene McKay gave me the original idea to take consulting one step further into publication and provided encouragement, advice, and ideas to help make it all happen. My most enthusiastic cheerleader for this latest project has been Stephanie Davis, to whom I am very grateful. Friends and professional acquaintances Jane Butler, Barbara Benson, and Frank Dinsmore provided some clarity in many corners of the broad range of SBA programs to contribute more accuracy to my work.

And I want to remember my dad, Joseph Henry Green (1919–2005), who taught me how to count money and the value of entrepreneurship.

Introduction

According to recent statistics, more than 99 percent of all business entities in the United States are small businesses. These businesses represent more than 50 percent of the private work force, over 40 percent of all private commercial sales, and in excess of 52 percent of the private-sector output.

Yet obtaining capital financing continues to be a challenge for most small businesses. During the past ten years, financial deregulation changed the landscape with respect to funding available to small businesses. Financing choices became more abundant due to the advent of many new nonregulated lenders and financial products, such as commercial mortgage-backed securities (CMBSs), which were created in the securities market. But conditions quickly changed as these innovative financing vehicles failed to retain investor confidence and actually contributed to the financial market collapse in late 2008.

In a classic case of too much money chasing too few deals, many originating lenders started lowering borrower qualification standards in order to grow business as the nation rebounded financially from 9/11. Finally by early 2008, investors began to question the credit quality and underwriting of these securities and the loans that backed them. Suddenly Wall Street could not fund a robust pipeline of commercial loans because of falling values on the CMBSs already held by the market.

Simultaneously the commercial banking sector was beginning to choke on a variety of problems. The money center banks were finding themselves squeezed by an amassing of unsold loans needing securitization. The economy began teetering on the edge of a liquidity crisis as the market for these securities dried up and the calls for credit default swap (CDS) redemptions went into high gear. Several major investment banks either failed or were forced into a quick sale. The major survivors sought refuge in the commercial banking system, and were granted charters within days of applying. Within ninety days, relatively small discount broker Raymond James became the nation's largest independent investment banking shop.

Much of the remainder of the banking industry quickly began choking on a real estate bubble, initially created by the collapse of the home lending market earlier in mid-2007, as sub-prime loan defaults rose sharply and investors began to reject investments in mortgage-backed securities (MBS). As new home construction and home resales fell off sharply in late 2007, the world entered a severe recession that affected virtually every business sector. Most immediate was the ripple effect in the commercial real estate market, which was reeling from rising vacancies, business bankruptcies, and plunging employment figures.

After a few relatively quiet years of a healthy banking sector, banks began to fail in mid-2008. As real estate values began to fall across the United States and bank capital bled, lending to small businesses evaporated almost overnight. The Federal Reserve and the FDIC were almost at open odds about how to address the problem, but meanwhile the economy continued to sink as there was no funding with which to spur growth in the small business sector.

At the time of this revision, it is still unclear as to what the federal government can or will do to restore the financing market for small businesses. In one very positive—albeit temporary—measure taken in Spring 2009, the federal stimulus program increased the SBA 7(a) guaranty on loans to up to 90 percent (from 75 percent), a move that incentivized banks with capital to make more loans. Additionally, for small business borrowers the guaranty fees on these loans was waived, saving the business up to $56,000. It remains to be seen as to whether that will remain in effect much longer.

Regardless, I felt it was time to revise *The SBA Loan Book* to bring it current with the many changes occurring in the SBA credit guaranty programs since 2005. I also wanted to advise readers how to tackle the much more challenging environment that small businesses currently face to obtain financing. Negotiating debt remains an art, and business owners should not be lulled into unrealistic expectations based on how much they borrowed from anyone in the past. There is a new set of rules in effect.

This book updates earlier editions in which I shared the rules to qualify for an SBA-guaranteed loan, and the basic information and strategies needed to succeed in getting the loan approved and closed. Most of the basic drill has not changed. What's different is the environment in which a business owner must navigate today.

If they read this book carefully and follow its advice closely, business owners will greatly improve their chances of getting an SBA loan approved. The conditions that can negatively alter the chances of approval are too numerous to cite here, but they are covered in Chapters 5 and 7. Efforts to borrow money will be more successful if the borrower develops a proposal with the lender's perspective in mind, and works back to what the business needs.

Certain attributes are especially helpful in obtaining financing, but none is more important to success than perseverance. In today's environment, you may put a lot of effort into preparing a proposal only to learn that the bank you're approaching is unable to fund any loans. You may even have to wait out the completion of a difficult business cycle and look for improvements in the macro economy before there is a chance to get funds. Wait, but don't wait idly.

Since the original edition in 1999, this book has served as a guide for more than 50,000 entrepreneurs to get started in the search for SBA financing. Its success has been due to the fact that the lessons, suggestions, and guidance offered here are not written in the abstract by a casual or theoretical observer, but by an active participant in the process. While my thirty years of firsthand experience in small business financing was not totally SBA related, guaranteed loans were probably about half of my lending. My understanding of this information is based on experience as a bank president and lender, as an independent commercial loan originator, and also as a borrower. I want to provide the reader with an updated version of what I have learned in originating, underwriting, and servicing small business loans.

Practical lessons about financing small businesses have to be learned over time. You can see it in such diverse places as construction sites, factories, power plants, automotive shops, convenience stores, archeological excavation sites, truck terminals, restaurant kitchens, day care centers, retail stores, insurance agencies, and machine shops. In each of these places someone is trying to perform an economic activity for a profitable outcome. There are less pleasant places where you can learn other lessons: equipment liquidation auctions, legal depositions, bankruptcy court, and even the courthouse steps on foreclosure day. All these locales are the kinds of places where you can see the positives and negatives of venturing into business.

This book provides a comprehensive guide to how a qualified borrower can successfully prepare for, apply for, and obtain a business loan. Throughout the text I have attempted to communicate the information in language that can be easily deciphered by the most inexperienced entrepreneur. The book incorporates general information about many disciplines in order to describe and detail the dynamics of commercial lending.

In its essence, finance can sometimes be very complex and sometimes be very simple. My goal is to collaborate with readers to provide information, direction, and expectations for the loan application process.

The book contains illustrations of several forms that are needed in various circumstances by participating borrowers in the SBA lending process. Many of these forms are official SBA documents, whiles others are tools built in Excel to better analyze and present information needed by your lender. All of these forms and more can be downloaded at no expense from my website *www.CharlesGreenCo.com* using the code: SBABOOK.

CHAPTER **1**

Loan Programs Offered by the SBA

Most business people would probably look to either strategic tax breaks or large public works projects for engines to spur economic development and boost our national economy. So think about the Small Business Administration in the same terms—an economic development agency that enables small businesses to more readily access business financing with longer repayment terms. These funds create jobs, develop communities, and spur economic activity that feeds families and generates taxes. Understanding the SBA program will ease your effort to take advantage of the benefits available for all eligible participants. You'll learn:

- ✦ How the SBA loan guaranty program works
- ✦ What options are available for SBA financing assistance
- ✦ Why SBA financing is one of the best options in today's economy

What Is the SBA?

"SBA" is the acronym for the U.S. Small Business Administration, an agency of the federal government established in 1953 to assist small business enterprises. Arguably the most important programs implemented by the agency are the loan assistance programs, which provide incentive to private sector commercial lenders (banks and certain licensed non-bank lenders) to extend long-term capital financing to qualified, eligible small businesses.

The SBA loan guaranty program has grown steadily over the years as a popular tool for small businesses to obtain capital financing. In 2009, with fluctuating economic conditions, difficult regulatory trends, and a collapse of the secondary market for guaranteed loans, the nation encountered a perfect storm. The agency experienced a rare but notable 37 percent reduction in the number of SBA loans funded (reduction of 30,811 loans), which translated into a 27 percent decline of loan volume ($5,175,000,000 decline).[1] But even in this disastrous year, the agency assisted with the creation of hundreds of thousands of jobs across thousands of communities in the United States.

Although the SBA conducts many programs to assist small businesses, the focus of this book is on the assistance provided by the flagship 7(a) Loan Guaranty Program, which provides a credit enhancement to participating lenders, and the 504 Loan Program, which provides subordinated financing directly to small businesses and is administered locally through SBA-licensed nonprofit Certified Development Companies (CDCs).

The regulations governing these loan programs and borrower's costs are subject to change from time to time. However, from this book you'll get a broad view of the program and financial requirements necessary to determine eligibility and qualifications for the borrower. Mainly, the book will help you in the efficient and effective development of an SBA loan application.

For a list and description of other programs and services conducted by the SBA, go to *www.sba.gov/aboutsba/sbaprograms/index.html.*

The Loan Guaranty Programs

The two primary loan guaranty programs that are currently offered by the SBA for small business financing are the 7(a) Loan Guaranty Program and the 504 Loan Program. They are governed by different regulations and are distinguished by: (1) eligibility standards, (2) restrictions on the use of loan proceeds, (3) repayment terms, and (4) the borrower's approval process. I describe these two programs in more detail below in order for you to understand what kind of funding can be obtained through the agency and to decipher which program may be more advantageous to your business.

---

1 U.S. Small Business Administration Summary of Performance and Financial Information, Fiscal Year 2009, found at *http://www.sba.gov/idc/groups/public/documents/ sba_homepage/serv_aboutsba_perf_summ.pdf.*

The 7(a) Loan Guaranty Program

The 7(a) loan program is SBA's primary loan program for helping start-up and existing businesses, providing funds for a variety of general business purposes. SBA does not make direct loans. Instead, it provides a credit enhancement to participating lending institutions in the form of a long-term loan guaranty. The costs of reimbursing banks for loan defaults is paid for from fees collected from participating small businesses getting loans and the lenders that fund them. While the guaranty reduces the risk to the lender, if you, the borrower, default, you must repay the entire debt.

Small businesses can obtain financing through the program for acquisition or improvement of assets (real estate, equipment, operating business concerns, etc.), refinancing existing debt, or working capital. Repayment terms are determined by the actual use of the loan proceeds according to limitations imposed on each purpose:

- ✧ Loans used to purchase, construct improvements on, or refinance real estate can be extended for up to a maximum of twenty-five years.
- ✧ Loans used to purchase equipment can be extended for up to a maximum of fifteen years (though usually limited to ten) or to the expected useful life of the equipment, whichever is shorter.
- ✧ Loans used to acquire an operating business concern can be extended for up to a maximum of ten years.
- ✧ Loans used to fund business working capital can be extended for up to a maximum of ten years.

Currently participating lenders are guaranteed repayment by the SBA for 75 percent of the total loan amount up to $2 million (80 percent for loans under $250,000) for a maximum loan guaranty of $1.5 million.

Change Is a Constant

The loan guaranty level is subject to change at any time when Congress decides such a modification is desirable or necessary. Contained within the American Recovery and Reinvestment Act of 2009 were provisions that temporarily increased the maximum guaranty to 90 percent of the loan (although the maximum guaranty amount remained $1.5 million). The obvious intended consequence was to encourage more lenders to approve more loans and enable more small businesses to get financing in an effort to stimulate economic growth during that difficult period.

You should determine the present status of guaranty limits at the onset of the application period to maximize your opportunities to get funding. Lenders may be willing to stretch a little in favor of borrower concessions if a higher loan guaranty is available.

Eligibility for borrowers to participate in the 7(a) program is limited by one of two factors: either their average annual revenues or their average employment. In accordance with federal law, as modified periodically by the Office of Management and Budget, the SBA determines eligibility for financing assistance by referring to the North American Industry Classification System (NAICS). The NAICS codes define what a "small" business is and determine the SBA eligibility of prospective borrowers.

Generally, most businesses that have an average total revenue over the previous three years of $7 million or less or have no more than 500 employees are eligible for SBA assistance. However, there is a wide range of limitations, based on industry. Average revenues can range from $750,000 to $35.5 million, and average employment can vary from 50 to 1,500. For one industry (power generation) the definition of "small" means producing less than 4 million megawatts of power!

While there are definitive qualifications for each industry, only one factor—revenue or employment—is used to measure whether a company is a "small" business or not.

One of the most attractive features of the 7(a) program is that the repayment terms provide for the full amortization of the loan proceeds. In other words, the borrower can repay the loan proceeds over the economic life of the asset being financed, or a reasonable period provided to repay borrowed working capital. Lenders cannot shorten the loan terms or use "balloon" notes, which may amortize loans for a longer term than the promissory note provides for repayment.

Most long-term commercial loans funded by banks are made for a three-, five-, or seven-year term, regardless of the purpose of the proceeds. If you are purchasing land and buildings but must repay over three years, obviously you are at a clear disadvantage and you'll face much more risk when you have to renegotiate the terms of that financing three years later.

By arranging for fully amortizing terms in the initial loan, you can better focus on growing business revenues and profits without the worry of changing terms. You can also avoid having to refinance the debt several times before repayment due to uncontrollable market conditions.

With few exceptions, lenders are restricted on the interest rates they can assess on 7(a) loans. Interest is generally negotiated between the borrower and lender based on the lender's cost of funds and analysis of the transaction risk. However, the SBA imposes rate caps on the interest the lender may charge. Rates can be fixed or variable. For variable rates, they may be pegged to the prime rate as published on the first day of each month in the *Wall Street Journal*; the one-month London Interbank Offered Rate (LIBOR) plus 3 percent; or the optional peg rate, which is published quarterly in the Federal Register.

- ✧ The prime rate is traditionally defined as the best rate offered by major U.S. banks to their prime commercial clients. Generally, over the past twenty years or more this rate has tracked the Fed Funds rate (interest rate paid to banks by the Federal Reserve Bank for overnight deposits) plus 3 percent.
- ✧ The LIBOR averages the rates paid by leading British banks for deposits from other banks worldwide. There are varying maturities offered. The SBA permits the lender to add an additional spread onto this rate as described below.
- ✧ The optional peg rate is a weighted average of rates the federal government pays for loans with maturities similar to the average SBA 7(a) loan. This rate is determined and published by the SBA in the Federal Register at the beginning of each fiscal quarter.

While there are exceptions in some of the Express and Special Lending programs, generally, the SBA limits lenders to the following maximum interest rates over one of the three rate indexes ("base") described above:

For loans less than $25,000, with a maturity of 7 years or less:	Base + 4.25%
For loans less than $25,000, with a maturity of 7 years or more:	Base + 4.75%
For loans $25,000–$50,000, with a maturity of 7 years or less:	Base + 3.25%
For loans $25,000–$50,000, with a maturity of 7 years or more:	Base + 3.75%
For loans more than $50,000, with a maturity of 7 years or less:	Base + 2.25%
For loans more than $50,000, with a maturity of 7 years or more:	Base + 2.75%

Variable interest rates may be adjusted at virtually any frequency negotiated by the lender and borrower, but most are reset either monthly or quarterly. SBA lets the lender decide so long as the change term is clearly defined in the promissory note.

Express Programs

The SBA Express programs offer streamlined and expedited loan procedures for particular groups of borrowers.

SBA Express

The SBA launched the Express Loan Program in an effort to accommodate lenders that were trying to fund smaller loans to smaller businesses but were finding the SBA processing requirements too onerous and expensive to be profitable.

Thus the SBA Express provides more flexibility to lenders that make these smaller loans by abbreviating the guaranty application, loosening collateral requirements, allowing lenders to use their own loan documents and procedures and charge higher interest rates, and promising a thirty-six-hour decision turnaround when lenders request a guaranty authorization. In exchange, the lender receives only a 50 percent guaranty from the SBA.

Express Loans offer small borrowers a flexible revolving or fixed-payment loan structure, depending on the lender's requirements, for a total of a seven-year term to repay the loan in full. Borrowers can repay the loan in full faster without penalty if they choose to amortize the loan from the beginning over seven years. Loans under this program are limited to $350,000.

The SBA Express has proven to be very popular with lenders and borrower and has become one of the most utilized financing options offered by the SBA.

Community Express Program

In October 2008, SBA introduced the newly restructured and enhanced Community Express Pilot Loan Program. Approved SBA lenders are authorized to adopt SBA's most streamlined and expedited loan procedures to provide a unique combination of financial and technical assistance to borrowers located in the nation's underserved communities.

Communities that are eligible include SBA's Historically Underutilized Business Zones (HUBZones) and those communities identified as distressed through the Community Reinvestment Act (CRA).

To encourage small businesses start-ups, SBA makes eligible loans of $25,000 or less for Community Express, regardless of where small businesses are located.

Because the SBA knows that the success of its loans to disadvantaged communities rests in large part on the technical assistance it renders the borrowers, the lenders have to document this assistance. If you request one of these loans, you have the option of using SBA's Small Business Training Network (SBTN) as well as such resources as Small Business Development Centers, SCORE (Service Corps of Retired Executives), Women's Business Centers, and Veterans Business Outreach Centers.

The Community Express Program offers borrowers a seven-year revolving line of credit for up to $250,000, with other typical 7(a) loan terms, such as interest rate restrictions. The exception is for loans under $25,000, which may be charged 2 percent higher rates. Lenders can use their own forms and are not required to have collateral on loans less than $25,000. For larger loans, the lender may use its own collateral policy. The SBA promises a thirty-six-hour decision turnaround when lenders request a guaranty authorization.

Patriot Express Program

If you or your co-owners are veterans, this may be the type of loan for you. The Patriot Express Program is designed for small businesses that are 51 percent or more owned by veterans or members of the military community. The maximum loan under this program is $500,000 and the guaranty follows the standard 7(a) percentages. This program combines many of the features of the other Express programs.

Borrowers under the Patriot Express Program must be eligible for SBA financing with every typical financial and personal qualification, but in addition must be 51 percent or more controlled by:

✧ A U.S. military veteran (other than dishonorably discharged)
✧ Active duty military, a potential retiree within twenty-four months of separation and discharging, or an active duty member within twelve months of discharge (TAP eligible)
✧ A reservist or National Guard member
✧ The current spouse of the above or the spouse of a service member or veteran who died of a service-connected disability

The Patriot Express Program offers borrowers a seven-year revolving line of credit for up to $500,000, with other typical 7(a) loan terms, such as interest rate restrictions (except for loans under $50,000, which may be charged 1 percent higher rates, or loans under $25,000, which may be charged 2 percent higher rates). Lenders can use their own forms and are not required to have collateral on loans less than $25,000. For loans up to $350,000, the lender may use its own collateral policy, but larger loans must take available collateral.

Like the other Express programs, the SBA promises a thirty-six-hour decision turnaround when lenders request a guaranty authorization.

Export Loan Programs

Since more than 70 percent of all U.S. exporters have less than twenty employees, the SBA has placed a high priority on providing financial assistance to help them develop or increase their export activities. There are a number of programs designed to serve these small businesses.

Export Express

The SBA Export Express Program provides exporters and lenders with a streamlined method to obtain SBA-guaranteed financing for loans and lines of credit up to $250,000, and the guaranty follows the standard 7(a) percentages. This program combines many of the features of the other Express programs.

The Export Express Program offers borrowers a seven-year revolving line of credit for up to $250,000, with other typical 7(a) loan terms, such as interest rate restrictions. Lenders make the credit decision, can use their own loan documentation forms, and are free to use their own collateral policies such as those on nonguaranteed loans. Quicker than the other Express programs, the SBA promises a twenty-four-hour decision turnaround when lenders request a guaranty authorization.

Export Working Capital Program

SBA's Export Working Capital Program (EWCP) loans are targeted for businesses that export and need additional working capital to support these sales. Participating lenders review and approve applications and submit the request to the SBA staff at the U.S. Export Assistance Center location servicing the exporter's geographical territory.

Exporting businesses can get up to a $2 million revolving credit facility through this program, which can be extended for up to twelve months. Loans carry a 90 percent SBA guaranty up to $1.5 million, and for larger loans, there is a companion guaranty that may be available from the Export-Import Bank for the gap. The interest rate may be fixed or variable and is negotiated between the lender and borrower.

The credit decision for these loans is made by the SBA, although lenders may use their own loan forms to document the transaction. The loans require all export-related inventory and receivables be pledged as collateral, as well as the personal guaranties of all 20+ percent owners. The SBA provides a five- to seven-day turnaround time to respond to the request for guaranty.

International Trade Loan Program

The International Trade Loan Program offers term loans to businesses that plan to start or continue exporting or that have been adversely affected by competition from imports. If you receive one of these loans, you must use the funds to enhance your position to compete. The program offers borrowers a maximum SBA-guaranteed portion of $1.75 million.

Funds may be used for the acquisition, construction, renovation, modernization, improvement, or expansion of long-term fixed assets or the refinancing of an existing loan used for these same purposes.

The maximum guaranty for this program follows the guidelines of the other 7(a) programs, with one important exception: borrowers using an International Trade Loan are able to exceed the typical amount of guaranty any one person qualifies for, which today equals $1.5 million. While the international trade loan itself is limited to a $1.5 million guaranty, borrowers may have a second SBA-guaranteed loan, so long as the combined guaranty does not exceed $1.75 million.

The interest rate may be fixed or variable and is negotiated between the lender and borrower, but the program restricts the maximum rate at prime plus 2.75 percent for loans with a maturity of seven or more years. As with most SBA programs, the lender makes the credit decisions, but the loan must be fully secured with collateral to the extent possible.

Rural Lender Advantage Program

The Small/Rural Lender Advantage (S/RLA) initiative by the SBA is designed to accommodate the unique loan-processing needs of small community and rural-based lenders, many of which make very few SBA loans. It is part of a broader SBA initiative to promote the economic development of local communities, particularly those facing the challenges of population loss, economic dislocation, and high unemployment. S/RLA encourages small community and rural lenders to partner with SBA by simplifying and streamlining loan application process and procedures, particularly for smaller SBA loans.

Key features of this program include:

✧ Streamlined loan application and processing for SBA loans of $150,000 or less, with limited additional information and analysis required for loans above $150,000
✧ A simplified SBA loan eligibility questionnaire to help small or occasional lenders meet SBA eligibility requirements
✧ Loans centrally processed through SBA's Standard 7(a) Loan Processing Center
✧ Lenders can transmit applications via fax and eventually online

Loans in this program are limited to $350,000 or less, and the standard 7(a) guaranty percentage applies. The interest rate may be fixed or variable, and is negotiated between the lender and borrower, but the program restricts the maximum rate at prime + 2.75 percent for loans with a maturity of seven or more years. The lender makes the credit decisions, but the loan must be fully secured with collateral to the extent possible.

Since this program is limited to lenders that averaged less than twenty SBA loans annually over the previous three years, the SBA reviews all loans for eligibility and credit underwriting. Guaranty decisions are generally turned around in three to five days in this program.

Special Purpose Loans

There are several special purpose loan programs under the umbrella of the 7(a) program that enable the borrower to qualify under certain conditions that may not otherwise be available. These special initiative programs are primarily intended to encourage and assist the private sector in accomplishing specific public policy objectives approved by Congress.

Community Adjustment and Investment Program

The Community Adjustment and Investment Program (CAIP) was established to assist U.S. companies doing business in areas of the country that have been negatively affected by the North American Free Trade Agreement (NAFTA). CAIP loans allow for the payment of fees on eligible loans, including the 7(a) Loan Guaranty Program guaranty fee and the 504 program guaranty and CDC and lender fees. Depending on the size of the loan, these fees can be sizeable. CAIP works with SBA to reduce borrower costs and increase the availability of these programs.

To be eligible for CAIP, the small business must reside in a county, or a defined area within a county, that is negatively affected by NAFTA. This is based on job losses and the unemployment rate of the county. The loan agreement also contains a job creation component. For 7(a) loans, one job has to be created for every $70,000 SBA guaranty. For 504 loans, one job has to be created for every $65,000 SBA guaranty.

As the NAFTA gets older, fewer businesses will be able to claim eligibility under this program, and it will probably be phased out over time.

CAPLines Program

This is an umbrella loan program designed to help small businesses with short-term and cyclical working capital needs. It offers five different types of credit lines: Seasonal, Contract, Builders, Standard Asset-Based, and Small Asset-Based.

✧ *Seasonal Line*—You must use proceeds from this line of credit solely to finance the seasonal increases of accounts receivable and inventory in your business (or in some cases associated increased labor costs). The loan can be revolving or nonrevolving, but you should repay it entirely by the end of the business cycle.

✧ *Contract Line*—This line of credit finances the direct labor and material cost associated with performing assignable contract(s) obtained by your business. The loan can be revolving or nonrevolving, but you should repay the associated borrowing from this line with the final payments from each associated contract.

✧ *Builders Line*—This line of credit is for small general contractors or builders constructing or renovating commercial or residential buildings. Proceeds can be used to finance direct labor and material costs. The building project (real estate) will serve as collateral for the loan, and the line of credit can be revolving or nonrevolving. As with the others, you should use the proceeds from the sale of the building to pay off the associated borrowing in full.

✧ *Standard Asset-Based Line*—This line of credit is a traditional asset-based revolving line of credit for businesses unable to meet credit standards associated with long-term credit. It provides financing for cyclical growth, as well as recurring and/or short-term working capital needs. You repay it by converting short-term assets (accounts receivable) into cash, which you then remit directly to the lender. The business continually draws from the line of credit based on its borrowing base of assets and repays the line as its cash cycle permits. This line generally is used by businesses that provide credit to other businesses by selling goods on open invoice. Because these loans require continual servicing and monitoring of collateral, additional fees may be charged by the lender to cover the extra costs.

✧ *Small Asset-Based Line*—This line of credit is an asset-based revolving line for smaller businesses and is limited to credit of up to $200,000. It operates like a standard asset-based line except that some of the stricter servicing requirements are waived, providing the business can consistently show repayment ability from cash flow for the full amount of the outstanding balance.

Employee Trusts Loan Program

This program is designed to provide financial assistance to Employee Stock Ownership Plans. The employee trust must be part of a plan sponsored by the employer company and qualified under regulations set by either the Internal Revenue Service Code (as an Employee Stock Ownership Plan, or ESOP) or the Department of Labor (the Employee Retirement Income Security Act, or ERISA). Applicants covered by the ERISA regulations must also secure an exemption from the Department of Labor regulations prohibiting certain loan transactions.

Pollution Control Loan Program

This program provides financing to eligible small businesses for the planning, design, or installation of a pollution control facility. This facility must prevent, reduce, abate, or control any form of pollution, including recycling. This program follows the guidelines for the 7(a) Loan Guaranty Program with the following exception: use of proceeds must be for fixed assets only.

Other Loan Programs

Military Reservists Loans

The Military Reservist Economic Injury Disaster Loan Program (MREIDL) provides funds to eligible small businesses to meet ordinary and necessary operating expenses that the business can't meet because an essential employee was "called up" to active duty in the military reserves. These loans are intended to help bridge the financial gap until the military reservist is able to return to the company. The loans are not to cover lost income or lost profits. MREIDL funds cannot be used to take the place of regular commercial debt, to refinance long-term debt, or to expand the business.

Federal law requires the SBA to determine whether credit in an amount needed to accomplish full recovery is available from nongovernment sources without creating an undue financial hardship to the applicant. Generally, SBA determines that over 90 percent of disaster loan applicants do not have sufficient financial resources to recover without the assistance of the federal government. When it passed the law creating these loans Congress intended that applicants with the financial capacity to fund their own recovery should do so and therefore shouldn't be eligible for MREIDL assistance.

These loans are underwritten with the full expectation of being repaid. Interest rates are fixed at 4 percent, and the loans are expected to be fully secured to the extent collateral is available. Repayment is limited to a maximum thirty-year term, but the SBA establishes the term based on its assessment of the installment payments the borrowers are able to repay. These loans are limited to $2 million, but the SBA has the authority to waive this limitation.

Types of Businesses Eligible for SBA Financing

Most every type of business and industry is eligible for SBA financing assistance, so long as they meet some basic qualifications:

- ✧ The business is operated for profit
- ✧ The business is engaged in, or proposes to do business in, the United States or its possessions
- ✧ The owners have a reasonable level of equity to invest
- ✧ The owners use alternative sources of financial resources, including personal assets, before seeking financial assistance

Some businesses and individuals require special consideration due to certain qualifications:

- ✧ Franchises are eligible except in situations where a franchisor retains power to control operations to such an extent as to be tantamount to an employment contract. The franchisee must have the right to profit from efforts commensurate with ownership.

✧ Recreational facilities and clubs are eligible provided: (a) the facilities are open to the general public, or (b) in membership-only situations, membership is not selectively denied to any particular group of individuals and the number of member-ships is not restricted either as a whole or by establishing maximum limits for particular groups.

✧ Farms and agricultural businesses are eligible. However, if you run such a business, you should first explore the Farm Service Agency (FSA) programs, particularly if you have a prior or existing relationship with FSA.

✧ Fishing vessels are eligible. However, those seeking funds for the construction or reconditioning of vessels with a cargo capacity of five tons or more must first request financing from the National Marine Fisheries Service (NMFS), a part of the Department of Commerce.

✧ Medical facilities (hospitals, clinics, emergency outpatient facilities, and medical and dental laboratories) are eligible. Convalescent and nursing homes are eligible, provided they are licensed by the appropriate government agency and ser-vices rendered go beyond those of room and board.

✧ An Eligible Passive Company (EPC) is a small entity that does not engage in regular and continuous business activity. For example, a business owner may decide to own the real estate that houses her business in a different corporation for tax, estate, or liability protection. If the business of that second company was solely to own the property and lease it to the owner's primary business, it would be an eligible passive com-pany and could get SBA financing. An EPC must use loan pro-ceeds to acquire or lease, and/or improve or renovate real or personal property that it leases to one or more operating com-panies for conducting that company's business. The EPC must comply with the conditions set forth in 13 CFR Sec 120.111, including that their lease with the operating company be in writing, that the operating company subordinate their lease to the SBA, that the operating company qualify as an eligible SBA borrower, and that any owner of 20 percent or more of the EPC and the operating company must personally guarantee the loan.

✧ If your business changes ownership and benefits from the change, you may be eligible for an SBA loan. In most cases, this benefit should be seen in promoting the sound development of the business or, perhaps, in preserving its existence when the former owner is retiring or changing careers. Loans cannot be made to help you purchase: (a) part of a business in which you have no present interest; or (b) part of an interest of a present and continuing owner. The SBA discourages loans to effect a change of ownership among members of the same family, and they will scrutinize such applications much more carefully.

✧ Legal aliens are eligible for SBA loans. However, the SBA will look at the type of status of the borrower (e.g., resident, lawful temporary resident, etc.) in determining the degree of risk relating to the continuity of the applicant's business. Excessive risk may be offset by full collateralization. You can discuss the various types of visas in more detail with your local SBA office. Use USCIS Form G-85 for verification of citizenship.

✧ Probation, parole, or indictment. The SBA won't accept applications from firms where a principal (any one of those required to submit a personal history statement, SBA Form 912) is currently incarcerated, on parole, probation, or under indictment; is a defendant in a criminal proceeding; or whose probation or parole is lifted expressly because it prohibits an SBA loan. On the other hand, if one of the principals has formerly been in prison but has served his or her sentence, the business would be eligible. Judgments concerning applicants who detail prison time on their personal history statement are made on a case-by-case evaluation of the nature, frequency, and timing of the offenses. If you answer a question on Form 912 in the affirmative, you'll have to submit fingerprint cards (available from the local SBA office) with your application.

Ineligible Businesses

There are a few types of businesses that are ineligible to receive financing assistance from the SBA. In general these business activities include those based on a passive investment, those engaged solely in financing third parties, or those operating a purely speculative business activity.

Ineligible businesses include those engaged in illegal activities, loan packaging, speculation, multi-sales distribution, gambling, investment or lending, or where the owner is on parole. Specific types of businesses not eligible include:

✧ Real estate investment firms, when the real property will be held for investment purposes.

✧ Firms involved in speculative activities that develop profits from fluctuations in price rather than through the normal course of trade (for example, wildcatting for oil and dealing in commodities futures), when these activities aren't part of the regular course of business.

✧ Dealers in rare coins and stamps.

✧ Firms involved in lending activities, such as banks, finance companies, factors, leasing companies, insurance companies (not agents), and any other firm whose stock in trade is money.

✧ Pyramid sales plans, where a participant's primary incentive is based on the sales made by an ever-increasing number of participants. Such products as cosmetics, household goods, and other soft goods lend themselves to this type of business.

✧ Firms involved in activities that are against the law in the jurisdiction where the business is located. Included in these activities are the production, servicing, or distribution of otherwise legal products that are to be used in connection with an illegal activity. If you're running a business selling drug paraphernalia or operating a motel that permits illegal prostitution, the SBA will not guarantee your loan.

✧ Gambling activities, including any business whose principal activity is gambling. While this precludes loans to racetracks, casinos, and similar enterprises, the rule does not restrict loans to otherwise eligible businesses, which obtain less than one-third of their annual gross income from either the sale of official state lottery tickets under a state license, or legal gambling activities licensed and supervised by a state authority.

✧ Charitable, religious, or other nonprofit institutions, government-owned corporations, consumer and marketing cooperatives, and churches and organizations promoting religious objectives are not eligible.

Other Loan Programs

The Microloan Program

If you are a small businesses with a need for a small short-term loan to be used for working capital or the purchase of inventory, supplies, furniture, fixtures, machinery, and/or equipment, you can apply for SBA's

Microloan Program. SBA makes funds available to specially designated intermediary lenders, which are nonprofit organizations with experience in lending and technical assistance. These intermediaries then make loans to eligible borrowers in amounts up to a maximum of $35,000. The average loan size is about $13,000. Applications are submitted to the local intermediary and all credit decisions are made on the local level.

More information about how to apply and finding local intermediaries can be obtained at *www.sba.gov/financialassistance/prospectivelenders/ micro/index.html.*

The CDC/504 Loan Program

The CDC/504 Loan Program is a long-term financing tool of the SBA specifically authorized by Congress to foster economic development, create or preserve jobs, and stimulate economic expansion. To be eligible, your small business must create or retain one job per $65,000 provided through the program (in the case of manufacturers, the goal is one job per $100,000). The 504 Program provides small businesses requiring "brick and mortar" financing with long-term, fixed-rate financing to acquire capital assets for expansion or modernization.

A Certified Development Company (CDC) is a private corporation authorized by the SBA to support and facilitate economic development in its community. CDCs work closely with SBA and private sector lenders to provide financing to small businesses through the 504 Loan Program. Although there are a few for-profit CDCs still around, today they must be organized as non-profit corporations. There are about 270 CDCs nationwide, and each are generally restricted to specific geographic areas.

Typically a 504 loan transaction will be structured to include:

✧ A loan secured from a private sector lender with a senior lien covering up to 50 percent of the total project cost

✧ A debenture secured through a CDC (backed by a 100 percent SBA guaranty) with a subordinated junior lien covering up to 40 percent of the total project costs

✧ An equity contribution from the borrower covering at minimum of 10 percent of the total project costs; however, if you're a new business or special facility owner, you'll probably be asked to contribute 15 percent

The loan terms for both the senior loan and CDC loan are usually twenty years for real estate loans or ten years for equipment, with a fully amortizing repayment schedule. The senior debt might be issued with a shorter ten-year term on real estate loans, however, depending on the borrower or lender's preference.

Generally the CDC works in cooperation with an SBA participating lender to determine eligibility, qualify the borrower, and structure financing for the applicant's financing. Proceeds from 504 loans are more restricted than other SBA financing programs and must be used solely for fixed-asset projects, such as:

✧ Purchasing land and improvements, including existing buildings and related development costs (grading, street improvements, utilities, parking lots, and landscaping)
✧ Construction of new facilities or modernizing, renovating, converting, or repurposing existing facilities
✧ Purchasing capital machinery and equipment (assets with an expected long-term useful life)
✧ Proceeds from 504 Program financing cannot be used for working capital, inventory, consolidating or repaying debt, or refinancing debt

To be eligible for a CDC/504 loan, the business must be operated for profit and fall within the size standards set by the SBA. Under the 504 Program, the business qualifies as "small" if it does not have a tangible net worth in excess of $7.5 million and does not have an average net income in excess of $2.5 million after taxes for the preceding two years. Or, the CDC has the option to use the size standards of the 7(a) program if they choose, to add flexibility to facilitating financing. Loans cannot be made to businesses engaged in speculation or investment in rental real estate.

The maximum SBA debenture for a typical project is $1.5 million when meeting the job-creating criteria or a community development goal. As we said above, generally, a business must create or retain one job for every $65,000 provided by the SBA-guaranteed portion of the transaction, except for small manufacturers, which have a $100,000 job creation or retention goal. However, the jobs creation requirement can be waived on all public policy and community development loans provided that the CDC has met their average job-creating goals. Jobs creation can also be waived on loans to small manufacturers that are not using the higher debenture amount.

The maximum SBA debenture for projects that meet one or more particular *public policy* goals is $2 million. These policy goals include:

- ✧ Business district revitalization
- ✧ Expansion of exports
- ✧ Expansion of minority business development
- ✧ Rural development
- ✧ Increasing productivity and competitiveness
- ✧ Restructuring due to federally mandated standards or policies
- ✧ Changes necessitated due to federal budget reductions
- ✧ Expansion of small business concerns owned and controlled by veterans (especially service-disabled veterans)
- ✧ Expansion of small business concerns owned and controlled by women
- ✧ Reduction of existing energy consumption by a minimum of 10 percent
- ✧ Increased use of sustainable designs to reduce environmental impact
- ✧ Upgrades to renewal energy sources
- ✧ Expansion into market with labor surplus
- ✧ Expansion of manufacturing jobs

Small Manufacturers

The maximum 504 debenture for small manufacturers is $4 million. A small manufacturer is defined as a company that has its primary business classified in sector 31, 32, or 33 of the NAICS and all of its production facilities located in the United States. To qualify for a $4 million 504 loan, the business must meet the definition of a small manufacturer and:

- ✧ Either create or retain at least one job per $100,000 guaranteed by the SBA or
- ✧ Improve the economy of the locality or achieve one or more public policy goals

Interest rates on 504 loans are pegged to an incremental spread above the current market rate for five-year and ten-year U.S. Treasury issues. The interest rates are fixed since the source of funds is from long-term debentures sold to investors. While that protects borrowers from an environment of rising interest rates, it also means that the rates will remain fixed if the market rates fall. There is a prepayment penalty to pay off a 504 loan ahead of maturity based on a yield maintenance calculation that is a function of the net rate paid to the investor. For clarity, ask the CDC to project that rate ahead of moving forward with the loan.

One obvious point to make is that fixing rates in a low market is a good opportunity. Even the prepayment penalties are much lower, reducing exposure to rising rates.

Interest rates on the senior financing must be negotiated with the participating lender and can be fixed or variable depending on their position.

Maturities on 504 loans can be ten or twenty years, depending on the use of funds. The SBA guaranty fee, CDC fee, and underwriting fees will total 2.15 percent and are included in the debenture balance. Other closing costs (attorneys, appraiser, etc.) for the 504 loans will be fairly constant but harder to quote as a percentage of the loan without identifying the size of the loan. These costs may be financed within the loan, depending on policies of the local CDC, which vary.

Generally, the project assets being financed are used as collateral, and other personal assets may be requested if the financed assets plus borrower's equity do not provide sufficient protection to the lender. This decision will usually factor on the historical financial performance of the business, management track record, and strength of the business plan. Personal guaranties of the principal owners are also required on all loans.

Applications for a CDC/504 loan may be initiated either directly with a CDC or through a participating SBA lender. The local SBA District Office can help borrowers identify the CDC in their area. A list of SBA District Offices can be found in the appendix.

Now that you've read this summary of the major loan programs available under the SBA, it's time to examine, briefly, how the basic loan structure works.

How the SBA Loan Guaranty Programs Work

Because the mechanics of the SBA loan guaranty program are often misunderstood by even some active participants, there is some criticism of the program from many directions and dissatisfaction from the businesses that do not get funding as quickly as they prefer or do not qualify for assistance. The program is actually a fairly well-managed endeavor of the federal government that provides needed assistance to the small business sector seeking to secure adequate long-term capital financing. In today's economic environment, it is needed more than ever.

In light of seemingly contradictory and often overlapping state and federal banking regulations, it is doubtful that the private sector would fulfill the demand for small business financing without assistance from the SBA. Lenders seek to make transactions with as little risk as possible, and banking regulators sure encourage this behavior in many ways. Nothing is as financially risky as a start-up small business concern that can leverage its capital 80–90 percent.

The SBA provides a solution to private sector lenders in form of a credit enhancement that permits them to extend credit to small businesses that would otherwise be considered too risky. By absorbing at least 50 percent of the risk of the deal with the backing of the U.S. government, the SBA gives lenders insurance coverage against the exposure to business catastrophe such that even their regulators cooperate.

As you've gathered from the preceding section, the SBA loan guaranty programs allow lenders to apply to the SBA for a guaranty based on eligibility standards that define the broad characteristics of the businesses permitted to receive this assistance. There are also some restrictions on how the proceeds of these loans may be used, which is something no taxpayer would want to be without.

Lenders provide the funding for these loans and always have direct exposure for a constant percentage of the outstanding principal balance—in other words they will have enough "skin in the game" to exercise prudence and good judgment. The lender will be the primary contact for the borrower in servicing the loan account.

Unless the loan is not repaid as agreed, you as the borrower may never be aware of the presence of the SBA after the loan closing. You are not involved directly with the agency unless there is a loan default. The agency may then be required to buy the guaranteed portion of the loan from the lender and, in limited instances, have to initiate loan collection efforts directly with you.

Since the agency rarely meets the borrower and never visits the business, the SBA must rely on the written application and the reported observations of the lender in order to approve the lender's request for a guaranty. The requirements for this application include an extensive list of information designed to ensure the borrower's compliance with myriad financial, regulatory, and business qualifications intended to reduce the lender's exposure to loss and adherence to program rules.

These loan guaranties are available to small business owners, regardless of age, gender, or ethnicity. When approved, the guaranty is provided under a standard SBA authorization agreement executed by the lender and the SBA, similar to the lender's loan agreement with the borrower. If you use the SBA program, you are not more susceptible to being scrutinized by or subject to extraordinary attention from any other federal agency unless you have not paid income taxes or have outstanding and unpaid child support payments, in which case extra attention is probably warranted.

Any federal or state chartered bank is capable of participating in the SBA loan guaranty programs. In addition, there are thirteen SBA-licensed nonbank lenders (SBLCs) that have the capability to make SBA-guaranteed loans.

All of these lenders have many benefits available to them through participation in the loan guaranty programs. For example, the financial guaranty permits lenders to enter into lending transactions with noncredit risks that otherwise might prevent them from being able to accommodate the borrower. These risks might involve the longer loan terms, the type of industry (such as recreational facilities or convenience stores), or the type of collateral used to secure the loan (such as single-purpose real estate improvements or specialized equipment).

In addition, since the SBA guaranty carries the full faith and credit of the U.S. federal government, lenders are able to sell the guaranteed portions of their loans to investors through an organized market, and that in turn provides liquidity back to the lender to originate new loans. This feature is particularly important to smaller community banks, which may have limited capital with which to leverage their operation.

The SBA loan guaranty programs are administered by over sixty district offices located throughout the country and are managed by a district director. Supervision of the 7(a) program and 504 program lending is managed by the Sacramento Loan Processing Center (SLPC). These districts are organized into ten regions, each of which are headed by a politically appointed regional director, who is involved with broader policy issues involving the agency.

The agency operates the loan guaranty programs under a transparent set of rules known as the Standard Operating Procedures (SOPs), all of which have been published in the Federal Register for review and comment in advance of implementation. As the agency has evolved into more of a service organization, which empowers lenders to play a more active role in the SBA process, lenders expect and usually get uniform implementation of the SOPs throughout every region in the country.

Regulatory authority for the Small Business Administration and the general regulations of its business credit programs are drawn from the Code of Federal Regulations, Volume 13, Business Credit and Assistance.

The SBA has developed an impressive website (*www.sba.gov*) that spells out the agency's programs, tools, and resources, and for the most part explains its rules and guidelines. The site also provides much good contact information for seeking assistance with the list of agency offices and resource centers. A list of more website resources can be found in the appendix.

CHAPTER **2**

Choosing the Best Loan Guaranty Option to Fund the Business

The good news is that you finally have plenty of financing options for your small business. The bad news is—you need to make sure to select the option that is really best for your business concern. In this chapter, we'll compare and examine the different characteristics of each program. You'll learn:

- ✧ 7(a) versus 504 loan—which one is really best for the deal?
- ✧ Specialty programs—is there advantage to the business?
- ✧ Loan versus line of credit—isn't it all just money?

Choices According to the Business Objective

Does the business need funding to build a new factory or finance a new contract? While that comparison seems easy to decipher, the differences in other business objectives are sometimes less obvious—and the appropriate financing less clear—and they require more study and consideration. Too many businesses borrow all the money available simply because it is offered, without considering their long-term objectives as part of the process. Business planning, strategic goals, and exit strategies get tossed aside sometimes because a banker making a cold call says his bank wants to make a business loan!

The broad choices of SBA financing tools provide solutions to many business challenges and opportunities but can also help small businesses make quick, wrong decisions. Bearing the long-term goals in mind at the onset of any financing consideration will, I hope, temper any short-term impulses to buy something that is not needed. A comparison of the SBA loan programs is mapped out on Table 2-1.

Loan Guaranty Program	Maximum Loan Amount	Restrictions on the Use of Loan Proceeds	Maximum Loan Term	Maximum Interest Rate
7(a)	$2 million	Acquire, remodel, expand, or construct real estate and improvements, purchase equipment or other capital assets, or working capital; refinance debt if justified	7–25 years, based on the use of loan proceeds	Prime + 2.75% (except loans under $50,000)
SBA Express	$350,000	Working capital	May be a 7-year-term loan or a revolving line of credit	
Community Express	$250,000	Working capital	May be a 7-year-term loan or a revolving line of credit	
Patriot Express	$500,000	See 7(a)	7–25 years based on the use of loan proceeds	
CAPLines	$2 million	Working capital	Revolving line of credit with up to a five-year term	
Export Working Capital Program	$2 million	Working capital for exporters	Revolving line of credit with up to a one-year term	
CDC/504	$2 million	Acquire or construct real estate and improvements, or capital assets for business	10 to 20 years, based on use of proceeds	
Microloans	$35,000	Purchase equipment or other assets or working capital (no repayment of existing debt)	Not to exceed 6 years	

A good starting point to evaluate which SBA loan program might be optimal for your business would be to begin with the eligible uses of these funds: buying a building, constructing a building, refinancing land and building debt, acquiring equipment or other capital assets, or working capital.

One of the most popular uses of SBA financing is for real estate and improvements (especially among lenders!). Recognizing that SBA-guaranteed funds cannot be used to acquire land without an immediate business use or to develop land and a building for speculative purposes, start with the nature of the real estate project.

Buying a Building

Either the 7(a), 504, or International Trade Loan Program can be used to finance the purchase of land and building for business use. Which one is the best choice will depend on some of the characteristics of the business. Here are some key differences to consider:

✧ 7(a) loan eligibility is restricted to businesses meeting either revenue or employment limitations according to size standards cited in the NAICS.

✧ 7(a) loans are restricted to $2 million total financing for the project.

✧ 7(a) loans do not have the jobs creation or preservation restriction that 504 loans require.

✧ 504 loan eligibility is restricted to businesses meeting either a maximum average net worth or business profit over the past three years, which is much less restrictive than the 7(a) program.

✧ 504 loans are usually negotiated with fixed interest rates, while most 7(a) loans have variable interest rates. However, on 504 loans, only the debenture is required to be fixed—the senior loan can be a variable rate. The borrower's choice of one or the other will depend on the current interest environment and the forecast for future economic growth. Be aware that the fixed interest rates on 504 loans also imply prepayment penalties if the senior loan (usually) or debenture is repaid earlier than scheduled. While the penalties are lower if the rate is lower, consideration should be given to how long the building will be suitable for the business.

✧ 504 loans generally have lower fees than 7(a) loans, unless Congress suspends 7(a) fees temporarily, as they did as part of the 2009 stimulus program.

✧ 504 loans can be much larger than 7(a) or International Trade loans. The maximum debenture (subordinated portion) can be up to $1.5 million (or $2 million for businesses meeting certain public policy objectives, and $4 million for certain manufacturing companies), which means the total project might be as much as $10 million, or more. The only limit is the practicality and judgment of the lender for eligible companies.

✧ International Trade loans have the same size qualifications as the 7(a) loans, but require a borrower to meet an additional program qualification of either starting an exporting business, continuing an exporting business, or having been previously adversely affected by competition from imports.

✧ International Trade loans are also restricted to $2 million for total project financing, but qualifying businesses can also couple this loan with a second SBA working capital loan for total guaranty eligibility of $1.75 million, so long as the working capital portion does not exceed $1.25 million.

Constructing a Building

Either the 7(a), 504, or International Trade Program can be used to finance the land and construction of improvements for business use. In this use of SBA lending programs, the lender may exert a preference for which program to employ. Borrowers should be sensitive to some of the same characteristics described above plus additional factors:

- ✧ 7(a) versus 504 qualifying business size standards for eligibility (see above).
- ✧ 7(a) versus 504 loan size limitations—$2 million versus unlimited (see above).
- ✧ 7(a) versus 504 interest rate options (see above).
- ✧ 7(a) loans offer essentially a one-step process whereas the construction loan is funded directly from one lender from beginning to end of construction. The loan is then converted to a permanent loan already scheduled on a long-term repayment schedule.
- ✧ 504 loans require two steps to complete construction financing. Usually the lender that has committed to funding the senior mortgage loan will provide construction financing. This loan may require an additional origination fee, and since it is not an SBA-guaranteed loan at that time, there is no restriction prohibiting such fees. Additionally, the lender's credit policy may not be as permissive as the 504 debenture funding and may have other requirements for the construction loan, such as additional collateral to be pledged during the construction period.
- ✧ Lenders may prefer 7(a) loans on transactions of $2 million or less, because a portion of their loan is guaranteed from the beginning of loan disbursements. When financing a construction loan with a 504 commitment, the lender is exposed without the guaranty until the debenture is funded and pays out the subordinated portion of the deal. That does not happen until the construction project is completed and the other borrower conditions defined at the beginning of the deal have been certified as being met.
- ✧ International Trade loan characteristics in this discussion mirror the 7(a) loan features, except as referenced earlier (see above).

Refinancing Land and Building

This choice of optimal loan programs is simple—the 7(a) and International Trade Loan programs permit refinancing real estate debt, and the 504 program only recently allowed refinancing as an eligible use, though it is restricted to 50 percent of the project.

✧ Refinancing existing debt with the 7(a) and International Trade Loan programs is subject to justification—the new loan must enable the business to lower its debt service payments by at least 10 percent to qualify for SBA assistance.

✧ The International Trade Loan Program requires the borrower to meet the additional program qualifications (see above).

✧ Refinancing land and building debt under both programs is limited to a $2 million maximum transaction for no more than a twenty-year term.

✧ 504 financing may work in situations where the borrower is expanding an existing project or perhaps trying to extract cash equity from assets for another purpose.

Purchasing Equipment or Other Capital Assets

Either the 7(a), 504, or International Trade Loan Program can be used to finance the purchase of equipment or other capital assets for business use. Borrowers should be sensitive to some of the same characteristics described above plus other factors:

✧ 7(a) versus 504 qualifying business size standards for eligibility (see above).

✧ 7(a) versus 504 loan size limitations—$2 million versus unlimited (see above).

✧ 7(a) versus 504 interest rate options (see above).

✧ 7(a) provides loan repayment terms of up to fifteen years or the useful life of the asset, whichever is less, although most loans are restricted to a ten-year repayment.

✧ 504 loans provide a loan repayment term of either ten or twenty years, depending on the useful life of the asset. A longer term will mean lower payments for the borrower.

Financing Working Capital

The 7(a) and related programs offer a wide array of choices for working capital financing. The 504 Loan Program cannot be used for working capital except as a use of 504 loan proceeds covering some of the closing costs associated with a 504 loan. Borrowers can navigate between the traditional 7(a) loan, Express, Export, CAPLine, or Microloan programs.

7(a) Program

The 7(a) Loan Guaranty Program offers loans up to $2 million with up to a ten-year (specifically for working capital) repayment term. Interest rates are capped at 2.25 percent over base rate for loans with a maturity of less than seven years, and 2.75 percent over base rate for loans with a maturity of more than seven years. Borrowers must meet 7(a) business size standards to be eligible.

SBA Express

The SBA Express Program offers a quick SBA decision turnaround with fewer lender documentation requirements necessary. It offers loans up to $350,000 with up to a seven-year repayment term. Interest rates can be up to 4.5 percent over base rate for loans over $50,000, and up to 6.5 percent for loans under $50,000. You must meet 7(a) business size standards to qualify.

Community Express

The Community Express Program offers a quick SBA decision turn-around with fewer lender documentation requirements necessary. It is targeted to enhancing lending in HUBZones (Historically Underutilized Business Zones). A critical component of this program is the requirement for the business to have received technical assistance to enhance opportunities to succeed. It offers loans up to $250,000 with up to a seven-year repayment term. Interest rates are capped according to 7(a) standards except for loans under $50,000, which may be higher. Borrowers must meet 7(a) business size standards to qualify.

Patriot Express

The Patriot Express Program offers a quick SBA decision turnaround with fewer lender documentation requirements necessary, and it is targeted at businesses with 51 percent or more ownership by military veterans or members of the military community. It offers loans up to $500,000 with up to a seven-year repayment term. Interest rates are capped according to 7(a) standards except for loans under $50,000, which may be higher. Borrowers must meet 7(a) business size standards to qualify.

Export Express

The Export Express Program offers a quick SBA decision turnaround with fewer lender documentation requirements necessary and targets businesses that export. It offers a revolving line of credit up to $250,000 with up to a seven-year repayment term. Interest rates are capped according to 7(a) standards, and borrowers must meet 7(a) business size standards to qualify.

Export Working Capital Program

The Export Working Capital Program targets businesses that are able to generate export sales. It offers a revolving line of credit up to $2 million for up to a twelve-month term. Interest rates are negotiated with the lender. Borrowers must meet 7(a) business size standards to qualify.

Rural Lender Advantage

The Rural Lender Advantage Program targets borrowers in smaller communities that often receive fewer SBA loans due to lower lender participation. It offers term loans up to $350,000 for up to a ten-year (specifically for working capital) repayment term. Interest rates are capped according to 7(a) standards, and borrowers must meet 7(a) business size standards to qualify.

CAPLines

The several options under the CAPLines Program offers a revolving line of credit of up to $2 million (except Small Asset-Based Line, which is limited to $200,000) with up to a five-year repayment term. Interest rates are capped according to 7(a) standards, and borrowers must meet 7(a) business size standards to qualify. The various options are best distinguished by the ultimate use of the loan proceeds:

- ✧ *Seasonal Line*—provides working capital for businesses with seasonal fluctuations of operating expenses that are later converted to cash
- ✧ *Contract Line*—provides working capital to businesses working on the completion of (a) contract(s) with a defined payment cycle
- ✧ *Builders Line*—provides working capital to construction businesses working on the completion of a specific building project
- ✧ *Standard Asset-Based Line*—provides a revolving facility of working capital to advance funds for business operations, and is repaid from the receivables collected in return
- ✧ *Small Asset-Based Line*—same as standard asset-based line, except geared toward businesses needing less than $200,000 and providing lower servicing costs

Microloans

The Microloan Program provides small, short-term loans to small businesses and certain nonprofit day care centers through intermediaries licensed by the SBA. Loans are limited to $35,000 and offer up to a six-year repayment term.

7(a) Loan Guaranty Program versus 504 Loan Program—Which Is Best?

Both the dominant programs offered by the SBA have their advocates. Both programs share many of the same characteristics: affordable, accessible financing provided with an SBA credit enhancement that make capital financing available to the riskiest sector of businesses in our economy—those generally with revenues of less than $10 million.

The differences in the two programs are important to all businesses though. Despite the specific differences between the programs' restrictions on the uses of funding, a very large number of businesses will qualify for both programs—specifically, businesses seeking SBA-assisted financing for acquiring or constructing improvements to real estate. Either of these two programs offer excellent financing vehicles compared to most conventional financing. Therefore you need to further explore specific program differences to decide which one is best for your situation. To help you, here is a closer examination of the program differences as they apply to many common business situations.

Collateral

One key distinction pointed out by 504 lenders is that this program only requires using the asset being financed as collateral, whereas the 7(a) program lender often requires that additional assets be pledged when available to lower leverage.

Variable Versus Fixed Interest Rates

Ask ten different bankers for a recommendation about variable versus fixed-rate loans, and you'll get eleven different answers. The different viewpoints reflect many differences in how transaction value and risks are evaluated by different people and their different experiences and expectations. A discussion of how lenders determine interest rates may shed some light on how transaction rates are established and the differences between fixed and variable rate choices. It also may give you more insight into negotiating rates with lenders.

Interest is, of course, the price paid by borrowers to lenders to rent capital over a set term of repayment. The Federal Reserve Board of Governors establishes targeted interest rates as the primary tool in effecting its monetary policy for the U.S. economy.

Good lenders will primarily price loans based on their assessment of the risk associated with repayment from each borrower. Therefore better transactions with lower risks generally are charged lower interest rates, and transactions with higher risks generally are charged higher interest rates.

Lenders also consider their own costs of capital while setting interest rates to ensure they infuse a sufficient premium over it to provide budgeted profits. After all, lenders are supposed to be for-profit enterprises, too. Lenders borrow funds from other parties in order to provide a majority of the monies they lend. Think about checking accounts, money market accounts, and certificates of deposits (CDs). These are liabilities to the lender that are in turn used to fund loans (assets) to lender clients. Most banks gather a majority of their funding from CDs, which are fixed-rate deposits with a defined term. Checking accounts and money market accounts are variable (or noninterest) accounts, but are constantly subject to an unannounced withdrawal.

Lenders seek to balance their loan portfolios with a mixture of variable and fixed interest rates so to hedge their own exposure to interest rate risks. If they are saturated with a mostly variable-rate loan portfolio, the condition is known as "asset sensitive" and exposes them to income losses should lending rates fall faster than they can adjust the cost of their funding. Likewise, if their portfolio is too weighted with fixed-rate loans, the condition is known as "liability sensitive." This latter condition exposes lenders to income losses in the event that interest rates on deposits increase faster than the lender can increase the yield on their loan portfolio.

By regular tracking of the level of variable and fixed-rate loans against the level of variable and fixed-rate deposits (called asset-liability management), lenders can balance their exposure in most interest rate environments to ensure that they do not face sudden losses of income when volatile changes occur. Well-managed lenders will generally offer borrowers a choice of variable or fixed-rate loans to remain competitive, but they have a specific yield target to ensure their portfolio is always priced in sync.

Variable interest rates are those that are tied to a base rate (e.g., *WSJ* prime rate, LIBOR, etc.) with an agreed-upon spread over (or under) the base rate, and an identified timetable as to when the rate will vary. For example, a lender may commonly offer a 7(a) loan at the *WSJ* prime rate plus 2 percent, adjusting quarterly. If the *WSJ* prime was 5 percent on the loan closing date, that quote would equate to a 7 percent interest rate on the loan. That rate would be reviewed on the first day of each succeeding quarter for a possible change in the *WSJ* prime.

The obvious advantage to you of a variable rate is that if rates decline, your cost of borrowing also declines. Conversely, the opposite is true when rates increase. Lenders like variable rates because they can maintain a constant profit margin over their costs of variable-priced deposits. You should take into consideration the following list of questions when weighing the desirability of choosing a variable rate loan:

1. *Do you want a 7(a) loan or a 504 loan?* Most 7(a) lenders are only going to offer a variable-rate option for a loan. This restriction has to do with their ability to resell the guaranteed portion of the loan. Variable loans sell for a better premium than fixed-rate loans. While the senior portion of the 504 loan can be a variable rate, the debenture portion can only be offered as fixed-rate financing.

2. *Which base rate is used?* It is important to understand the different base rates offered and become familiar with how they are established, their volatility, and what their movement trends have been over the past few years.

3. *What is the lender's spread over the base rate?* Comparing rates with another lender's offer may be insightful as to their competitiveness.

4. *How often will the rate be reviewed for variance?* Whether the rate is subject to change monthly, quarterly, or annuallyshould impact the borrower's decision about accepting a variable rate.

5. *What is your exit strategy for the business?* What you plan for the business over the next three and next ten years is germane to your interest rate selection. Will the business raise more capital and expand, be sold, or just focus on thriving in its current mode?

6. *What do leading economists project for the U.S. economy and interest rates over the next twelve months and beyond?* While there are no guaranties that what they say will happen, it is smart to at least be aware of what experts are saying about where interest rates may go in the months and years ahead.

Fixed interest rates are those that are set at the onset of the loan and maintained at the same level until maturity. Lenders manage loans priced at fixed rates by attempting to source their funding with fixed-rate liabilities with similar terms. When providing 7(a) or 504 loans for twenty or twenty-five years, that matching becomes more challenging.

The obvious advantage of a fixed rate to you is that there is a predictable cost of funding for the loan for the life of the loan. You are not exposed to rate increases that can quickly reduce profits, particularly during a period of stagnant or declining revenues. The obvious downside is that you will miss a declining rate environment, when the costs of borrowing can decline and potentially save your business a lot of money and permit it to repay the financing faster. You should take into consideration the following list of questions when weighing the desirability of choosing a fixed-rate loan:

7. *Do you want a 7(a) loan or a 504 loan?* As we said above, most 7(a) lenders are only going to offer a variable rate option for a loan.

8. *What is the premium paid over a variable rate offer for the same loan?* It is not reasonable to expect that borrowers will be offered the same rate for their choice of variable or fixed rates. Generally, fixed rates are offered at a premium over the variable rate in return for eliminating some of the rate exposure the borrower would have faced over the life of the loan. Note the premium and evaluate carefully whether this fixed rate premium payment is worth eliminating the exposure to future rate variations.

9. *What is the penalty to repay this loan ahead of maturity?* Since lenders must match the fixed-rate loan with fixed-rate funding of their own, there are usually penalties for repaying a fixed-rate loan early. Get familiar with those penalty clauses and calculations before agreeing to the loan. Business conditions can change in a very short period, and a loan can change from desirable to undesirable in a matter of months. Know what the cost of such a change would be before agreeing to accept fixed-rate financing.

10. *What is your exit strategy for the business?* What you plan for the business over the next three and next ten years is germane to your interest rate selection. Will the business raise more capital and expand, be sold, or just focus on thriving in its current mode?

11. *What do leading economists project for the U.S. economy and interest rates over the next twelve months and beyond?* While there are no guarantees that what they say will happen, it is smart to at least be aware of what experts are saying about where interest rates may go in the months and years ahead.

Variable Versus Fixed Interest Rates: My Choice

After reading this section you should at least be able to better distinguish some of the characteristics and dynamics behind interest rate choices. While many factors will contribute to your ultimate choice, including the lender's propensity to tilt that choice to their preference, I offer the following advice based on my career as a lender: When offered a reasonable variable-rate option, choose it.

Generally interest rates are increased when the economy is very robust and the Fed is trying to cool things down to avoid inflation. It is likely that your business will also be doing well and can afford the higher interest costs during these periods. As the economy slows, rates will begin to fall and a variably priced loan cost falls with it.

Disciplined lenders will price a loan according to the factors mentioned above—their cost of funds and assessment of transaction risk. They won't negotiate with you unless they are in a competitive situation and really want to buy your business or have baked in some wiggle room to concede.

Fixed rates are always more expensive on Day One of the loan, when the outstanding balance is usually at its highest and just begins to amortize. There is a huge financial premium to be paid for the comfort of knowing that the rate will never change. What you don't know is whether the business will want or need the financing as long as is required to let the prepayment penalty period elapse. Think of the many variables that could change and cause your business to reconsider the need for or desirability of that obligation: you could die, sell the business, or the business could really take off.

Variable-rate financing offers a lower rate when the loan is at its highest value. With casual tracking during the past twenty years variable rates always remained lower than the fixed-rate option more than 70 percent of the time. And consider that toward the last half of the loan, even if the variable rate were higher than the fixed option, your cash out of pocket over the life of the loan could still be lower.

Most importantly, the repayment of the entire loan at any time without a penalty means that you won't have to pay extra penalties for unforeseen changes in the business strategy. If you later decide that the existing loan agreement is not the best available, you can refinance it with another lender.

A final topic to mention so as to explain some circumstances that can arise regarding fixed-rate loans and your banker's flexibility: "troubled debt restructure" (TDR). Troubled debt restructure is a term used by bank regulators to describe a loan account where the borrower's financial condition is weakened to the point that the bank concedes to easier terms to keep loan payments being made and avoid default.

Let's suppose you locked in a fixed rate at 7 percent when the WSJ Prime was at 5.5 percent and the economy takes a turn for the worse. Say then that the WSJ Prime rate falls to 3.25 percent over the course of a few months and your business is feeling the declining economy.

Like many business owners, to adjust for the falling profits in your business you will ask your banker to renegotiate your rate in light of changing market conditions. For instance, you could ask that the rate be lowered to 5 percent. This is higher than the WSJ Prime but a bit lower than the rate was when you locked it in. Still, it gives you some relief.

Once classified as a TDR, the bank must write down any differential between the value of the loan's collateral and the balance of the loan. The bank will have to further impair the loan balance by an amount equal to the present value of the expected future cash flow of the loan repayments, based on the company's present financial conditions. Under some conditions, the bank may have to stop accruing interest altogether.

The TDR discussion is included here just to highlight another advantage of a variable interest rate, which would have let the loan's interest rate fall automatically. With a fixed rate, the bank has to perform more evaluation and possibly make significant write downs on your loan, even though it may be performing as agreed upon.

Repayment Terms

Given that you will face more restrictions in the use of 504 loan proceeds than of 7(a) loans, my comparison of repayment terms between the two programs is focused strictly on real estate financing. With a 504 loan, the repayment term of the debenture (subordinated) portion is twenty years. The senior portion must be at least ten years, but could be longer if the lender decides to make that option available. The 7(a) loan in contrast has a twenty-five year repayment term limit.

The typical five-year differential between the loan terms means that, assuming the loans have similar features, your payments on a 7(a) loan will usually be lower, while the total financing cost on a 504 loan will generally be lower. You should analyze the differences in choices when deciding which program to use if your project is eligible for both.

For example, consider a $1 million loan where the 7(a) average variable rate over its twenty-five year term exactly equals the combined fixed rate of the senior and subordinated 504 loans over a twenty year term. For this case, 7 percent is the rate used to compare both programs (although at this writing, the 504 debenture rate is 5.29 percent):

	Monthly Loan Payment	Total Interest Paid over Life of Loan
7(a) Loan	$7,068	$1,120,338
504 Loan	$7,753	$860,717

For a monthly payment saving of $685 per month, you'll spend $259,621 more in interest costs over the life of the loan.

Now look at the difference if the senior loan of the 504 financing is changed to a twenty-five year repayment term while the subordinated portion remains at twenty years:

	Monthly Loan Payment	Total Interest Paid over Life of Loan
7(a) Loan	$7,068	$1,120,338
504 Loan	$7,373	$1,004,951

Similarly, for a 504 payment reduction of $305 per month, the 504 borrower will spend an additional $115,387 over the life of the loan.

These examples are fairly severe and contain some assumptions that may never occur, but they help remind us that the term matters and debt costs a lot of money. Sometimes getting a longer term is very helpful in that it lowers the monthly repayment required, but there is a tangible cost to that convenience.

The best course of action may be to try to get the best of both worlds: the 7(a) loan term clearly offers more flexibility, and with discipline, you can increase payments later, when cash flow permits, to accelerate the loan repayment without penalty to lower the interest expense later in the loan term.

The 504 term requires more cash flow than the 7(a) but for stronger borrowers that is a welcome reduction in borrowing costs over the life of the loan. Sometimes the senior debt will not have a prepayment penalty and can be reduced faster.

Transaction Complexity?

Compared to 504 loans, the 7(a) program is simpler if you meet the qualification standards. The lender determines whether the business transaction makes sense, whether the borrower meets their credit standards, and then applies to the SBA for the guaranty. Once approved, the lender closes the loan with required documents and funds credit accordingly. The lender's proceeds are guaranteed directly by the SBA, which interfaces only with the lender.

With a 504 loan, the transaction has to be approved by the lender, a CDC, and the SBA, which interfaces with the CDC rather than the lender. Once the transaction is closed, the proceeds will be provided from the next debenture pool, which may be funded days or weeks later. There are twice as many documents to sign since there are two elements in the financing for the business—a senior loan and a subordinated loan. Thereafter, there are two payments each month and two parties to provide ongoing financial information to during the life of the loan.

Certainly 504 offers benefits to many more businesses than the 7(a) program due to its expanded qualification size standards, lower costs, and credit limits, but there are conditions that make it less attractive for smaller concerns if they happen to qualify for both programs.

Loan Versus Line-of-Credit Financing

Many of the financing options described under the 7(a) program are "lines of credit" rather than loans. Since I've seen many business owners confused by the difference between these two financing vehicles, it's worthwhile to take time to discuss them.

Obviously, a "loan" is a generic description used to encompass a number of different financing structures. Generally it refers to the extension of credit. However, used in association with the SBA programs, the word "loan" refers specifically to a "term loan," or a loan made for a specific term of years, with repayment spread out in equal installments over that period ("equal installments" relative to the variations in the interest rate during that period, of course).

But a "revolving line of credit" is a credit facility that has a specific credit limit, is available for a specific use and repayment period, and may include more specific restrictions on the borrower by the lender. Due to the higher costs and additional restrictions, you should make sure you fully grasp the expectations of the lender when utilizing this kind of credit facility, or you'll face more difficult situations trying to avoid default. Here are some of the specific terms involved:

Revolving Loan Limits

A revolving line of credit (RLOC) is a financing vehicle that makes a specified loan sum available to the borrower for use as working capital. The word "revolving" refers to the fact that the funds can be advanced to the borrower, repaid, and then advanced again. In many businesses, this borrow–repay–borrow again cycle may repeat itself several times during the term of the line. RLOCs are generally provided to businesses that sell to their clients on credit or open account. In other words, RLOCs are a substitute credit for credit that borrowers are extending to others.

For larger RLOCs, lenders use "fund control" procedures to assure that the funds are used and repaid according to the agreed-upon conditions. The lender strictly monitors and controls all advances and repayments through its direct control of all of the borrower's cash accounts. Payments received by the borrower for sums owed to it are deposited into these control accounts that are subsequently released only upon the approval by the lender.

Use of Line-of-Credit Proceeds

The lender usually sets specific limitations on the use of line-of-credit loan proceeds. Alternatively, such use is restricted to defined advances on certain of the borrower's collateral assets (though these may not exist at the time the line of credit is created). For example, most RLOCs are secured by the business accounts receivable (A/R). The lender will advance funds as a percentage of the receivable balance. As a borrower, you can draw on these funds up to the limit, but as the receivables are collected (and deposited directly into your controlled cash accounts), your lender will use those funds to repay the balances outstanding on the line of credit.

If you've applied for a line of credit in order to build, before lending money the lending institution will generally require an inspection of the facility you're constructing to assure themselves that all of the advanced funds have actually been used on the project.

Repayment Term

Lines of credit have various repayment terms that range from one to seven years. The shorter-term RLOCs generally are more project or contract specific, while the longer-term facilities are intended to cover many business cycles in the hope that the business can accumulate profits and wean itself off borrowed capital.

Line-of-Credit Restrictions

RLOC funding is intended to cover the business's direct cost of goods sold (COGS). It is specifically *not* intended for the acquisition of assets, repayment of debts, or payment of overhead of a business. This distinction is important. The payment of COGS means that the business is employing funds directly to generate revenues. It is manufacturing goods, fulfilling a contract, meeting payroll, or buying raw materials. The upshot of the expenses should be the creation of an account receivable. Other uses of the funds would require a longer term to repay than the normal cash cycle of generating revenues and would have to be repaid from business profits. With RLOC, you're repaying the lender from gross receipts. Obviously your business must be generating profits constantly to cover operating overhead and other capital expenses.

Use of a line of credit is highly structured and you must use it in a disciplined manner. Borrowers subject themselves to a high degree of lender control, and the lender can, without notice, cut off your funds or freeze your cash and accounts. You should view these credit facilities as a way to create business scale over a certain period and then reduce and close your line of credit. Due to the heavy servicing requirements, which you'll ultimately pay for, the costs are very high, and tangibly reduce the profits of the business. Therefore, you should plan to accumulate capital from profits that will permit you to eventually achieve self-financing business growth without reliance on RLOC facilities.

CHAPTER **3**

Understanding Business Lending

Understanding the process of getting a loan is as important as being qualified for a loan. In this chapter, we'll explore the mechanics of dealing with a small business lender and learn:

- ✧ How lenders evaluate the loan
- ✧ What to expect from the process
- ✧ The financial mechanics of projecting income and expenses

Putting the Process in Perspective

Borrowers are frequently frustrated with lenders who may sometimes seem disinterested in considering business loan proposals. Equally upsetting is the seemingly lengthy amount of time required to move through the application process. You may also be dissatisfied with the conservative approach lenders use to underwrite business loans. These situations are very common and originate from a number of factors.

Primarily, understand that lenders are very averse to the risk of loan losses. Their job is to make loan investments in situations where risk is minimal and repayment is as assured as they can make it, within competitive boundaries. For the risks that lenders elect to accept, they will protect themselves by requiring multiple sources of repayment of their loan.

In recent years, bank lenders have been bogged down with an enormous amount of bureaucratic requirements to document loans, client dealings, and transaction records. Lenders are responsible for providing a paper trail of all their decisions for eventual review by internal and external auditors and by government regulators.

The Cost of Lending

The time and effort to pacify bank regulators and comply with federal banking rules have become a disproportionately large cost of doing business, interfering with the lender's capability to meet the needs of customers. In 1998, the Comptroller of the Currency estimated that 14 percent of an average bank's operating costs were directly attributable to the cost of compliance with various laws and regulations. And that was before the Gramm-Leach-Bliley Act, Sarbanes-Oxley Act, and the Patriot Act added many more layers of red tape on the banking industry!

Challenges to getting credit from a lender:

◆ **Lenders tend to avoid risks.**

◆ **Lenders require multiple repayment sources.**

◆ **Lenders must deal with the burden of regulatory oversight.**

◆ **Lenders have documentation responsibilities.**

When lenders seem too conservative, they are responding to conditions that support their position, which can contribute to your frustration. But keep in mind the following points.

First, the lender is in business, too. The lender has a responsibility to provide a financial return for its shareholders by obtaining funds from depositors or investors and then prudently lending these funds to responsible borrowers. Lenders must contend with the continually changing cost of funds and with competition from other regulated and nonregulated financial institutions. They must also produce a motivated and competent business development and support staff to create a portfolio of prudent loan investments in a rapidly changing economy. In addition, banks have the burden of federal or state regulators to manage.

Second, most loan officers spend their lending careers focused on evaluating and underwriting thousands of various business entities. They know a little bit about everything, but not much about any one thing. Because small business loan officers are usually not specialists, they will have only an outsider's limited perspective of the dynamics of the hundreds of small business industries. They will act single-mindedly to protect the interest of the institution that employs them.

There are many lenders who do an exemplary job of evaluating transaction proposals according to the guidelines that their institution has chosen. But many loan officers have had to deal with great ideas that went wrong and with individuals who tried to defraud them. All lenders have been subjected to exaggerations, ineptness, and imprudence on the part of borrowers they trusted. So don't blame them if they're cautious—it's born of experience.

Some lenders, particularly many large regional banks, simply have a very low tolerance for the risks of commercial loans to small businesses. Their policy is to accommodate opportunities in the market so long as their funds have absolutely minimal risk concerning repayment, which is tantamount to almost not lending to small businesses. If you're seeking loans, you should accept that position and confine your search primarily to smaller banks or nonbank lenders with a more accommodating posture toward the small business market.

When applying for a business loan, you'll be required to provide considerable information designed to educate the lender on every aspect of your business. The purpose of this requirement is to enable the lender to evaluate your business—its management, performance, products or services, and prospects for success. But, most importantly, the lender must be convinced that you understand your own business and industry, and that you are capable of using this knowledge to succeed in your chosen field.

Therefore, when you're preparing your loan application, you should focus on information that shows you're a good manager. Is the business earning money? How strong and reliable is the cash flow? What are the long-term trends of the financial results and how predictably will they continue?

This information protects you as well as the lender, and may prevent the business from borrowing into failure. Closer examination may give you notice of impending problems, providing time to change strategies and alter the business course if necessary.

The lender is an enterprise in the business of renting capital. Loans are made only in situations where the likelihood of being repaid is very high. By not being an investor, the lender avoids the risks often taken by small businesses or by venture capitalists. Lenders will always require more than one exit strategy to get the loan proceeds out of the business, usually involving collateral fully covering the loan and personal guaranties.

The protection a lender requires for a loan provides a safeguard for the borrower as well, in the form of a second opinion of the business. While lenders are seldom experts in the borrower's industry, many will have extensive general business experience that may be helpful to the borrower's situation.

> **The lender will ask for an immense volume of documentation without regard to the effort needed to provide it or its usefulness once obtained. Just get it and eliminate one reason the lender could turn down the request.**

How the Lender Views a Loan Application

Lenders earn the majority of their revenue from loan interest. The lender's primary job is to make and collect good loans. However, it is easy to lose money by extending loans in a haphazard way, so lenders have developed strategies to reduce the risks associated with loans.

Most lenders use a formal loan policy to define the types of loans and the method of administering them. These policies may be based on the particular expertise the lender employs or on the prevalent industries in the lender's geographic region. Lending money to finance oil and gas wells in west Texas requires a different expertise than lending against a wheat harvest in Kansas. Lenders will generally work with what they're familiar with in order to control the risk of their portfolio.

In a loan application the lender is seeking information. This information may be as trivial as the borrower's federal tax identification number or as detailed as a projection of how fast the inventory will turn over during the next two years on a given sales trajectory. All of this information helps the lender assess the business. How well the borrower has performed in the past is generally used as a fair indicator of how well the borrower will operate in the future.

The lender has to be convinced that borrowers understand not only their products and services but also other external factors that affect their businesses. The borrower must know not only the science of flipping hamburgers but also how traffic count on their street relates to sales.

A frequent complaint about lenders involves the time taken to evaluate a loan proposal. Although many lenders may seem inordinately slow, a thorough analysis of a business does require time. Mistakes are generally made by not taking enough time rather than taking too much. The loan officer's job performance will be graded more severely for loan losses than for loan successes.

Lenders may often seem disinterested in the critical time requirements of your loan request. But urgency does not relieve the loan officer of the inherent responsibilities of underwriting. When you demand an answer too soon, that answer is always going to be negative.

The better prepared you are with pertinent information, the faster the lender can address the loan request. Since the loan officer's job is not to organize your paperwork, delivering incomplete, disarranged information to the lender will slow down the review of any request or even cause the application to be rejected.

Your loan request is similar to a company's effort to sell a product. In many respects, the lender is investing in people and in the value of management. The personalities of the borrower and the lender must be compatible or the relationship will not last very long.

When listening to the comments of the loan officer, you need to be patient with the lender's lack of understanding, excitement, or enthusiasm. When the loan officer raises concerns, objections, or questions, respond directly with measured information specific to the question.

Although a commercial loan is a financial transaction, it is ultimately a relationship between lender and borrower. The key to success is the reciprocal comfort level between the people involved.

The Five Cs of Lending

Commercial lending is an art, not a science. Based on the information provided and confirmed, lenders have a responsibility to make lending decisions that are consistent with the parameters and limitations of their institution and with the principles of prudent lending. Stretching these principles beyond their limitations is not good business and carries enormous risks that are not worth taking for either party. Most denied loan requests lack a key ingredient that would make the lender confident that the funds could be repaid from the operations of the business.

Lenders test each loan application against five elementary lending criteria to determine the strength of the proposed deal. There is no magic formula or defined minimum standard of these criteria for the borrower to attain. In order to consider the loan request seriously, the lender has to be comfortable with the combined, subjective strength of these criteria.

If the borrower has an acute weakness in any of these criteria, that deficiency may or may not be overcome with a stronger position in one of the remaining categories. It depends on the relative strengths and weaknesses of the borrower as a whole.

In considering your loan application, the lender will look at

- ✧ Capacity
- ✧ Capital
- ✧ Collateral
- ✧ Credit
- ✧ Character

Capacity

Using this criteria, the lender attempts to determine whether you have the qualifications, wherewithal, or "capacity" to borrow the sum requested. Are you operating within the confines of your abilities? Or are you attempting to accomplish something beyond your limitations? Do your position in the market, experience in the industry, and track record in business make the lender confident that you will use the loan proceeds to produce the projected results?

The lender will carefully consider whether you demonstrate sufficient effort, resolve, ingenuity, and perseverance to manage and coordinate the tasks necessary to generate sufficient profits to repay the loan. If you've previously obtained and repaid a loan of only $20,000, that accomplishment alone does not automatically justify your capacity for a subsequent loan of $2 million in the same industry.

Further, lenders will evaluate your new loan request by reviewing the ability of your current operation to cover existing obligations. If your cash flow is barely able to manage today's business, lenders will avoid the risk of increasing the pressure on your funding merely on the hope that your new idea will succeed. If your present cash flow coverage for existing debt plus the proposed funding does not exceed 1.25 times more than current revenues, you are probably not going to be approved in a tight economy.

Sometimes borrowers fail to pass this test because they have more ambition than talent. The lender must draw these conclusions for better or for worse from the limited information provided within the application and from a few meetings with the borrower. A borrower's resume, past accomplishments, references, and ability to communicate a credible strategy, as well as a demonstration of prior financial successes, can contribute significantly to establishing the capacity to obtain a business loan.

Capital

When you ask lenders to be involved in a transaction, they must quantify the adequacy of your investment. The lender will always limit its leverage, or the amount of funding as a percentage of the total funding, in a deal and require you to have a meaningful amount of capital at risk. This limit will ensure that the owner is committed to the venture and reduces the lender's exposure to loss.

Capital is defined as the portion of the total business investment that you, the borrower, contribute. Different lenders have different requirements for the minimum capital contributions from borrowers in different situations. These varying capital requirements depend on the use of proceeds, the availability, reliability and value of collateral, and the history and nature of the business operation.

As a company's profits grow, the lender will watch its equity or net worth position. Lenders expect that the company's owners will permit some earnings to be retained by the business accordingly, rather than constantly drawing down all of the profits with dividends and distributions. While this equity-building process may cause you to pay more taxes and limit the growth of personal income, it is a reasonable expectation if you want to borrow money for your business to finance its

---

Ability versus Ambition

Lender will have to judge whether borrower has the capacity to succeed.

The business must always generate a portion of its capital funds internally—at any stage, it is smart for the business and required by the lender.

growth. The business must provide a measure of its own financing to provide a growing revenue base. This strategy makes good long-term sense for the business and for you.

Though generally unpopular with small business owners, the lender's requirement to contribute internally generated capital is significant since growth will present a new set of financial demands on the company. As sales grow, businesses invariably need new locations, new equipment, or additional working capital to absorb increasing receivable and inventory balances. Retaining these profits in the business will provide a vital part of this essential funding and reduces future borrowing requirements.

Collateral

This criteria quantifies your ability to support the loan request with tangible assets that will guarantee the loan by providing the lender with a secondary source of repayment. Lenders usually require that the loan be supported by assets valued on a discounted basis. This discounted value provides the lender with a safe margin to cover the time and costs of converting depreciated assets into cash, should that ever be necessary.

Typically, at a minimum the lender will secure the loan with your assets being financed. But sometimes the lender is requested to finance a sum reflecting a higher leverage than the discounted value of the financed assets. And sometimes the loan is for even more than the actual cost of the financed assets, because the ancillary costs involved with the acquisition become part of the requested loan proceeds. And always you are purchasing an asset that the lender could not readily liquidate without incurring expenses.

In these circumstances, lenders will require you to encumber additional assets that are not part of the transaction. This precaution ensures that the lender has a comfortable margin of value from which to be repaid if the business operations do not provide sufficient profits. The lender will discount the market value of the collateral assets so as to maintain an adequate excess margin to cover the loan balance at any point in your repayment schedule along with the costs projected to convert the collateral to cash.

The excess margin is required to ensure that asset values always equal or exceed the balance of the loan, commensurate with the schedule on which the loan principal is repaid and the period over which the asset is normally depreciated. As the borrower, you will generally be required to provide a minimum of 100 percent collateral coverage over the entire term of the loan.

Credit

The lender will always review your previous experience as a borrower. Studying your credit history discloses whether you or your busi-

By placing a lien on the borrower's assets, the lender ensures that they have more than one way to get a loan repaid in the event of default.

Lenders view how well the borrower's previous loans have been repaid as indicative of how well the next one will perform.

ness have paid previous borrowings as agreed. The credit report also discloses whether the business or you have (or have had) civil judgments awarded against them, unpaid tax liabilities, liens against their assets, or ever sought protection under bankruptcy proceedings.

While clearly not an absolute indicator of how well the business will perform in the future, this information tells the lender how you've performed in the past. If the information is negative, they may assume that you're unsuitable for an extension of credit. The report may also reveal that you have not overcome earlier difficulties. Poor performance with previous lenders may indicate that you don't take the responsibility of repayment seriously.

Character

Character may be the most important assessment the lender can make about the loan applicant. Regardless of the positive attributes of your capacity, capital, collateral, and credit, if you don't demonstrate integrity and appear trustworthy to the lender, they'll refuse any proposal you make.

Character is the most subjective criteria. Not only is it difficult to define, it is difficult to assess. There is no checklist available to guide the lender's sensitivity to quantifying someone's good character, particularly when the other party is a new acquaintance.

The lender has to observe and study you to evaluate your personal qualities and characteristics. The lender must watch for potential flaws in your attitude, conversation, perspective, or opinion about business ethics, responsibility, and commitment.

Your character is important because it reveals intent. If the loan officer senses that you are ambivalent toward fulfilling responsibilities under the proposed business deal, there is a character problem. The loan officer must believe that you embrace a moral obligation to repay the loan, superseding even the legal agreement to do so.

When a lender does not feel comfortable with your character as a borrower, this information generally will not be directly communicated to you. The loan request will often be denied for different reasons, because the loan officer may have difficulty defending a subjective decision without definitive proof. This ambiguity is part of the intangible matrix of underwriting commercial loans.

In the real world of our diverse society, it is sometimes difficult for persons of different origins to communicate effectively to each other. This situation can lead to misinterpretations of words and actions, making it hard for one ethnic group to become comfortable with another. These culture differences certainly permeate the lending environment. The borrower and lender must be sensitive to such differ-

> The lender must be confident of the borrower's intention and commitment to repay a loan. Character counts.

ences; they must invest extra time developing a business relationship to establish comfort and confidence in each other and explore language, expression, and cultural mores to find a common ground on which to establish a positive business relationship.

How Loans Are Approved

As financial institutions grow from hometown neighbors into national conglomerates, the ability of an individual to single-handedly approve a commercial loan has all but vanished. Loan authority—the internal lending capacity a financial institution delegates to an individual to approve loans—has virtually disappeared from any lending representative that interfaces directly with the borrower.

Most loan or business development officers simply manage the process to respond to customer requests and originate loans outside the lender's client base. When an attractive loan request is submitted, the loan officer compiles the borrower's application data, evaluates it for eligibility, and verifies the accuracy of this information. If the loan officer concludes that the borrower's request has merit and is consistent with the lender's loan criteria, the deal is forwarded on for formal consideration by someone with the authority to make an actual credit decision.

Depending on the size of the organization and the size of the loan request, sufficient credit authority to make a decision may go through several layers of credit review to render a final answer. The two primary structures used by most lenders to make credit decisions are the loan committee and designated chain of credit authority.

Loan committees are usually organized groups that meet regularly to consider various loan proposals offered by the lender's loan originators. The size of the lending institution usually determines the size and composition of the loan committee. In small-to-medium-sized institutions, the loan committee will be composed of the senior management, the senior credit officer, and often several outside directors.

The loan committee hears all proposals and discusses each one according to the merits of the information presented. The person sponsoring the loan application usually presents the loan request and defends it against any questions or critique from the committee. Although the presenter should be supportive of the transaction, this commitment may have its limitations.

The committee process can become somewhat political. Failure to support loan proposals introduced by other committee members can cost reciprocal support for one's own loan proposals. This system can

> Loan approval is rarely granted directly by the lender's representative to the client. But rather, getting a loan approved requires the successful presentation by the representative internally to the credit authority or loan committee on behalf of the borrower.

obviously be flawed with personalities, institutional hierarchies, and the dynamics of corporate ambitions.

With the designated chain of credit authority, experienced credit underwriters are vested with incremental levels of authority and are responsible to impartially evaluate and decide upon requests. There may be many levels of credit authority through which transactions must be approved, depending on the amount of money involved. Persons vested with credit authority are typically insulated from direct contact with borrowers and depend entirely on information filtered through the business development officer.

In too many lending institutions, the chances of deal success can be negatively affected by poor communication skills of the individual sponsoring the loan request. Loan requests stand a better chance of success if the business development person can effectively articulate the positive attributes of the transaction to the credit authority. Often, ineffective translation of a loan proposal slows down or eliminates viable opportunities in the loan approval rituals. This weakness in the process is bad for both the borrower and the lender.

Lenders rarely get fired for being too conservative, and it is always easier to find a reason not to make a loan. Sometimes people who hold credit authority will seem to actually compete with their peers to be the most conservative underwriter. In such cases, lending is unnecessarily restricted and the institution pays a heavy price—sluggish growth and the loss of potential income.

With most lenders, credit authority is vested among underwriters or committees that are not personally involved with originating the transaction. This process has advantages and disadvantages.

On the positive side, the lender is able to evaluate the proposed loan in a vacuum without the excitement, hype, and emotional appeal often created by the borrower to convince the lender to approve the loan. Arguably, lenders can make sound credit decisions without these other factors. Borrowers can be confident that an affirmative reply in such circumstances reflects the lender's recognition of a solid financial investment and commitment to a business relationship.

On the negative side, a laboratory approach to the borrower's loan request makes it difficult for the lender to consider legitimate contributing factors that may not be reflected on the financial ratios. Sometimes, extraneous factors off the balance sheet can compensate for a less than glorious financial history, when the lender is struggling through a review of the numbers. Success must start somewhere. A newer company may fail to earn money instantly for a variety of reasons; without an explanation that takes those reasons into account, lenders sometimes miss opportunities to invest in good loan transactions. Emerging companies may not have sterling financial histories, but may have a bright future based on market factors, new products, or premium locations not accounted for on its financial statement.

Getting SBA Approval

After the lender approves the credit request, the transaction may have to be forwarded to the SBA for additional credit review and for the loan guaranty request of the lender to be considered. The lender's status with the SBA determines the level of scrutiny under which the loan and guaranty requests are treated. There are three distinct lender classifications utilized by the SBA.

Preferred Lender Program (PLP)

This designation is the highest classification conferred on lenders by which the SBA delegates the credit approval and eligibility assessment to the lender. Using PLP, the lender notifies the agency of a loan approval granted under the program criteria and submits documentation verifying borrower eligibility. With this status, lenders are usually capable of completing the SBA authorization process in twenty-four hours.

Lenders qualify for PLP status by having an exceptional performance record with a steady loan volume, good payment currency on their SBA loans, and low default rates. These attributes confirm that PLP lenders are better equipped to lend through the SBA guaranty programs than less-experienced participating lenders.

Certified Lender Program (CLP)

This lender designation provides accelerated processing for 7(a) loan guaranty requests, but in return the lender agrees to perform more thorough financial analysis and assumes additional servicing responsibilities for the life of the loan.

Lenders qualify for CLP status by having a consistent performance record of good loan volume and low default rates. Utilizing a CLP lender ensures the borrower of faster processing by the SBA and suggests that the borrower is dealing with a more experienced SBA lender. Generally credit and guaranty requests under the CLP program are responded to within three days of submission.

SBA loan guaranty approval turnaround time (best case):

PLP lenders—
24 hours

CLP lenders—
3 days

GP lenders—
15 days target
(but may take up
to 45 days depending
on application)

General Program Lender (GP)

All chartered banks are eligible to participate in the SBA 7(a) Loan Guaranty Program upon entering into a formal agreement with the SBA setting forth their covenants to comply with the program regulations.

Most lenders participate under this classification of the program, which requires the lender to submit loan guaranty applications to one of the agency's two processing centers in Citrus Heights, CA, or Hazard, KY, for review on a first-come, first-served basis. Applications not completed according to agency requirements are screened out and returned to the lender for necessary modifications.

The SBA evaluates the transaction based solely on the merits demonstrated in the documentation prepared and submitted by the lender. SBA staff members do not visit or contact the applicant business. The participating lender is required to respond to any questions the SBA may have regarding the guaranty application and provide any additional information requested.

While each SBA district office is somewhat different, all offices are generally reasonable in their loan approval. Except for lenders with a poor track record with the SBA, the agency usually assumes that the lender has the capacity to make prudent credit decisions. However, the SBA will review the lender's credit decision for reasonableness and accuracy.

In addition, the SBA will seek to ensure that the borrower is eligible for participation and that the proposed transaction is an acceptable use of proceeds under the SBA regulations as defined by the program's standard operating procedures.

Approval of the loan request by the lender does not guarantee automatic SBA approval. But if the lender is well acquainted with the SBA program, and if the lender does not make any substantive errors in qualifying the proposal, the borrower can assume that SBA approval is probable.

What Is the Business of the Borrower?

One of the fundamental determinants of the lender's review of the business loan request is evaluating the industry in which the business operates. There are many inherent characteristics in various business categories that create risks for a lender. Many lenders will actually avoid loans to specific industries if the relative risks are perceived to be beyond what the lender is willing to accept.

Before seeking financing, you should understand how you will be viewed as an industry from the lender's perspective. For instance, small business lenders may feel more confident financing a convenience store that sells gasoline than financing an oil and gas exploration company. The risks associated with each of these businesses are dramatically different though both operate in related industries.

Positioning your business in a more positive light in its industry helps you by elevating the lender's perception and magnifies the appeal of the transaction. For example, instead of limiting a company's description as a "hamburger stand," broaden the depiction to define the business as a "food service provider."

This heightened characterization can effectively communicate the actual maneuverability of a business that owns a grill and a kitchen and has patrons regularly appearing to purchase food. As a food service provider, you verify that you have the flexibility to modify your business strategy and product mix according to unforeseen changes in the macro and micro economy. That is to say you can switch from hamburgers to chicken sandwiches if necessary to follow current trends in dining preferences or in response to something more drastic like an E. coli outbreak.

Knowing how lenders perceive and evaluate the borrower's industry and business can assist in planning the approach necessary to obtain credit. Where is the business within the life cycle of its industry? How will the business exploit its position and opportunity? This preparation will help you define the risks that the lender will have to address. Explain your strategy to reduce the obvious risks facing the lender. If you incorporate these concepts into the loan application, the loan will be easier to approve.

Lenders will evaluate your industry life cycle to determine whether your business is beyond its financial peak (such as manufacturing buggy whips) or whether your business is too new to be an acceptable risk (such as manufacturing battery-powered automobiles). Lenders prudently prefer to finance an industry that still has strong growth potential for the products or services it provides, certainly well before its marketing peak has occurred.

Lenders will be wary of you if your business attempts to serve too many specialized markets from a limited operating base. For example, a dry cleaner/car wash/convenience store/cappuccino bar with live music represents a unique business plan probably destined to fail. Such an operation could not have adequate focus, effective marketing, or cost efficiencies sufficient to generate regular profits. Define your business in specific terms so that the lender clearly understands what product or service you're trying to deliver.

Always present a clear definition of the business in the broadest terms possible, so to accentuate the company's role in the larger economy and flexibility of navigating the future.

How Is the Business Organized?

Business entities may be organized in one of four different legal forms, which may affect how a lender analyzes a loan request. Each business form has distinct legal characteristics and tax attributes. Selecting the appropriate form of business entity is an important decision and you should make it at the time you establish your company, preferably with the advice of an attorney and accountant. Each business form is eligible for financing assistance from the SBA.

Proprietorship

This form of business organization is for individuals who have chosen to sell products or provide services without the creation of a separate legal entity. The business is embodied in the efforts of the individual, who may use a distinctive business name or title, which is usually preceded with "d/b/a," which stands for "doing business as." The business name does not carry protection from duplication, and the individual carries full legal and financial liability for all acts of the enterprise. A proprietor's income is described as business income on Schedule C of the IRS form 1040.

Partnership

This form of business organization is for two or more individuals who choose to formalize their business relationship in a registered partnership. Partnerships may be defined as general or limited, each of which provides distinct definitions of the responsibilities of the individual partners.

In brief, general partnerships divide the responsibility of their activities equally among the partners on a prorated or percentage of ownership basis. Limited partnerships may limit the responsibility and liability of the limited partners for the activities of the partnership. Limited partnerships have a general partner who accepts the personal liability for the actions of the partnership.

Partnerships are usually taxed by prorating any gains or losses among the partners, as provided for in the partnership agreement. Consult an attorney for additional information.

Corporation

This form of business organization is a distinct business entity organized by one or more individual "shareholders," who have certain rights under the protection of the corporate entity. Generally, shareholders are not exposed to any of the liabilities of the corporation unless they purposely elect to personally guarantee specific liabilities of the corporation.

Four types of business organization:

✧ **Proprietorship—** doing business as an individual without protection of a legal entity.
✧ **Partnership—** sets forth ownership and responsibility of each partner and pass-through taxation based on percentage of ownership.
✧ **Corporation—** affords liability protection to owners, but may create second level of taxation.
✧ **Limited Liability Company—** combines best tax features of partnership and liability protection of a corporation, which may benefit newer companies.

The two primary forms of corporations are the "C" corporation and the "S" or "subchapter S" corporation. Although similar, these corporate forms differ in that an S corporation is intended to provide smaller companies (those with less than 100 shareholders) the advantage of lower tax obligations by passing profits or losses through to the shareholders on a pro rata distribution based on ownership percentage, similar to a partnership. In contrast, C corporation earnings are taxable and the shareholders are also taxed on any distributions or dividends paid out by the corporation. Distributions and dividends paid by C corporations to shareholders are not deductible from the corporation's taxable income, thereby causing the distributed monies to be taxed twice. Consult an attorney for additional information.

Limited Liability Company

In recent years, many states have created an entity known as a Limited Liability Company (LLC), which combines the favorable liability protection of a corporation and the favorable taxation attributes of a partnership. Owners of LLC interests are known as "members," and the controlling members may be described as "managing members."

LLCs have grown in popularity due to the flexibility they afford to members, particularly related to tax treatment and protection of all investors equally. These organizations are frequently used in the Eligible Passive Borrower ("EPB") structure described later in the book. One particular advantage LLCs have over subchapter S corporations is the ability to have a wider variety of ownership without restriction as to the number of investors.

Why Borrow Money?

Debt is expensive and represents an additional business risk for the company seeking to obtain it. In conjunction with the normal business risks associated with building new facilities or launching new products, borrowing money involves compounding a new layer of management— the lender. Your new lending partner may not be as patient as you want, particularly if your plans go awry. The lender may have higher expectations for the financial results than management or the market can deliver in a given time frame.

Before seeking to borrow funds you should carefully consider all the implications of debt because of the potential risk of not succeeding. Rather than maximizing your available leverage, consider the advantages of minimizing the level of borrowed monies in order to reduce your company's exposure to default.

Defining the exact reason your business requires a loan is the first step toward the application process. Qualified borrowers lose precious time and credibility by not establishing a succinct financing proposition to explain how much funding is needed and how it will be used. Unfocused borrowers make lenders nervous. It is impossible to feel confident about a business that wants to acquire a large, imprecise loan to sink into an enterprise without defining how it will be absorbed and what results are intended.

You must be able to specify exactly why you need financing and exactly what the intended impact will be on your enterprise. Failure to articulate this information reflects either unprepared or inadequate management, or the existence of another agenda in which the lender should not participate.

Time is frequently wasted by small business owners seeking to borrow money from the wrong lender through their failure to define the kind of money they need. Too many institutions reject these inappropriate applications without referring borrowers to the correct lender.

Understanding that certain lenders service specific types of loans can make the search for financing much easier and more successful. The six most common reasons for business owners to borrow money through the SBA guaranty programs are:

- ✧ Real estate loans
- ✧ Business "start-up" loans
- ✧ Equipment loans
- ✧ Business acquisition loans
- ✧ Working capital loans
- ✧ Refinancing existing debt

Each of these reasons requires distinctive underwriting and repayment terms.

Real Estate Loans

Whether for acquisition, construction, or the construction of improvements, real estate loans are the most popular loans for most small business lenders. These are typically long-term loans that on the average have the safest collateral available to lenders. SBA-guaranteed loans for commercial real estate provide up to a twenty-five year amortization of principal and interest.

Business "Start-up" Loans

Start-up financing is needed by some borrowers to supplement their own equity contributions when launching a new business. Most lenders require the borrower to have strong collateral or other compensating factors to justify the risks involved with this kind of financing. Start-up money is hard to obtain if the borrower cannot supply a 25 to 35 percent personal cash contribution to the total financing needed.

SBA financing for start-up businesses can be amortized over a long term, based on the use of loan proceeds, as described in other loan purposes discussed in this section. As the most difficult financing to obtain, start-up loans can test the new business owner's resolve to create a new business.

Equipment Loans

Equipment loans are term loans that provide funding to purchase equipment assets. They are usually repaid over a term of no more than the expected useful life of the equipment. SBA loans for equipment usually offer a ten-year amortization of principal and interest, although loans may be amortized for up to fifteen years for certain major equipment assets if that term is consistent with the useful life of the asset.

Business Acquisition Loans

Funds from an SBA-guaranteed lender can be borrowed to purchase an existing business. Such acquisitions can be either "asset" purchases or "stock" purchases, depending on the legal agreement of the buyer and seller. The leverage on these loans will vary widely among lenders, and will also depend on the targeted business's particular industry. The willingness of a lender to finance business acquisitions will rest primarily on the prior success of that entity and the ability of the borrower to provide a secondary source of repayment if the business is not laden with substantive capital assets. Unless real estate is being acquired as part of the transaction, these loans can only be amortized over a maximum term of ten years.

Working Capital Loans

Monies used by the business as operating cash to produce profitable revenues is called "working capital." So long as the borrower can provide assets as collateral, loans can usually include funds for working capital, which are repaid over a long term. Loans for this purpose are essentially a substitute for capital and provide time for businesses to

Have a well-thought-out plan before applying for a business loan, including how much is needed, how it will be used, and precisely how it will create enough profits to repay the loan in a reasonable time.

accumulate profits to provide for their own working capital. SBA loans for working capital are amortized over a maximum of seven years.

Refinancing Existing Debt

SBA funds can be used to refinance existing debt for businesses, so long as the original loan proceeds were used for eligible purposes, and the previous debt was extended on "unreasonable terms." Defining "unreasonable terms" generally implies that the term of the loan was too short, the pricing too high, or the collateral coverage was unnecessarily overreaching.

To determine whether certain business debt can be refinanced, the lender must establish that the new SBA-guaranteed loan could be used to lower the existing debt service by an aggregate 10 percent from the existing repayment schedule(s). Any loan with a balloon payment shorter than its amortization is automatically eligible.

So far as excessive collateral, the lender must judge as to whether too much collateral was required at the time that the original loan was extended, without regard to values based on asset appreciation or the ensuing reduction of debt.

Adjusting the Borrower's Attitude

You'll be better prepared to negotiate a debt relationship when you recognize the dynamics of the loan application process and set your expectations accordingly. Approaching the process with a realistic attitude enhances your loan application and increases your chances of success.

You might prepare yourself for the worst possible scenario, summed up in an old banker's axiom called the "Golden Rule: "Those with the gold make the rules." During the application process, you'll provide an enormous volume of information, answer many laborious questions, and be scrutinized over trivial details of your company and your personal financial affairs. This repetitive and tedious process is not intended to target you. Rather it's a necessary process required to define the lender's risk.

After all, you're requesting a service that requires subjective qualification and objective quantification. One business (you) is asking another business (the lender) for a non-equity investment of time and funding. The application process, by necessity, is arduous but meaningful. Most lenders evaluate hundreds if not thousands of loan requests every year.

Plan ahead and initiate the loan request weeks if not months before you will need the money. By rushing the process at the last minute, you will dampen the lender's enthusiasm about the loan request and create suspicions that you're distorting or concealing facts. Even if you're approved for a loan, missteps in the application or approval process can weaken your relationship with the lender from the beginning, which may haunt you later.

Information is a powerful tool for supporting the business loan application. Your understanding of your industry, competition, market, and even the greater economy can support the representations you may be depending on to boost your loan request. This pertinent data will make the lender more confident about your capability to repay the loan.

The lender's frontline business developer with whom you directly interface may not possess the same business acumen and often will not have as much business experience as you. But the lender has chosen this person to perform an important screening process for eliminating the numerous proposals that are undefined or unrealistic.

Recognizing the difficulty of the lender's role does not ease the effort that you may be required to put in to educate a novice lender, but you will benefit from approaching the relationship understanding the dynamics of the lender's role. You need cooperation and patience throughout this process to successfully obtain a loan.

Researching the Lending Market

The best source of information to find small business financing is definitely not creative TV advertising, clever radio ads, or glossy magazine ads.

A practical rule is that the lenders with the fanciest advertising may be the most difficult lenders from which to get a loan. Why do the largest banks spend so much money on advertising when they already have a high public profile and their branches seem to be everywhere? One reason is that, in comparison to their smaller competitors, these larger banks have more stringent credit standards and they turn down a higher percentage of loan applications. Therefore, these lenders need a larger stream of applications in order to find the loan requests they will approve.

How should you find a lender that is interested in small businesses? Research the market for lenders that address the small business sector. One good place to start this research is at the website of the nearest SBA District Office. A complete list of SBA District Offices is included in the appendix.

The SBA can provide contact information for the local lenders that participate in the SBA loan guaranty program.

You should interview the commercial loan officers from several local lenders to determine if they make small business loans. Prior to applying for a loan, determine if the lender would seriously consider the specific kind of transaction you're seeking. Which lender would be most likely to favorably consider your loan proposal?

Be aware that some lenders may not be in optimum financial condition. Following the investment market collapse in 2008 and the residential and commercial property bubble, many banks are not performing well, and many have already failed. While poor management, bad investments, and unsound business practices accounted for some of these failures, others were just unable to counteract the effects of problems among their particular client base.

There are many sources of information to learn about the financial health of a particular bank. One independent source is Bauer Financial Reports, Inc., which monitors the performance of banks and rates them according to their financial condition and performance. Their "star" reports are available to the public by visiting their website at *www .bauerfinancial.com.*

The Federal Deposit Insurance Corporation (FDIC) is another excellent source of information. On their website (*www.fdic.com*) anyone can determine if the bank is under any kind of regulatory action or can review the bank's financial statement ("Call Report") posted quarterly.

Getting a Second Opinion

It is always a good idea to test the loan application on your closest advisors before submitting it to a lender for review. Sometimes in the rush to complete the voluminous set of documents, you can lose sight of errors in providing support information or omissions in detailing plans and projections. Having other parties review this data before it is submitted to the lender can reduce your chances of mistakes and hopefully eliminate embarrassing inaccuracies.

If your business is a larger one, you may have staff that can be assigned the task to review specific sections of the information to proof the work for errors or omissions. For example, the marketing department can review the presentation of the company's marketing plan, while the operations department can review a description of the company's production details. This exercise will also separate you from

Banker's Golden Rule:

Those with the gold make the rules.

The best source of SBA-guaranteed loans is generally from smaller ($100 million–$400 million assets) community banks and SBA-licensed small business lending companies (SBLCs) that really specialize in SBA lending.

the documents for a few days, improving your focus, and ensuring the clarity of important details.

After each section has been reviewed with the input from each appropriate department, the executive officers responsible for sourcing these funds should review the entire set of data one last time for thoroughness and accuracy.

If a business does not have people in positions capable of providing this level of review, you might ask your company's CPA, business advisor, or loan consultant to review the application information. *Always* get a second opinion on the proposal before it leaves your office.

Giving the Application a Trial Run

In its formative stages test the application in a preliminary interview with a lender. This exploratory meeting is not intended to establish a banking relationship between you and the lender; rather use it to define general parameters of the proposed loan.

In these discussions, talk (not write) about the proposed loan, regarding its size, term, use of proceeds, and collateral. In response, the lender will indicate the feasibility and limitations of the loan transaction.

Since this preliminary discussion is designed to assist with preparation of a final proposal, you don't need to select the most appropriate lender. Nor should you leave any written information in the lender's files that may affect how the lender would structure the proposed loan or that could be compared to an amended application.

If there are any special circumstances that you would need to explain or that would require additional attention, save this information for the end of the discussion. Keep the conversation positive: how the lender would approach the deal and what could be done. Once the potential for a deal is determined, you can introduce other conditions to determine how the lender can work with or around them.

Because this exercise is intended to be a trial run to access the lending community, avoid committing to a particular loan request until you learn how the lender reacts. Thereby you'll gain insight and information about changes that would strengthen a particular application strategy.

Expect that lenders will understandably refuse to be specific about their willingness to finance the transactions until you provide more information in writing. This reaction need not eliminate a lender from the prospect list. Instead it should prompt you to interview different lenders from whom information might be obtained.

Have advisors review a loan application for a second opinion to ensure accuracy, completeness, and focus before submitting it to a lender.

Timing Is Important

To maximize the impact of your presentation of a loan proposal, smart scheduling is important and can be based on calculated criteria. Make an appointment to see the lender, rather than arriving unexpectedly. Without discussing the proposal over the phone, tell the loan officer the purpose of the appointment and how much time you will need to present the loan request. A prepared borrower needs a minimum of an hour of the loan officer's full attention without interruption. Timing the presentation is essential to maximizing its impact and increasing your chances of approval.

Most loan officers appreciate this planning in order to reserve sufficient time to focus on what you want to discuss. Requesting an appointment will communicate that you are serious about the presentation and that you expect the loan officer's undivided attention.

When setting an appointment with a loan officer, recognize that some meeting times can be better than others. For example, if the lender is a bank, the first and fifteenth days of the month may be disadvantageous if the lending officer also has other banking responsibilities to support the bank lobby traffic. Those two days are the busiest days of the month for retail banks, due to payroll deposits, government check cashing, and benefit payment receipts. The lender could be constantly interrupted with frivolous questions and check approvals for other clients.

Avoid Mondays and Fridays. Loan officers are often subjected to more demands on these days, due to the natural interruption of workflow caused by the weekend. They seem to have more continuous control of their time Tuesday through Thursday. Within this time frame, morning meetings are more favorable than afternoon meetings.

Although many people are impressed when treated to lunch by a banker, the invitation does not indicate any elevation of the borrower's desirability to the lender. In addition, lunch meetings are usually too congested with the distractions of loud noise, food service, and the lack of privacy to get the full attention you need for the loan proposal. Trying to share any written information in that scenario is problematic. At this stage of a loan proposal, you need the quiet and seclusion of an office.

It is possible to determine—and avoid—times when lenders are being audited by their regulators. During the audit, which usually lasts from two to three weeks, the lender is often deluged with information requests from these auditors, which could make this period a difficult one for you to get the lender's full attention.

Practice makes perfect. Trying the draft proposal out verbally on different lenders increases the borrower's confidence and provides information about various policies, practices, and preferences of the local lending market.

Of course, the primary determinant of when the applicant can meet with the loan officer is when your business permits. Important duties at the business must be the primary and controlling priorities.

Projecting the Revenues, Expenses, and Income

Financing is based on a simple principle: Lenders always require the borrower to agree that the loan will be repaid. At the time the loan request is submitted, the lender will evaluate your ability to repay the loan with funds generated by the business. This analysis is integral to your ability to get a loan.

The lender will expect you to provide realistic projections about how the proceeds of the loan will be invested to generate revenues for your business. Further, you should identify the costs the business will incur to produce these revenues, and calculate the resulting profits from which you will repay the loan.

The integrity and reasonableness of these projections are often the most important factors in granting loan approval. In constructing these financial projections, you must be honest not only with the lender but also with yourself; representing unrealistic figures is unethical and self-defeating.

The lender is usually not an expert in your field and may not recognize exaggerated revenue projections or inadequate expense estimates. Failure to be prudent and exercise good judgment can place the company and your own financial stability at risk if you borrow money that cannot be paid back as scheduled.

Financial projections take into account the estimated operating results of the business for a defined period in the future. Most lenders require operating results projected for a minimum of two years. It is useful to project the first twelve months on a month-to-month basis, in order to demonstrate the immediate effects of the borrowed money on the current business cash cycle. Projecting financial results beyond twenty-four months is difficult, due to multiple factors and economic cycles that you can't anticipate or easily predict.

In developing the operating projections, use a model that resembles the business profit/loss statement (sometimes referred to as a pro forma) and insert the estimated figures accordingly. The starting date of the projections should coincide with the date of your next fiscal year.

Written details of significant revenue sources, COGS, and major expenses are very desirable and necessary to explain and substantiate the estimates. Rather than overloading this worksheet with rows

> **Meet with the lender when they can most likely give prospective borrowers unhurried, uninterrupted time.**

of itemized minutia, the projection model will be easier to read if you streamline it by combining the many small detailed accounts into larger revenue and expense categories.

For example, the many different expenses of hiring, compensating, motivating, providing benefits to, and paying taxes for employees should be projected as "Salaries" rather than detailed into several line items. This larger, general category would include all salary related expenses such as payroll taxes, unemployment insurance premiums, employee benefits, employee insurance costs, payroll processing costs, and other direct expenses attributable to the employment costs of the business.

You can detail specific accounts of the "Salaries" expense category in schedules, which can be readily found if requested. Meanwhile they won't distract from the main information. This exercise helps you organize information better and keeps the lender focused on the big picture.

Providing the lender with line-by-line calculations of the expected revenues or expenses could create many unnecessary, extraneous questions, as well as confuse the lender as to exactly what your revenue or costs are. You don't want the lender to micromanage the business or to lose sight of the overall projected results.

Producing this projection model will assist in your planning and subject the proposal to a financial litmus test. The most important guideline is to be realistic. You need to demonstrate confidence in the projected revenues and costs necessary to produce business income.

A simple profit/loss projection model is shown in Illustration 3-A. It is easy to use this model to estimate your results by adding the specific revenue and expense estimates. If you create this in a spreadsheet program like Excel, calculations can be automated and the projection worksheet becomes a powerful tool for the business.

Most projection models include these categories:

Income

Sales/Revenues—Monies expected to be received by the business in payment for services provided or products sold to its customers.

Cost of Goods Sold (COGS)—Expenses that represent a direct cost associated with producing or acquiring the products or services sold by the business. (If the borrower is not sure about which expenses to include here, consult the company's accountant.)

Gross profit—The result of subtracting the COGS from the Sales/Revenues.

Realistic, detailed revenue/expense projections will define the feasibility of a loan proposal for the borrower and lender.

Expenses

Salaries—Labor costs (except the direct labor cost included in the COGS), FICA tax payments, unemployment taxes, benefit insurance, other employee benefits, and other costs incurred by the business to acquire labor.

Management salaries—Optional entry to define the labor expense of the company's management. Lenders are often interested in how well the borrower plans to reward management and owners.

Administrative—Costs associated with managing the operation, such as office supplies, petty cash, refreshments, light equipment maintenance, copier supplies, and other small expenses associated with the administrative functions of the borrower.

Advertising—Costs of marketing and advertising the business, such as brochures, newspaper ads, website ads, radio and television commercials, yellow pages ads, corporate gifts, direct mail, telemarketing, and other promotion efforts.

Bank fees—Costs of banking fees (except interest on loans). Typically, a business that might incur large bank fees is one that issues a large number of checks, requires a significant volume of cash inventory, makes frequent deposits, or utilizes a merchant account for credit card processing. This line item should be used only if the estimated expenses are expected to exceed 3 percent of the company's total expenses. Otherwise, they should be included in administrative expenses.

Depreciation/Amortization—Noncash expenses based on the useful life of capital assets or the acceptable amortization period recommended by the CPA. These expenses affect the profitability of the business, but not the cash flow. The sum of these entries is added back to the company's net income when projecting the operation's cash flow.

Entertainment/Travel—Costs of entertaining prospective clients, traveling for any business nature, such as sales calls, service calls, or trade conferences, or other general purposes not attributable to the direct production of income. This line item should be used only if the estimated expenses are expected to exceed 3 percent of the company's total expenses. Otherwise, they should be included in administrative expenses.

Equipment—Costs of purchasing light equipment assets that are acquired with the entire expense recognized in the same year, or equipment leasing costs. Equipment maintenance and repair expenses should be included in this sum. This line item should be

Profit/Loss Projections

Company _____   Date _____

	YEAR 1	% sales	YEAR 2	% sales
Total Revenues	_____	100%	_____	100%
Cost of Goods Sold	_____	_____	_____	_____
Gross Profit (Revenues minus COGS)	_____	_____	_____	_____
Expenses				
Salaries	_____	_____	_____	_____
Management Salaries	_____	_____	_____	_____
Administrative	_____	_____	_____	_____
Advertising	_____	_____	_____	_____
Bank Fees	_____	_____	_____	_____
Depreciation	_____	_____	_____	_____
Entertainment & Travel	_____	_____	_____	_____
Equipment Rental	_____	_____	_____	_____
Insurance	_____	_____	_____	_____
Postage & Courier	_____	_____	_____	_____
Professional Fees	_____	_____	_____	_____
Rent/Occupancy (including utilities)	_____	_____	_____	_____
Telephone	_____	_____	_____	_____
Miscellaneous	_____	_____	_____	_____
Miscellaneous	_____	_____	_____	_____
Miscellaneous	_____	_____	_____	_____
Other	_____	_____	_____	_____
Other	_____	_____	_____	_____
Interest—Senior Debt	_____	_____	_____	_____
Interest—Sub. Debt	_____	_____	_____	_____
Earnings Before Taxes (Gross Profit minus total expenses)	_____	_____	_____	_____
ADD BACK:				
Interest Expense	_____		_____	
Depreciation	_____		_____	
Cash For Debt Service (earnings + interest + depreciation + amortization)	_____		_____	
Total Annual Debt Payments (interest + principal loan payments)	_____		_____	
Debt Service Coverage ("cash for debt service" divided by "total debt payments")	_____ x		_____ x	

ILLUSTRATION 3-A

used only if the estimated expenses are expected to exceed 3 percent of the company's total expenses. Otherwise, they should be included in administrative or miscellaneous expenses.

Insurance—Expenses for general liability insurance, property and casualty insurance, auto insurance, workers' compensation, and any other insurance expenses of the business (except employee benefit insurance). This line item should be used only if the estimated expenses are expected to exceed 3 percent of the company's total expenses. Otherwise, they should be included in administrative expenses.

Postage/Courier—Costs of postage, postage equipment, courier fees (UPS, FedEx, etc.), and special handling costs (such as certified mail). This line item should be used only if the estimated expenses are expected to exceed 3 percent of the company's total expenses. Otherwise, they should be included in administrative expenses.

Professional fees—Costs of any professional services anticipated for the business, such as legal, accounting, tax, information technology, management consulting, etc.

Rent/Occupancy—Costs of occupancy, including rent, CAM (Common Area Maintenance) charges, utilities, real estate taxes, repairs, facility maintenance, and any other expenses associated with the business premises.

Telephone/Internet—Costs of the basic telephone service, long distance, answering services, communication equipment rental, Internet service, DSL, cable, WiFi, and any other expenses related to providing telephone or Internet communications for the business.

Miscellaneous—Various costs that are not defined in the other categories but that must be recognized. This entry should be relatively small. If it exceeds 7 percent of the expenses projected, then additional categories should be introduced for any group of costs that total comparably with the other categories used in the projections.

Total operating expenses—Total the sum of projected expenses.

Operating Profit—Gross profit minus total expenses also referred to as Earnings Before Interest and Taxes (EBIT).

Interest—Interest costs expected to be incurred for all debt balances during the period. Be sure to use the actual interest rate and loan amortization schedule for all balances, and calculate the proposed financing according to the terms requested.

Income taxes—Federal and state income taxes, based on expected profits. (Note: Most lenders are not interested in income tax projections, due to many variables that make reliable estimates difficult to calculate.)
Net Profit—Operating profit less interest and income taxes.

Projecting Cash Flow

Income projections will provide you with the expected profits (or losses) of your business. The next step is to develop a cash flow projection.

In the traditional cash flow model, the noncash expenses (depreciation and amortization) and interest expenses are added to the company's net profit. This calculation provides a quick summary of the total cash available to service the projected debt. This figure is derived as follows:

Net Profit + Depreciation & Amortization + Interest Expenses = Gross Cash Flow

With this calculation, the lender will be primarily interested in determining the ratio of your available cash to the total debt payments required to make payments on the proposed loan. The *Debt Service Coverage Ratio* is calculated as follows:

$$\frac{\text{Cash Flow Available for Debt Service}}{\text{Total Principal \& Interest Payments}}$$

This ratio measures a company's ability to meet its scheduled obligations and to service its debt with its projected cash flow. By comparing your cash available to the required debt payments, this ratio indicates how well you are managing your existing debt and your capacity to take on new loans. If this ratio is less than 1.0x, then you are not projected to have sufficient cash to meet your existing or projected payments.

Most lenders require this ratio to be a minimum of 1.25x, or higher, depending on their loan policy and the borrower's situation. If the cash flow projections do not result in an adequate Debt Service Coverage Ratio, you are likely suggesting a loan that you cannot repay. At this point of planning, you will need to review all of your revenue and expense estimates. If you cannot reconcile these figures according to your best estimate of your cash flow, then you will have to reduce the loan request to a level that can be serviced by the profits produced with a smaller loan.

A useful management tool to incorporate this level of evaluation into your business planning is to develop a month-to-month cash flow projection model, which tracks revenues and expenses in monthly increments. The traditional cash flow model discussed above does not account for accounts receivable (credit sales), trade accounts (credit purchases), and other variables that will affect the company's cash flow.

Using a month-to-month pro forma will enable you to account for all such variables and to be more accurate in predicting the cash flows of the business cycle. A detailed legend is necessary for explaining all of your assumptions in developing the pro forma.

Illustration 3-B shows a commonly used cash flow projection model. It is easy to modify this model to match your own financial reporting simply by changing the revenue or expense entries to match your company's financial statement. Other variables that have an impact on your cash flow should also be included.

One more detail to know about cash flow evaluations and the bank's evaluation of your likely ability to repay a loan priced with variable rate funding: The bank underwriter will "shock test" your cash flow numbers to take into account how your historic and projected results would perform if your interest rate increased 1 to 2 percent. While they probably won't expect that you could cover your debt with a 1.25x ratio after adding 2 percent to your interest rate, they may have a baseline limit they will watch for, like say a 1.0x ratio after the shock.

Other Financial Analysis

Lenders may use a number of financial ratios in analyzing your financial position to determine the relative financial strength of the business. They use various calculations to measure the liquidity (cash on hand compared to cash required), leverage (ratio of equity financing to debt financing), operating (profitability), and coverage (funding available to service future debt obligations—shown above), of the business in comparison to a composite of other businesses of similar size in your industry.

Depending on your financial acumen and the depth of analysis you are willing to perform, you yourself can calculate these ratios on your company's financial results to get a better understanding of how the operation is performing from several angles. This insight will be instructive as to what reaction you should expected from the lender's evaluation of the financing proposal. Inclusion of this analysis in any proposal would be a positive demonstration that your business has a good handle on its financial management and helpful to the loan proposal by accentuating the financial strength of the business.

The most commonly used financial ratios to evaluate small companies are discussed below with an explanation of how they are calculated and what information they provide. There are no right or wrong ratios; these figures measure the borrower's financial position in relative terms, which can be compared to other businesses. Most lenders use the Risk

Management Association (RMA) Annual Statement Studies as a guideline for industry norms in comparatively analyzing financial ratios.

The RMA Studies gather voluntary submissions of financial statements from thousands of businesses in every industry, as defined by the NAICS. These financial statements are compiled and averaged to determine the median and mean of operating standards for every industry each year. These results are published by NAICS category in order to provide information about the relative financial condition and performance of each industrial sector.

The Annual Statement Studies offer business owners a comparative analysis of how their business measures up to its industry peers. Nonmembers can purchase them from RMA at their website. Go to: *www.rmahq.org/RMA/RMAUniverse/ProductsandServices/RMABookstore/ Downloads/StatementStudiesSIC/*.

Liquidity Ratios

Liquidity ratios refer to measurements of a company's current assets to meet its current liabilities when due. Evaluating these components of the balance sheet will help you understand the adequacy of working capital at the current level of sales, and predict how your business will fare with changes in revenues.

Current Ratio

The current ratio is a rough measurement of a company's ability to pay its current liabilities with its current assets. "Current" refers to company assets that are either in cash or will be converted to cash within twelve months, or company liabilities that must be paid within twelve months. The ratio measures the relative strength or weakness of the working capital outlook, which is the result of dividing the current assets by the current liabilities.

With a 1.0x ratio, the business has exactly the amount of cash it needs to cover its liabilities. A higher ratio means the business has excess cash available to meet its liabilities over the next twelve months. The composition and quality of current assets are critically important to understanding the liquidity of a business. This ratio is calculated as follows:

$$\frac{\textbf{Total Current Assets}}{\textbf{Total Current Liabilities}}$$

Quick Ratio (Acid Test)

Dubbed the "acid test," the quick ratio provides a more strenuous test of liquidity, based on existing cash assets and cash equivalents, which will quickly be converted to cash in the current period. For most

Monthly Cash Flow Projection

Company _____ Date _____

	MONTH											
	1	2	3	4	5	6	7	8	9	10	11	12
1. Cash on Hand												
Receipts												
2. Sales Revenues												
3. Other Revenues												
4. Other Cash Injection												
5. Cash Available (Add lines 1–4)												
Payments												
6. Purchases/COGS												
7. Salaries												
8. Mgt. Salaries												
9. PR Taxes/Benefits												
10. Administration												
11. Advertising												
12. Bank Fees												
13. Depreciation												
14. Entertain./Travel												
15. Equipment Rental												
16. Insurance												
17. Postage/Courier												
18. Professional Fees												
19. Rent/Occupancy												
20. Telephone												
21. Miscellaneous												
22. Miscellaneous												
23. Other												
24. Other												
25. Interest (Sen. Debt)												
26. Interest (Sub. Debt)												
Subtotal Payments (Add lines 6–26)												
27. Principal Pyt (Sen.)												
28. Principal Pyt (Sub.)												
29. Total Cash Payments (Add lines 6–28)												
Cash Remaining (Line 5 minus line 29)												

ILLUSTRATION 3-B

businesses, this definition means that accounts receivable can be used in this calculation but inventory cannot. If the resulting ratio is significantly lower than the current ratio, it probably means that the business is relying heavily on the conversion of inventory to liquidate current liabilities, rather than converting previous sales to cash.

This ratio is calculated as follows:

$$\frac{\text{Cash \& Equivalents \& Receivables}}{\text{Total Current Liabilities}}$$

Sales/Receivables Ratio

The sales/receivables ratio measures the number of times the accounts receivable "turn over" during the year. If a company's ratio equals twelve, that means that the receivables turn over twelve times a year, or are fully paid about every thirty days. A higher ratio is desirable because it means that there is a shorter time between the sale and cash collection. If a company's ratio is smaller than the rest of its industry, then the quality of the company's receivables or the company's credit and collection policies may need to be examined.

Warning!

This ratio may not be a good analytical tool for companies with a high seasonal fluctuation of sales or those that have a high proportion of cash sales to total sales. It also only measures receivables to net sales at one point during the course of the fiscal year. Reviewing this ratio over a period of several months and determining an average figure is a more effective way to track this ratio with more confidence.

This ratio is calculated as follows:

$$\frac{\text{Net Sales}}{\text{Trade Receivables (net)}}$$

Day's Receivables

The day's receivables ratio defines the average number of days required to collect an account receivable. Higher ratios (25+ days) are indicative that the company's clients are dragging out payments and more likely to become past due (depending on terms offered). This ratio may be indicative of the control a company is able to exercise over clients with its credit and collections policy, or the quality of its accounts.

This ratio is calculated as follows:

$$\frac{365}{\textbf{Sales/Receivables Ratio}}$$

COGS/Inventory

The COGS/inventory ratio measures the number of times the inventory "turns over" during the year. If a company's ratio equals twelve, that means that the inventory turns over twelve times a year, or about every thirty days. A higher ratio is desirable and indicates that the inventory is turning over more often, which usually means the company has better liquidity and/or good merchandising. If a company's ratio is smaller than the rest of its industry's, then the company's inventory may not be selling, may be obsolete, or may be overstocked.

Warning!

This ratio may not be a good analytical tool for companies with a high seasonal fluctuation of sales. It also only measures inventory to cost of sales at one point during the fiscal year. Reviewing this ratio over a period of several months and determining an average figure is a more effective way to track this ratio with more confidence.

This ratio is calculated as follows:

$$\frac{\textbf{Cost of Sales}}{\textbf{Inventory}}$$

Day's Inventory

The day's inventory ratio expresses the COGS/inventory ratio in the average number of days required to use the inventory on hand. This ratio may be indicative of the quality of inventory management or the quality of the inventory.

This ratio is calculated as follows:

$$\frac{365}{\textbf{COGS/Inventory Ratio}}$$

COGS/Payables

The COGS/payables ratio measures the number of times the company's trade payables "turn over" during the year. The larger this ratio, the shorter the time between the company's purchase of goods and subsequent payment. If the company's ratio is lower than the industry average, then there may be a liquidity problem causing the company to pay its bills slowly. Lower ratios also may be caused by generous sales terms provided by suppliers or disputed invoices.

Warning!

This ratio may not be a good analytical tool for companies with a high seasonal fluctuation of sales. It also only measures one day's payables to cost of sales. Reviewing this ratio over a period of several months and determining an average figure is a more effective way to track this ratio with more confidence.

This ratio is calculated as follows:

$$\frac{\text{COGS}}{\text{Trade Payables}}$$

Leverage Ratios

Leverage ratios refer to measurements of the protection a company's assets provide for the obligations held by its creditors. Higher leveraged firms reflect a heavier reliance on external financing. Evaluating these components of the balance sheet will help you understand the vulnerability of your company to a downturn or its future access to external financing.

Fixed/Worth

The fixed/worth ratio compares the size of a business's investment in fixed assets (land, building, and equipment) relative to its tangible net worth. By measuring the portion of equity that is employed in fixed investments, a lender can evaluate how easy (or difficult) it will be to convert a company's capital to cash if necessary. Therefore, a lower ratio indicates that more of the net worth is represented in more current assets.

This ratio is calculated as follows:

$$\frac{\text{Net Fixed Assets}}{\text{Tangible Net Worth}}$$

Debt/Worth

The debt/worth ratio compares the size of a business's tangible capital financing (internal) to a lender's debt financing (external). By determining the relative investment that the owners provide in relation to the company's debt, the ratio defines the degree of risk that the lender assumes. The larger the ratio, the more risk that is assumed externally.

This ratio is calculated as follows:

$$\frac{\text{Total Liabilities}}{\text{Tangible Net Worth}}$$

Operating Ratios

Operating ratios refer to measurements of management's performance through the production of profits.

Percentage of Profit Before Taxes/Total Assets

The percentage of profits before taxes/total assets ratio measures the pretax financial return against total assets, which reflects the efficiency with which management is employing the company's assets to produce a profit.

Warning!

This ratio may not be a good analytical tool for companies with heavily depreciated assets, large amounts of intangible assets, or unusual fluctuations of revenue or expenses. It also only measures one period's profit to total assets. Reviewing this ratio over several periods and determining an average figure is a more effective way to track this ratio with more confidence.

This ratio is calculated as follows:

$$\frac{\text{Profit Before Taxes}}{\text{Total Assets} \times 100}$$

Percentage of Profit Before Taxes/Tangible Net Worth

The percentage of profits before taxes/tangible net worth ratio measures the pretax financial return against tangible net worth, which reflects the efficiency with which management is employing the company's capital to produce a profit.

Warning!

This ratio may not be a good analytical tool for companies with heavily depreciated assets, large amounts of intangible assets, or unusual fluctuations of revenue or expenses. It also only measures one period's profit to tangible net worth. Reviewing this ratio over several periods and determining an average figure is a more effective way to track this ratio with more confidence.

This ratio is calculated as follows:

$$\frac{\text{Profit Before Taxes}}{\text{Tangible Net Worth}} \times 100$$

Sales/Total Assets

The sales/total assets ratio measures the company's revenues against its total assets, which reflects the efficiency with which management is employing the company's assets to produce revenues.

Warning!

This ratio may not be a good analytical tool for companies with heavily depreciated assets or labor-intensive operations. It also only measures one period's sales to total assets. Reviewing this ratio over several periods and determining an average figure is a more effective way to track this ratio with more confidence.

This ratio is calculated as follows:

$$\frac{\text{Net Sales}}{\text{Total Assets}}$$

"Figures never lie, so figure a lot of liars."

—Unknown

A problem with many of these ratios is that they may be skewed by business circumstances that distort the results. It is always a good idea to determine the root cause of any numbers that do not compare favorably with industry standards or the past trends of the business.

Be mindful (and remind the lender) that there are no good or bad ratios; they are always relative. Even if your financial performance is very impressive, the company may not compare well with the RMA results because of extraordinary local reasons that cannot be reflected in the study. These studies alone should not determine whether the loan proposal is approved or rejected. The information is useful for understanding how a company compares to the average ratios of other companies in the same business. Based on this data, you can explain differences between your company's performance and the industry norms, good or bad.

CHAPTER **4**

Compiling a Winning
Loan Proposal

The most dreaded part of applying for a business loan is the mountain of paperwork requested by the lender—most of which may seem redundant, unnecessary, and ultimately unread. This chapter defines most of the information that is being sought by the lender and explains why it's really necessary. You'll learn:

✧ What information is needed and why
✧ How to organize it best
✧ How to recognize and explain any limitations

Getting Organized

When applying for a business loan, people are often surprised about the extensive list of information that is required by the lender. This information is intended to provide the lender with details about such items as the amount of the borrower's loan request, status of the business, use of the loan proceeds, value of collateral assets, and financial condition of the business and business owners.

The size of the loan proposal will not necessarily enlarge or reduce the list of required information. The need for the lender to understand your situation, financial condition, and prospects for repayment is constant, whether the loan is for thousands or millions of dollars. The degree of scrutiny could be greater on larger transactions, but your command of this information is always important, regardless of the size of the loan proposal.

There is no universal list of required application documents, since every deal is different. The suggested list of information presented in this chapter is fairly comprehensive, but it may be either too inclusive or exclusive of items needed for any particular loan application. That's because no two loan transactions are alike—the lender, the borrower, the business, and the situation are unique in every transaction.

Hundreds of variables can change the information requirements of the lender. Even the lender will not know everything that is needed until the review process is completed.

Applying for a business loan requires you to educate the lender about the business and its owners with a customized set of standard documents, some of which are prepared specifically for each particular application. These documents will disclose a considerable amount of information from which the lender will determine whether you qualify for a loan in accordance with the lender's criteria.

This chapter defines many items frequently requested by lenders, describes exactly what the lender is looking for, and discusses why this information is needed. Further, it will suggest how to anticipate questions and be prepared to answer them in advance of meeting the lender. Attention to the details of this process will enhance your loan application and accelerate the lender's response.

Most of the information, documents, and records you will need are detailed in this chapter, organized in specific categories and in the logical order for discussing these topics with the lender when you present the loan proposal. I recommend that you introduce the proposal to the lender in person in order to benefit from the most effective and persuasive technique for obtaining loan approval—your impressive selling skills. However, it will be necessary to leave the lender with a written summary of the proposal along with the plethora of documentation to support the proposal. The loan officer can refer back to the information you provided when he or she begins to review the specifics of the request and answers questions from the decision makers.

In the lender's eyes, your level of preparation and degree of cooperation will be indicative of how desirable you will be as a customer. If it is difficult to get you to respond to requests for documentation and information before the loan is approved and closed, the lender will assume that it will be even more difficult to get such information after the loan is funded. When you're responsive and cooperative in meeting these information requests, you're demonstrating willingness to be part of a relationship, and you have bolstered your efforts to be seriously considered for the proposed loan.

**Be Prepared
—Boy Scout Motto**

Much of the data suggested in this chapter may not exist in the form of a specific document. For purposes of supplying required information to the lender, generating memoranda is an effective way to document the facts, figures, and information in writing. Provide complete, concise information with accuracy and clarity and in a logical sequence.

You'll undermine the information you're providing to support your business when it contains grammatical errors, misspelled words, and incoherent ideas. With the high-quality word processing software now available you can avoid and eliminate many of these errors, even if you're not an experienced writer. There is no excuse for poorly written information communicated incorrectly and haphazardly.

When supplying information to the lender, assume that the lender does not understand the industry jargon or common abbreviations. Explain any technical terms and methodologies to ensure that the lender can follow the reasoning of your loan proposal. For example, a lender that doesn't understand how local health ordinances mandate certain minimum standards for food processing may not recognize how you can justify the costly expenditures required to build a commercial kitchen. By assuming that the lender has no familiarity with the business, your application can communicate precisely what you want to accomplish and how you propose to pay for it.

Too many small businesses pay thousands of dollars annually to accountants and CPAs for the preparation of financial statements without truly understanding what this information discloses. The lender will carefully study your balance sheet, income statement, and cash flow statement. By analyzing financial trends and ratios of the historical and current financial statements, the lender will assess the financial strength of your company and will even compare it to other companies in the industry. After determining the positive (or negative) trends of these results, the lender must weigh the risks of lending money to you. The lender is primarily interested in your ability to produce future funds to repay the loan.

In addition, the lender will check your company's credit history, appraise the collateral, check references, verify account balances, and test the reasonableness of financial projections of future performance in order to quantify the risk associated with providing funding to your business.

When initiating the application process for a business loan, it is essential for you to have a detailed command of all of the requested documentation so to be ready to respond to the lender's questions and conclusions. Sometimes a business will have periods of lower performance, or other events will occur that will raise the concern of the lender. Be prepared to discuss those exceptions and to produce analysis to support the alternative explanation. By anticipating the need for these items, you can demonstrate your relevant management skills and competence in managing the business's financial affairs.

The lender will need information in several distinct categories. Although there is no official format, your assemblage of documentation should be organized to assist the lender in cataloging the information more easily and evaluating it quickly. This is more efficient and in better sequence than submitting information in a business plan format.

Due to the typically large volume of material, it is more useful to arrange the information in a series of large open-ended folders, rather than using ring binders, clamps, or color-coded tabs. This system permits the lender to access and to file each section independently. Much of the information may have to be copied for various parties to review and file it, and this duplication can be done more easily if the documents are not bound in any way.

It is important to provide clean, clear documents that are entirely legible. Review everything prior to submission to eliminate incorrect compilation, incomplete pages, poor copy reproduction, or out-of-sequence documents. These logistic errors cause confusion and distract the lender from the business information you're submitting.

Never submit original documents, such as the company's various contracts. Any copied document can be authenticated, if necessary, with a dated original signature on the margin of the cover page.

Finally, if you cannot produce a particular document or other information requested by the lender on demand, it's important to provide an honest, direct explanation with a legitimate reason and a time frame for availability. If, for example, company operations are overloaded at that moment and no one can stop to prepare the information, you'll be demonstrating that the business priorities are in correct order.

It is a mistake to blame the unavailability of information on the company's accountant, attorney, bookkeeper, or any other party. If you can't manage these parties (and you're the one who's paying them for professional assistance), how can you manage other operations to repay the lender's loan?

If information is not available due to reasons that cannot be resolved immediately, then consider delaying the initiation of the loan application. For example, if you're not able to obtain the most recent financial statements because the accountant has not been paid for last year's financial statement, then you're wise to wait. Your credibility would be damaged if the lender were to learn that the company's invoices are significantly past due.

Categorized organization of information will permit the lender to absorb as much or as little information as is needed. The format suggested below accommodates faster evaluation and consideration in the loan review process.

Do You Need a Business Plan?

How do companies use business plans? Too often, business owners put a business plan together only when seeking external financing from lenders or investors. Business plans should provide information on the short- and intermediate-term strategies for accomplishing long-term goals. Business plans should detail how financial, operational, marketing, and human resources will be converted into a successful and profitable venture. Business plans should be used as a road map to determine the destination and then measure results against projections.

Many people are obsessed with business plans—particularly those who charge exorbitant fees to prepare them. Business plans are very good tools that can assist business owners and managers to plan better and target results better. And when an existing business is seeking to obtain additional financing, a business plan can be a very good document to communicate how the company plans to build on the results they have compiled to that point in its operating history. *But the plan itself is not a sufficient substitute for everything else needed by the lender.*

If you've put together a business plan merely to justify financing, then it has limited utility or value for both you and the lender. If the lender requires a business plan, then you probably haven't made a clear case about what your business goals are. That being the case, you should invest the time to produce a plan. But it would also be in your interest to continue to use and regularly update the plan after the financing is obtained.

> **Ensure that all documentation is easily accessed without binding or staples. Use clamps or paper clips to make lender handling and duplication easier.**

Borrower Beware!

Many lenders have had the unfortunate experience of entering into discussions with a borrower who was using false, exaggerated, or misleading information to obtain credit. Whether or not the ploy succeeded, the effects are often felt by legitimate borrowers, whose applications are subsequently scrutinized with even more diligence and suspicion. While under normal circumstances there is a natural inclination toward trusting people, lenders must be prepared to confirm everything.

Unless actual loan losses have been incurred, many lenders may be hesitant to prosecute loan applicants who have used false information to obtain their loan. But the federal government is not so hesitant, and the SBA's Inspector General is available to investigate any attempt to defraud the agency with false or misleading information. These cases are prosecuted by a U.S. attorney, who has virtually unlimited resources to pursue such matters. Most federal prosecutors have almost perfect conviction rates.

For those individuals who are flippant about the integrity of their business dealings, or who willingly try to obtain an SBA loan with fraudulent information, these actions can carry heavy penalties. It is a federal crime to submit false information in order to induce a lender and the SBA to provide business financing. If caught in such an attempt, one can be sure of criminal prosecution. If convicted, one may be punished with up to twenty years in prison and a fine of as much as $1 million plus restitution.

Borrowers certify the accuracy and completeness of the information they submit in the SBA Business Loan Application. Covenants contained there acknowledge that the information is provided by the borrower in order to obtain loan approval. Borrowers also affirm that they have not made payments to anyone within the government for assistance with the loan application, nor will they hire anyone employed by the agency for a period of two years after the loan is approved.

In 1994, the SBA began to verify each borrower's personal and business income tax returns with the Internal Revenue Service. There have been many instances of fictitious tax returns submitted to the agency by fraudulent loan applicants, resulting in significant loan losses. Lenders now confirm that the income tax returns submitted with loan applications are the same as those income tax returns submitted to the IRS to report income.

> "The only good loan is one that's paid back."
>
> E. Guice Potter Sr.
> (1970–1994)
> President
> Commercial National Bank
> Anniston, AL

Business Loan Proposal

Produce information addressed to the lender that clearly sets forth the exact loan proposal you're requesting.

Many of the items listed below involve professional preparation, such as appraisals or environmental reports, which require engagement of a qualified third-party consultant. Lenders will generally approve loans subject to the information that will be provided for in these reports. You won't be required to spend any money for this information until you are assured that the loan is approved, subject to specific condition that will be confirmed by the consultants. These items are marked below with an asterisk (*).

At a minimum, the loan proposal should include the following components that are applicable to the business or its owners:

General Information
Loan purpose
Loan justification
Proposed loan structure
Use of proceeds
Collateral information
Application form

Personal Information
Date of birth
Social security number
Place of birth
Citizenship
Current/previous address
Military record
Spouse information
Other business interests
Regulatory questions

Business Information
Business name
Address
Taxpayer ID
Date established
Number of employees
Name of bank
Previous SBA debt
Business indebtedness
Business owners
Regulatory questions
Business history
Organizational chart
Key employee resumes
Credit authorization
Lease agreements

Business organization
    documentation
Identification of loan consultant

  For Partnership:
    Partnership agreement
    List of partners
    Certificate of good standing
    Certificate as to partners

  For Corporation:
    Articles of incorporation
    By-laws
    Corporate seal
    Corporate resolution
    List of corporate officers
    Certificate of good standing

  For Limited Liability
    Company:
    Articles of organization
    LLC operating agreement
    List of LLC members

Financial Information
Personal financial statement
Personal tax returns, 3 yrs.
Year-end financial statements,
    3 yrs.
Interim financial statement
Net worth reconciliation
Financial statement analysis
A/R aging report
Inventory aging
A/P aging report
Business tax returns, 3 yrs.

P/L projections, 2 yrs.
12-month cash flow pro forma
Balance sheet pro forma

Collateral Information
Real Property Collateral
Legal description
Appraisal (*)
Property Deed
Survey (*)
Location map
Engineering report (*)
Environment report (*)
Environment Questionnaire
Photographs
Lease agreements
Sales contracts
Insurance coverage

Personal Property Collateral
Description:
  Manufacturer
  Date acquired
  Cost
  Serial numbers
  Location
Appraisal (*)
Photographs
Price quotations

Automotive Collateral
Description:
  Manufacturer
  Date acquired
  Cost
  Serial numbers
  Mileage (or log hours)
  Registration no.
Title
Appraisal (*)
Photographs

Securities Collateral
Brokerage statements
Schedule of closely held securities

Notes Receivable Collateral
Description:
  Name of debtor
  Balance of the note
  Interest rate
  Repayment terms
  Collateral
  Current status
Collateral values
Copy of notes

Depository Account Collateral
Description:
  Name of depository
  Name on account
  Type of account
  Account balances
  Interest rate on account
  Maturity of account
Account statements

Accounts Receivable/Inventory
  Collateral
A/R aging
Bad debt schedule
Inventory report
Obsolete inventory
Inventory valuation
Borrowing base certificate
Customer lists

Cash Surrender Value Collateral
Copy of policy
Policy declaration
Assignment form

Marketing Information

What are the products or services of the business?

How does the business operate?

Who is the typical customer for products or services?

How does the business advertise?

Who is the competition?

How will the borrower increase revenues?

Miscellaneous Information

Affiliates

Year-end financial statements, 3 yrs.

Interim financial statement

Ownership schedule

Legal entity documents

Construction Loans

Performance bond (*)

AIA contract

Cost breakdown

Boundary survey (*)

Sealed construction plans (*)

Construction specifications

Soil reports (*)

Construction schedule

Building permits (*)

Builder's Risk Insurance (*)

Utility service confirmation

Zoning verification letter

Franchise Businesses

Franchise information

Franchise agreement (*)

Uniform Franchise Offering Circular

Special Assets

Contracts

Lottery awards

Trusts

Tax-exempt bonds

SBA Documents

Business loan application (**)

Statements required by law (**)

Statement of financial need (**)

Statement of personal history (**)

Compensation agreement (**)

Assurance of compliance for non-discrimination (**)

Certificate for regarding debarment (**)

Request for transcript of tax form (**)

(**)—Items marked with double asterisk are typically furnished and prepared by lender.

A detailed discussion of each of these documentation requirements is contained in the following pages. If any of the recommended items are not applicable to your business or loan request, disregard it when compiling this information.

General Information

Purpose of the loan. The lender wants a concise statement of exactly why you want to borrow money. It is important to provide the lender with an explanation of the purpose of the loan and where all of the funds will be spent. Do not be surprised if the lender is not satisfied with your statement that you merely want to purchase an asset.

The lender will require a thorough explanation as to what you're seeking to accomplish with the asset. You may want to buy a new forklift, in order to increase productivity in warehouse operations by lowering labor costs and reducing the exposure to job-related injuries. It is important for the lender to understand the costs savings that may effectively pay for the forklift.

Justification of the loan. A prepared borrower will produce a statement explaining how a business loan guaranteed by the U.S. Small Business Administration is the best source of the funds being requested. The lender may be aware of alternative sources for the financing and will want to test whether you've considered them as well. Be prepared to explain why this loan is the most advantageous source of financing, due to more reasonable costs, better terms, higher leverage, or other factors that made you choose to apply for the loan. Often this information is specifically requested by the SBA.

As part of justifying use of the SBA, be specific as to how you have determined the amount of the loan request and consequently how much equity you will contribute to the transaction. If there is a logical reason to limit the company's investment, be sure to identify it to the lender. Otherwise, be prepared for the lender to insist that you contribute a higher sum into the transaction if you have the resources.

Proposed structure of the loan. Propose how the loan should be structured at the time the loan request is submitted and provide your reasoning. Loan structure refers to the conditions and terms that define the transaction between you and the lender.

You have the best opportunity to influence the loan structure at the opening of negotiations. By introducing your preferences up front, you set the tone for discussions and are likely to get a better deal by demonstrating concern on these issues than by waiting to allow the lender to offer its own terms.

Lenders often do not appreciate the borrower's desire to maintain cash reserves, especially when part of the loan request is specified for that purpose. Be prepared to walk away from that part of the proposal, since most lenders do not feel it is prudent to fund cash that they cannot be assured is used in the manner requested and may wind up enlarging the lender's loss exposure.

The lender will always have the ultimate leverage in determining the loan terms. But your suggestion of reasonable terms in the proposal is an important communication to the lender that influences the tone for the loan negotiations. Components of the loan structure should include:

✧ *Loan amount*—Specify exactly how much money you want, and be ready to defend it with supporting information.
✧ *Loan term*—Define the period over which you want to repay the loan. Remember, maximum repayment periods are established by the SBA.
✧ *Interest rate*—It never hurts to ask for lower rates, but be realistic about how much risk the deal presents to the lender. Real estate loans are generally safer than equipment loans; equipment loans are generally safer than working capital loans. Interest rate should be a function of the lender's risk.

Be sure you know how to calculate the loan payment using the amount, interest rate, and repayment term requested before initiating negotiations about the loan structure. Being able to accurately determine the payment is essential so that you can be certain that the requested loan and terms can be comfortably managed within your predicted cash flow. There is no sense in requesting or agreeing to terms under which you can't perform.

There are several financial software programs that provide loan amortization formulas, such as Lotus 123 or Microsoft Excel. Alternatively, you may choose to invest in a business calculator to accomplish this task.

Use of loan proceeds. Your loan proposal must include a specific schedule that defines how and when the proceeds of the loan will be used. If you don't specifically declare exactly how much is needed, the lender will decide based on limited information, which will slow down the approval process and may lower the approved loan.

The lender deserves to know precisely where every dollar goes. When you're purchasing an asset, this number is easy to define. But, if you seek to borrow a portion of the funds for working capital, specifying where these funds will be applied is a little more difficult.

Produce a detailed month-to-month cash flow projection for working capital financing, predicting how and when the cash proceeds will be used, and describe the expected expenses or purchases that will be paid. It is easier for you to restrict the use of working capital proceeds to larger-ticket items such as inventory, contracted services, or other major costs that the lender can identify without as much documentation.

Produce accurate documentation that details how the loan will be used. The SBA requires lender verification of the use of proceeds, such as copies of notes being refinanced (along with the original settlement statement or security agreement), purchase contracts, construction contracts, bills of sale, price quotes, or other documents that back up the uses of funds.

If there is working capital in the transaction, prepare a schedule of where these funds will be applied. Most lenders require borrowers to provide paid receipts to justify working capital needs and will hold back loan funds to reimburse you after the costs are incurred. If you're requesting to finance the transaction costs associated with the loan, you should seek assistance from the lender to determine exactly what these costs will be before submitting the final proposal.

Collateral. Define what assets are available to reasonably secure the loan. Collateral is very important to the lender because it defines a tangible alternative repayment source for the lender to the normal liquidation of a loan expected from business profits. The lender will typically require at least 100 percent coverage of the loan value, using asset values discounted to provide for liquidation expenses and carrying costs.

For example, if you're purchasing a building with the loan proceeds, the lender will discount the loan amount from the property's appraised value in order to determine a collateral advance value. If the lender's loan policy defines an advance rate of 75 percent on commercial real estate, the lender will reduce the value of the property's appraised value by 25 percent to determine the collateral value. On that basis, the lender will lend you up to 75 percent of the cost of the building (or percentage of appraised value, whichever is lower). Should you require a greater sum, the lender may consider a larger loan but will require you to pledge additional assets in order to fully secure the extra funds.

Most commercial property lenders advance up to 80 percent of the lower value of the subject real estate, but that figure varies depending on the lender's loan policy, the type of property improvements, and the condition of the local real estate market. Unimproved real estate is usually only financed for 50 percent of its value.

Lenders generally value equipment and furniture at 50 percent of cost, and give little or no value to leasehold improvements or fixtures unless the real estate also secures the loan. Accounts receivable and inventory (current assets) are of little, if any, value to term loan lenders. Current assets can disappear too fast to be considered dependable secondary sources of repayment.

Loan application form. Some lenders require that you submit a loan application form that is unique to the lender. This application is not to be confused with the SBA Business Loan Application. Many lenders choose to use an in-house application form that requests basic information and includes language that requires the borrower to warrant the accuracy of the information provided.

This document is sometimes used by certain lenders as an internal document to move the deal into its loan approval process. Be cooperative with such requests, even if compliance duplicates information you've already provided. The information gathered on such forms generally assists the lender in an orderly movement of information to other parts of its organization.

Special information. If there are special circumstances, negative or positive, that affect your access to financing, present these circumstances to the lender at an early stage of the application process. With increasing frequency, borrowers have extraordinary conditions that require special handling by the lender on a case-by-case basis.

During the past several years, thousands of persons with great character and impeccable credit have encountered conditions beyond their control that have tarnished otherwise perfect financial histories. The unpredictable economy, particularly in the periods after the 2007–2009 financial crisis, led to many unavoidable bankruptcies and property foreclosures. Add to that a soaring divorce rate, which has affected thousands of business owners, and you can see why average credit scores have gone down nationally. Still, these situations do not necessarily reflect issues with these individuals' characters, willingness to repay their loans, or business capability.

Lenders will discover these conditions early during their due diligence procedures, so it is better for you to introduce the topic and provide a full explanation up front. This voluntary revelation removes any suspicion of the lender that you may have attempted to hide this information. It also provides a legitimate forum in which to enhance the lender's understanding of any such events before any preconceived notions come to mind.

Be thoughtful about how and when you broach this subject with your lenders. First, you need to get the lender interested in the deal. Introduction of any special information too early may end the chances of getting a fair hearing. Once the lender has enough data to genuinely express interest in a deal, introduce any unrelated but relevant situations that need explanation and initiate a dialogue about how a loan can be granted in light of the negative history.

There is a more detailed discussion about several potential circumstances that may need explanation by borrowers, and suggestions on how to approach that conversation later in Chapter 5.

Personal Information

The lender will require personal information about each individual who owns an interest in the business entity and each party planning to guarantee the proposed loan. This information is designed to assist the lender and SBA to confirm that each individual is eligible for SBA participation.

The information covers a broad range of facts that are pertinent to your qualification to participate in SBA financing. Certain disclosures could result in further review by other government agencies. Specifically, if you or any of your co-owners have been arrested for or convicted of a crime, other than minor traffic offenses, SBA regulations require an FBI review of this information to confirm that you have completed all sentencing requirements. Prior conviction of a felony does not necessarily deem an individual ineligible for SBA financing, but all terms of the sentencing must have been completed, including probation and payment of fines, in order for financing to be considered.

The information required on each individual involved includes:

Date of birth. Federal law prohibits a person's age from being used as a qualification (or disqualification) for obtaining a loan. The individual's date of birth is used to verify identification.

Social security number. This information is required to verify identification.

Place of birth. This information is required to verify identification and citizenship.

Declaration of citizenship. The individuals are required to declare their country of citizenship. If any individual is not a U.S. citizen, proof of alien status must be provided. Foreign citizens must have at least a Legal Permanent Resident (LPR) status, also known as "permanent resident aliens" status (green card) to qualify for SBA assistance. Current proof from the INS establishing this status must be furnished at the time of application. Proof is obtainable by submitting a copy of both sides of the holder's green card to the lender, who will forward copies to the INS with Form G-845 and the borrower's written authorization for verification.

Non-LPR individuals may be eligible to participate in SBA-assisted transactions only when they own less than 51 percent of the enterprise and the loan is fully secured for the life of the loan.

Current home address and occupancy dates. This information is required for lender and SBA to determine residency and verify credit history.

Previous home address and occupancy dates. This information is required as per SBA regulations to validate other financial records submitted.

Declaration of military service. This information is required as per SBA regulations.

Name of spouse and spouse's social security number. This information is required as per SBA regulations.

List of affiliated business interests (in which a 20 percent+ interest is owned). This information is required as per SBA regulations to confirm the eligibility of the borrower. If any such interests exist, it will be necessary to produce financial information for each such business to determine the cumulative effect these other businesses have on the eligibility of the proposed transaction.

Regulatory character questions. A written response is required to answer any affirmative replies to these questions:

✧ Are you presently under indictment, on parole, or probation?
✧ Have you ever been charged with or arrested for any criminal offense other than a minor motor vehicle violation?
✧ Have you ever been convicted, placed on pretrial diversion, or placed on any form of probation, including adjudication withheld pending probation, for any criminal offense other than a minor motor vehicle violation?
✧ Have you ever been involved in bankruptcy or insolvency proceedings?
✧ Are you involved in any pending lawsuits?
✧ Do you or your spouse or any member of your household, or anyone who owns, manages, or directs your business or their spouses or members of their households, work for the Small Business Administration, Small Business Advisory Council, SCORE or ACE, any federal agency, or the participating lender?

Positive reply to any of these questions does not automatically disqualify the applicant from SBA assistance or alter their eligibility. A positive reply to the questions concerning criminal arrests or convictions will mean that the applicant must provide two sets of fingerprint cards (on SBA specific cards!) which are submitted to the FBI for a brief background check. FBI processing may be waived for minor offenses, subject to approval of the SBA district director.

The SBA requires that anyone having such an offense in his or her past for which the record was sealed, expunged, or is otherwise unavailable also provide complete disclosure.

Most of the information compiled to answer these questions is required to complete the SBA Form 4 (the Business Loan Application) and Form 912 (the Statement of Personal History), which are found in Illustrations 4-A and 4-B, respectively.

			OMB Approval No: 3245-0016
			Expiration Date: 11/30/04

U.S. Small Business Administration

APPLICATION FOR BUSINESS LOAN

Individual	Full Address

Name of Applicant Business		Tax I.D. No. or SSN

Full Street Address of Business		Tel. No. (inc. A/C)

City	County	State	Zip	Number of Employees (Including subsidiaries and affiliates)
Type of Business		Date Business Established		At Time of Application ____
Bank of Business Account and Address				If Loan is Approved ____
				Subsidiaries or Affiliates (Separate for above) ____

Use of Proceeds: (Enter Gross Dollar Amounts Rounded to the Nearest Hundreds)	Loan Requested		Loan Request
Land Acquisition		Payoff SBA Loan	
New Construction/ Expansion Repair		Payoff Bank Loan (Non SBA Associated	
Acquisition and/or Repair of Machinery and Equipment		Other Debt Payment (Non SBA Associated)	
Inventory Purchase		All Other	
Working Capital (including Accounts Payable)		Total Loan Requested	
Acquisition of Existing Business		Term of Loan - (Requested Mat.)	____ Yrs.

PREVIOUS SBA OR OTHER FEDERAL GOVERNMENT DEBT: If you or any principals or affiliates have 1) ever requested Government Financing or 2) are delinquent on the repayment of any Federal Debt complete the following:

Name of Agency	Original Amount of Loan	Date of Request	Approved or Declined	Balance	Current or Past Due
	$			$	
	$			$	

ASSISTANCE List the name(s) and occupation of anyone who assisted in the preparation of this form, other than applicant.

Name and Occupation	Address	Total Fees Paid	Fees Due
Name and Occupation	Address	Total Fees Paid	Fees Due

Note: The estimated burden completing this form is 12.0 hours per response. You will not be required to respond to any collection of information unless it displays a currently valid OMB approval number. Comments on the burden should be sent to U.S. Small Business Administration, Chief, AIB, 409 3rd St., S.W., Washington, D.C. 20416 and Desk Office for Small Business Administration, Office of Management and Budget, New Executive Office Building, room 10202 Washington, D.C. 20503. OMB Approval (3245-0016). **PLEASE DO NOT SEND FORMS TO OMB.**
SUBMIT COMPLETED APPLICATION TO LENDER OF CHOICE

SBA Form 4 (8-01) Use Previous Edition Until Exhausted

Federal Recycling Program   Printed on Recycled Paper

Page 1

This form was electronically produced by Elite Federal Forms, Inc.

ILLUSTRATION 4-A

ALL EXHIBITS MUST BE SIGNED AND DATED BY PERSON SIGNING THIS FORM

BUSINESS INDEBTEDNESS: Furnish the following information on all installment debts, contracts, notes, and mortgages payable. Indicate by an asterisk (*) items to be paid by loan proceeds and reason for paying them (present balance should agree with the latest balance sheet submitted).

To Whom Payable	Original Amount	Original Date	Present Balance	Rate of Interest	Maturity Date	Monthly Payment	Security	Current or Past Due
Acct. #	$		$			$		
Acct. #	$		$			$		
Acct. #	$		$			$		
Acct. #	$		$			$		
Acct. #	$		$			$		

MANAGEMENT (Proprietor, partners, officers, directors, all holders of outstanding stock – 100% of ownership must be shown). Use separate sheet if necessary.

Name and Social Security Number and Position Title	Complete Address	%Owned	*Military Service From To	*Sex

Race*: American Indian/Alaska Native ☐   Black/African-Amer. ☐   Asian ☐   Native Hawaiian/Pacific Islander ☐   White ☐   **Ethnicity*** Hisp./Latino ☐   Not Hisp./Latino ☐

Race*: American Indian/Alaska Native ☐   Black/African-Amer. ☐   Asian ☐   Native Hawaiian/Pacific Islander ☐   White ☐   **Ethnicity*** Hisp./Latino ☐   Not Hisp./Latino ☐

Race*: American Indian/Alaska Native ☐   Black/African-Amer. ☐   Asian ☐   Native Hawaiian/Pacific Islander ☐   White ☐   **Ethnicity*** Hisp./Latino ☐   Not Hisp./Latino ☐

Race*: American Indian/Alaska Native ☐   Black/African-Amer. ☐   Asian ☐   Native Hawaiian/Pacific Islander ☐   White ☐   **Ethnicity*** Hisp./Latino ☐   Not Hisp./Latino ☐

*This data is collected for statistical purpose only. It has no bearing on the credit decision to approve or decline this application. One or more boxes may be selected.

THE FOLLOWING EXHIBITS MUST BE COMPLETED WHERE APPLICABLE. ALL QUESTIONS ANSWERED ARE MADE A PART OF THE APPLICATION.

For Guarantee Loans please provide an original and one copy (Photocopy is Acceptable) of the Application Form, and all Exhibits to the participating lender. For Direct Loans submit one original copy of the application and Exhibits to SBA.

1. Submit SBA Form 912 (Statement of Personal History) for each type of individual that the Form 912 requires.

2. If your collateral consists of (A) Land and Building, (B) Machinery and Equipment, (C) Furniture and Fixtures, (D) Accounts *Receivable*, (E) Inventory, (F) Other, please provide an itemized list (labeled Exhibit A) that contains serial and identification numbers for all articles that had an Original value of greater than $500. Include a legal description of Real Estate Offered as collateral.

3. Furnish a signed current personal balance sheet (SBA Form 413 may be used for this purpose) for each stockholder (with 20% or greater ownership), partner, officer, and owner. Include the assets and liabilities of the spouse and any close relatives living in the household. Also, include your Social Security Number. The date should be the same as the most recent business financial statement. Label it Exhibit B.

4. Include the financial statements listed below: a,b,c for the last three years; also a,b,c, and d as of the same date, - current within 90 days of filing the application; and statement e, if applicable. Label it Exhibit C (Contact SBA for referral if assistance with preparation is wanted.) **All** information must be signed and dated.

a. Balance Sheet
b. Profit and Loss Statement (if not available, explain why and substitute Federal income tax forms)
c. Reconciliation of Net Worth
d. Aging of Accounts Receivable and Payable (summary not detailed)
e. Projection of earnings for at least one year where financial statements for the last three years are unavailable or when SBA requests them.

5. Provide a brief history of your company and a paragraph describing the expected benefits it will receive from the loan. Label it Exhibit D.

6. Provide a brief description similar to a resume of the education, technical and business background for all the people listed under Management. Label it Exhibit E.

ILLUSTRATION 4-A

ALL EXHIBITS MUST BE SIGNED AND DATED BY PERSON SIGNING THIS FORM

7. Submit the names, addresses, tax I.D. number(EIN or SSN), and current personal balance sheet(s) of any co-signers and/or guarantors for the loan who are not otherwise affiliated with the business as Exhibit F.

8. Include a list of any machinery or equipment or other non-real estate assets to be purchased with loan proceeds and the cost of each item as quoted by the seller as Exhibit G. Include the seller's name and address.

9. Have you or any officers of your company ever been involved in bankruptcy or insolvency proceedings? If so, please provide the details as Exhibit H.
If none, check here: Yes   No

10. Are you or your business involved in any pending lawsuits? If yes, provide the details as Exhibit I.
If none, check here: Yes | No

11. Do you or your spouse or any member of your household, or anyone who owns, manages or directs your business or their spouses or members of their households work for the Small Business Administration, Small Business Advisory Council, SCORE or ACE, any Federal Agency, or the participating lender? If so, please provide the name and address of the person and the office where employed. Label this Exhibit J.
If none, check here:

12. Does your business, its owners or majority stockholders own or have a controlling interest in other businesses? If yes, please provide their names and the relationship with your company along with a current balance sheet and operating statement for each. This should be Exhibit K.

13. Do you buy from, sell to, or use the services of any concern in which someone in your company has a significant financial interest? If yes, provide details on a separate sheet of paper labeled Exhibit L.

14. If your business is a franchise, include a copy of the franchise agreement and a copy of the FTC disclosure statement supplied to you by the Franchisor. Please include it as Exhibit M.

CONSTRUCTION LOANS ONLY

15. Include as a separate exhibit (Exhibit N) the estimated cost of the project and a statement of the source of any additional funds.

16. Provide copies of preliminary construction plans and specifications. Include them as Exhibit O. Final plans will be required prior to disbursement.

EXPORT LOANS

17. Does your business presently engage in Export Trade?
Check here: Yes | No

18. Will you be using proceeds from this loan to support your company's exports?
Check here: Yes | No

19. Would you like information on Exporting?
Check here: Yes   No

AGREEMENTS AND CERTIFICATIONS

Agreements of non-employment of SBA Personnel: I agree that if SBA approves this loan application I will not, for at least two years, hire as an employee or consultant anyone that was employed by SBA during the one year period prior to the disbursement of the loan.

Certification: I certify: (a) I have not paid anyone connected with the Federal Government for help in getting this loan. I also agree to report to the SBA office of the Inspector General, Washington, DC 20416 any Federal Government employee who offers, in return for any type of compensation, to help get this loan approved.

(b) All information in this application and the Exhibits are true and complete to the best of my knowledge and are submitted to SBA so SBA can decide whether to grant a loan or participate with a lending institution in a loan to me. I agree to pay for or reimburse SBA for the cost of any surveys, title or mortgage examinations, appraisals, credit reports, etc., performed by non-SBA personnel provided I have given my consent-

(c) I understand that I need not pay anybody to deal with SBA. I have read and understand SBA Form 159, which explains SBA policy on representatives and their fees.

(d) As consideration for any Management, Technical, and Business Development Assistance that may be provided, I waive all claims against SBA and its consultants.

If you knowingly make a false statement or overvalue a security to obtain a guaranteed loan from SBA, you can be fined up to $10,000 and/or imprisoned for not more than five years under 18 usc 1001; if submitted to a Federally insured institution, under 18 USC 1014 by Imprisonment of not more than twenty years and/or a fine of not more than $1,000,000. I authorize the SBA's Office of Inspector General to request criminal record information about me from criminal justice agencies for the purpose of determining my eligibility for programs authorized by the Small Business Act, as amended.

If Applicant is a proprietor or general partner, sign below:

By: _____

If Applicant is a Corporation, sign below:

_____
Corporate Name and Seal   Date

By: _____
                    Signature of President

Attested by: _____
                    Signature of Corporate Secretary

SUBMIT COMPLETED APPLICATION TO LENDER OF CHOICE

ILLUSTRATION 4-A

APPLICANT'S CERTIFICATION

By my signature, I certify that I have read and received a copy of the "STATEMENTS REQUIRED BY LAW AND EXECUTIVE ORDER" which was attached to this application. My signature represents my agreement to comply with the approval of my loan request and to comply, whenever applicable, with the hazard insurance, lead-based paint, civil rights or other limitations in this notice.

Each proprietor, each General Partner, each Limited Partner or Stockholder owning 20% or more, each Guarantor and the spouse of each of these must sign. Each person should sign only once.

Business Name: _____

By: _____

    Signature and Title   Date

Guarantors:

_____

Signature and Title   Date

_____

Signature and Title   Date

_____

Signature and Title   Date

_____

Signature and Title   Date

_____

Signature and Title   Date

_____

Signature and Title   Date

_____

Signature and Title   Date

SBA Form 4 (8-01) Use Previous Edition Until Exhausted   Page 4

PART 2

ILLUSTRATION 4-A

OMB Approval No.: 3245-0016
Expiration Date: 11/30/2004

U.S. SMALL BUSINESS ADMINISTRATION
SCHEDULE OF COLLATERAL
Exhibit A

Applicant		
Street Address		
City	**State**	**Zip Code**

LIST ALL COLLATERAL TO BE USED AS SECURITY FOR THIS LOAN

Section I - REAL ESTATE

Attach a copy of the deed(s) containing a full legal description of the land and show the location (street address) and city where the deed(s) is recorded. Following the address below, give a brief description of the improvements, such as size, type of construction, use, number of stories, and present condition (use additional sheet if more space is required).

LIST PARCELS OF REAL ESTATE

Address	Year Acquired	Original Cost	Market Value	Amount of Lien	Name of Lienholder

Description(s)

SBA Form 4, Schedule A (8-01) Previous Editions Obsolete

Federal Recycling Program ♻ *Printed on Recycled Paper*

This form was electronically produced by Elite Federal Forms, Inc.

SUBMIT COMPLETED APPLICATION TO LENDER OF CHOICE

ILLUSTRATION 4-A

SECTION II - PERSONAL PROPERTY

All items listed herein must show manufacturer or make, model, year, and serial number. Items with no serial number must be clearly identified (use additional sheet if more space is required).

Description - Show Manufacturer, Model, Serial No.	Year Acquired	Original Cost	Market Value	Current Lien Balance	Name of Lienholder

All information contained herein is TRUE and CORRECT to the best of my knowldege. **If you knowingly make a false statement or overvalue a security to obtain a guaranteed loan from SBA, you can be fined up to $10,000 and/or imprisoned for not more than five years under 18 usc 1001; if submitted to a Federally Insured Institution, under 18 USC 1014 by Imprisonment of not more than twenty years and/or a fine of not more than $1,000,000.** I authorize the SBA's Office of Inspector General to request criminal record information about me from criminal justice agencies for the purpose of determining my eligibility for programs authorized by the Small Business Act, as amended.

Name _____   Date _____

Name _____   Date _____

NOTE: The estimated burden for completing this form is 2.25 hours per response. You will not be required to respond to collection of information unless it displays a currently valid OMB approval number. Comments on the burden should be sent to U.S. Small Business Administration, Chief, AIB, 409 3rd St., SW, Washington, D.C. 20416 and Desk Officer for Small Business Administration, Office of Management and Budget, New Executive Office Building, Room 10202, Washington, D.C. 20503. **OMB Approval (3245-0016). PLEASE DO NOT SEND FORMS TO OMB.**

SBA Form 4, Schedule A (8-01) Previous Editions Obsolete

ILLUSTRATION 4-A

Return Executed Copies 1, 2, and 3 to SBA

OMB APPROVAL NO.3245-0178
Expiration Date:9/30/2006

United States of America

SMALL BUSINESS ADMINISTRATION

STATEMENT OF PERSONAL HISTORY

Please Read Carefully - Print or Type

Each member of the small business or the development company requesting assistance must submit this form in TRIPLICATE for filing with the SBA application. This form must be filled out and submitted:

1. By the proprietor, if a sole proprietorship.

2. By each partner, if a partnership.

3. By each officer, director, and additionally by each holder of 20% or more of the ownership stock, if a corporation, limited liability company, or a development company.

Name and Address of Applicant (Firm Name)(Street, City, State, and ZIP Code)

SBA District/Disaster Area Office

Amount Applied for (when applicable) | File No. (if known)

1. Personal Statement of: (State name in full, if no middle name, state (NMN), or if initial only, indicate initial.) List all former names used, and dates each name was used. Use separate sheet if necessary.

First   Middle   Last

2. Give the percentage of ownership or stocked owned or to be owned in the small business or the development company

Social Security No.

3. Date of Birth (Month, day, and year)

4. Place of Birth: (City & State or Foreign Country)

Name and Address of participating lender or surety co. (when applicable and known)

5. U.S. Citizen? ☐ YES ☐ NO
If No, are you a Lawful ☐ YES ☐ NO
Permanent resident alien:
If non- U.S. citizen provide alien registration number:

6. Present residence address:
From:
To:
Address:

Most recent prior address (omit if over 10 years ago):
From:
To:
Address:

Home Telephone No. (Include A/C):
Business Telephone No. (Include A/C):

PLEASE SEE REVERSE SIDE FOR EXPLANATION REGARDING DISCLOSURE OF INFORMATION AND THE USES OF SUCH INFORMATION.

IT IS IMPORTANT THAT THE NEXT THREE QUESTIONS BE ANSWERED COMPLETELY. AN ARREST OR CONVICTION RECORD WILL NOT NECESSARILY DISQUALIFY YOU; HOWEVER, AN UNTRUTHFUL ANSWER WILL CAUSE YOUR APPLICATION TO BE DENIED.

IF YOU ANSWER "YES" TO 7, 8, OR 9, FURNISH DETAILS ON A SEPARATE SHEET. INCLUDE DATES, LOCATION, FINES, SENTENCES, WHETHER MISDEMEANOR OR FELONY, DATES OF PAROLE/PROBATION, UNPAID FINES OR PENALTIES, NAME(S) UNDER WHICH CHARGED, AND ANY OTHER PERTINENT INFORMATION.

7. Are you presently under indictment, on parole or probation?

☐ Yes ☐ No   (If yes, indicate date parole or probation is to expire.)

8. Have you ever been charged with and or arrested for any criminal offense other than a minor motor vehicle violation? Include offenses which have been dismissed, discharged, or not prosecuted (All arrests and charges must be disclosed and explained on an attached sheet.)

☐ Yes ☐ No

9. Have you ever been convicted, placed on pretrial diversion, or placed on any form of probation, including adjudication withheld pending probation, for any criminal offense other than a minor vehicle violation?

☐ Yes ☐ No

10. I authorize the Small Business Administration Office of Inspector General to request criminal record information about me from criminal justice agencies for the purpose of determining my eligibility for programs authorized by the Small Business Act, and the Small Business Investment Act.

CAUTION: Knowingly making a false statement on this form is a violation of Federal law and could result in criminal prosecution, significant civil penalties, and a denial of your loan, surety bond, or other program participation. A false statement is punishable under 18 USC 1001 by imprisonment of not more than five years and/or a fine of not more than $10,000; under 15 USC 645 by imprisonment of not more than two years and/or a fine of not more than $5,000; and, if submitted to a Federally insured institution, under 18 USC 1014 by imprisonment of not more than thirty years and/or a fine of not more than $1,000,000.

Signature | Title | Date

Agency Use Only

11. ☐ Fingerprints Waived

☐ Fingerprints Required

Date Sent to OIG _____

Date   Approving Authority

Date   Approving Authority

12. ☐ Cleared for Processing   Date   Approving Authority

13. ☐ Request a Character Evaluation   Date   Approving Authority

(Required whenever 7, 8 or 9 are answered "yes" even if cleared for processing.)

PLEASE NOTE: The estimated burden for completing this form is 15 minutes per re sponse.   You are not required to respond to any collection of information unless it displays a currently valid OMB approval number. Comments on the burden should be sent to U.S. Small Business Administration, Chief, AIB, 409 3rd St., S.W., Washington D.C. 20416 and Desk Officer for the Small Business Administration, Office of Management and Budget, New Executive Office Building, Room 10202, Washington, D.C. 20503. OMB Approval 3245-0178. **PLEASE DO NOT SEND FORMS TO OMB.**

SBA 912 (10-03) SOP 5010.4 Previous Edition Obsolete

This form was electronically produced by Elite Federal Forms, Inc.

ILLUSTRATION 4-B

Business Information

The lender will require administrative information about you in order to evaluate the proposed loan. This information is designed to help the lender establish your eligibility for SBA participation. It also provides the lender with information from which can be determined how your company is organized and the depth of your operations.

Registered business name. The lender needs to know the exact legal name under which your business is legally registered, along with any trade names or d/b/a (aka doing business as) under which the company operates. The legal business name is what is usually registered with the secretary of state, and includes designation of corporation, partnership, or LLC. The trade name refers to all businesses that operate under a name different than that under which they are legally organized, such as "ABC Corporation d/b/a Bernie's Rib Shack." Such secondary name registration is typically required with the local superior court.

Address(es) of business. The lender will need to know the exact mailing address and principal location of the business, as well as a list of any other offices, stores, plants, warehouses, or other sites used by the business in the course of normal operations. Principal telephone numbers of the business must also be submitted.

Employer Identification Mumber (EIN). Lenders need this information for verification of the business identification.

Date established. Identify the date on which the business was established.

Number of employees. The lender will require that you define how many persons the company employs, including all affiliated businesses and subsidiaries. In addition, you'll be asked to estimate the number of employees that you will add if the proposed financing is approved. This information may be necessary to ensure your eligibility.

Name and address of principal bank. The lender will request the name and address of your principal depository bank.

Previous SBA/government debt. You must disclose any previous loans requested or obtained through the SBA or other federal agencies, the amount, the date of request, whether or not it was approved, what the current balance is, and the loan's current status.

Identify professionals assisting you. If you are using any professional assistance for the preparation of the SBA application, this information must be disclosed to the SBA, along with a disclosure of any fees paid or agreed on for these services. This requirement includes "packaging fees" or any consulting charges incurred for the gathering or preparing of your information or identification of a lender by a third party. Points, referral fees, and arbitrary fees determined solely by the loan balance and not determined by specified, detailed duties provided on your behalf are usually not permitted in conjunction with SBA loans.

Schedule of business debt. Provide a schedule of all outstanding business loans, which should reconcile with the most recent interim financial statement submitted to the lender.

List of business owners. The lender needs a complete list of the individual owners of the business, with names, social security numbers, addresses, and their respective percentage of ownership. In addition, the SBA requests to know whether the named individuals completed any military service (along with the period of service). The SBA is interested in the voluntary ethnic and gender classifications of the individuals it serves, but by law borrowers are not required or compelled to contribute this information.

Regulatory questions. A written response is required to answer any affirmative replies to these questions:

✧ Has any officer of the business ever been involved in bankruptcy or insolvency proceedings?
✧ Is the business involved in any pending lawsuits?
✧ Does the business own a 20 percent or more interest in other businesses?
✧ Does the business presently engage in export trade?
✧ Does the business intend to begin exporting as a result of this loan?

History of the business. The lender can understand the business better if you can provide some narrative about the history of your business. Discuss what led to the founding of the company and some of the achievements that have been accomplished since the business began operating.

Some relevant information includes the revenue growth record of the company, business locations, key employees, and historical results. This section should detail the products or services offered by the company, describe the market the company seeks to address, and identify the company's competition.

Organizational chart. This document will provide a graphic demonstration that defines the business entity's chain of command or lines of authority. It is important to the lender to understand the flow of authority and the various positions used by the company to accomplish its mission.

Resumes of key employees and owners. The lender can have more confidence in your plans if you provide good information about the key people in the organization who will direct the company's efforts. This information should give details that go beyond the organizational chart and identify the specific functions of each person as they relate to the business's operation and each person's experience that will enable them to perform these functions.

A resume quantifies the background, education, and experience of each individual on hand at the business to accomplish its mission. This information is easier to interpret if prepared in a standard format with the same layout and style for each person.

In larger transactions, particularly since SBA loans have longer terms, the lender will be concerned about executive management succession, which can be addressed with this section of information.

Credit authorization. Provide the lender with written authorization to obtain credit reports for each owner, shareholder, or partner who will be guaranteeing the requested loan, but it is not legally required. An example of such an authorization can be found in Illustration 4-C.

Authorization to Release Information

I/We hereby authorize the release to _____ of any and all information they may require at any time for any purpose related to our credit transaction with them. I/We further authorize _____ to release such information to any entity they deem necessary for any purpose related to our credit transaction with them.

I/We hereby certify that the enclosed information (plus any attachments or exhibits) is valid and correct to the best of my/our knowledge.

I/We hereby acknowledge that all loan approvals will be in writing and subject to the terms and conditions set forth in a commitment letter signed by an officer of _____ .

Name _____

Address _____

City, State, Zip _____

Social Security # _____ Date of Birth _____

_____   _____
Signature   *Date*

Name _____

Address _____

City, State, Zip _____

Social Security # _____ Date of Birth _____

_____   _____
Signature   *Date*

ILLUSTRATION 4-C

The credit report is intended to disclose to the lender the past credit history of the individuals and other pertinent background information that may be pertinent to evaluating each person. This information is needed for the lender to determine whether the individuals have satisfactorily managed earlier credit relationships or whether there are unresolved issues or problems that would cause the lender to question the likelihood of being repaid. The credit report also reveals if there are any matters of public record regarding the individuals, such as judgments, tax liens, bankruptcies, or debts under collection.

Lease agreements. If you occupy leased premises, the lender will require a copy of the lease agreement. The lender will require your lease to either have a sufficient term remaining or have an option to renew for a period not less than the number of months until the maturity date of the subject loan.

Business organization documentation. The lender needs documentation that describes any legal registration under which you have organized to conduct business. There are four primary legal structures under which a commercial business can organize: a sole proprietorship (which usually requires no registration), partnership, corporation, and limited liability company.

If you are operating as a *sole proprietorship*, a distinct legal entity has not been created to distinguish the individual owner from the business enterprise. Therefore, the business does not require any administrative or legal filing, except a name registration if the business operates under a name different from its owner, which would be filed with the local superior court.

If the business is organized as a *partnership*, you need the following documentation:

✧ *Partnership agreement*—The lender will require that you provide a copy of the partnership agreement with any amendments.
✧ *List of partners*—The lender will require a complete list of the partners that is representative of 100 percent ownership of the partnership. This list should include the names, addresses, percentage of ownership, and status of the interests (general or limited).
✧ *Certificate of good standing*—The lender will require a certificate of good standing for the partnership, which is usually issued by the secretary of state in the home state of the business, which regulates legal entities. This certificate provides confir-

mation that the partnership is duly recognized by the state and authorized to conduct business.

✧ *Certificate as to Partners*—Provide the lender with a Certificate as to Partners, which attests to the authority of the partnership to enter into the loan agreement. You can use SBA Form 160A to satisfy this requirement. A copy of this form is found in Illustration 4-D.

If your business is organized as a *corporation*, the following documentation is required:

✧ *Articles of incorporation*—This document is used to register a corporation with the state, to be legally registered and recognized as a legal entity.

✧ *By-laws*—This document is adopted by its shareholders at the time of incorporation to set forth the official rules that govern the corporation.

✧ *Corporate seal*—Many states require that a corporation have an embossed seal that produces a distinctive imprint of the corporation's name and organization date. In states where required, lenders will direct corporate borrowers to use their seal on particular documents in order to confirm the corporate authority of any signer.

✧ *Corporate resolution*—The lender will request a corporate resolution confirming that the corporation's board of directors has authorized the company to enter into the proposed loan. SBA Form 160 can be used to satisfy this requirement. A copy of this form is found in Illustration 4-E.

✧ *List of corporate officers*—The lender will require a current list of corporate officers (those persons who hold a legal corporate position as defined in the by-laws).

✧ *Certificate of good standing*—The lender will require a certificate of good standing for the corporation, which is usually issued by the secretary of state in the home state of the business, which regulates legal entities. This certificate provides confirmation that the corporation is duly recognized by the state and authorized to conduct business.

If the business is organized as a *limited liability company* ("LLC"), the following documentation is required:

U.S. SMALL BUSINESS ADMINISTRATION

CERTIFICATE AS TO PARTNERS

SBA LOAN NO.

We, the undersigned, are general partners doing business under the firm name and style of _____

_____ and constitute all the partners thereof.

Acts done in the name of or on behalf of the firm, by any one of us shall be binding on said firm and each and all of us.

This statement is signed and the foregoing representations are made in order to induce the _____

_____ (hereinafter called "Lender") or the Small Business Administration (hereinafter called "SBA"):

1. To consider applications for a loan or loans to said firm when signed by any one of us.
2. To make a loan or loans to said firm against a promissory note or promissory notes signed in the firm name by any one of us.
3. To accept as security for the payment of such note or notes any collateral which may be offered by any one of us.
4. To consider applications signed in the firm name by any one of us for any renewals or extensions for all or any part of such loan or loans and any other loan or loans heretofore or hereafter made by Lender or SBA to said firm.
5. To accept any other instruments or agreements of said firm which may be required by Lender or SBA in connection with such loan, renewals, or extensions when signed by any one of us.

Any indebtedness heretofore contracted and any contracts or agreements heretofore made with Lender or SBA on behalf of said firm and all acts of partners or agents of said firm in connection with said indebtedness or said contracts or agreements are hereby ratified and confirmed, and we do hereby certify that THERE IS ATTACHED HERETO A TRUE COPY OF OUR AGREEMENT OF PARTNERSHIP.

Each of the undersigned is authorized to mortgage and/or pledge all or any part of the property, real, personal, or mixed, of said firm as security for any such loan.

This statement and representations made herein are in no way intended to exclude the general authority of each partner as to any acts not specifically mentioned or to limit the power of any one of us to bind said firm and each and every one of us individually.

Lender or SBA is authorized to rely upon the aforesaid statements until receipt of written notice of any change.

Signed this _____ day of_____ _____

_____	_____
(Typewrite Name)	(Signature)
_____	_____
(Typewrite Name)	(Signature)
_____	_____
(Typewrite Name)	(Signature)
_____	_____
(Typewrite Name)	(Signature)
_____	_____
(Typewrite Name)	(Signature)
_____	_____
(Typewrite Name)	(Signature)
_____	_____
(Typewrite Name)	(Signature)
_____	_____
(Typewrite Name)	(Signature)

State of _____)

County of _____)ss:

On this_____ day of_____ _____ , before me personally

_____ and _____ and _____ and

_____ and _____ and _____ and

_____ and _____ and _____

to be known to be the persons described in an who executed the foregoing instrument, and acknowledged that they executed the same as their free act and deed.

My commission expires _____

_____

Notary Public

NOTE: If this form of notarial certificate cannot be used in the State in question, the form should be properly modified.

SBA FORM 160A (11-87) Use 12-84 edition until exhausted ♻

This form was electronically produced by Elite Federal Forms, Inc.

ILLUSTRATION 4-D

U.S. SMALL BUSINESS ADMINISTRATION

RESOLUTION OF BOARD OF DIRECTORS OF

SBA LOAN NO

(For Corporate Applicants)

_____

(Name of Applicant)

(1) RESOLVED, that the officers of this corporation named below, or any one of them, or their, or any one of their, duly elected or appointed successors in office, be and they are hereby authorized and empowered in the name and on behalf of this corporation and under its corporate seal to execute and deliver to the _____
(hereinafter called "Lender") or the Small Business Administration (hereinafter called "SBA"), as the case may be, in the form required by Lender or SBA, the following documents: (a) application for a loan or loans, the total thereof not to exceed in principal amount $ _____ , maturing upon such date or dates and bearing interest at such rate or rates as may be prescribed by Lender or SBA; (b) applications for any renewals or extensions of all or any part of such loan or loans and of any other loans, heretofore or hereafter made by Lender or SBA to this corporation; (c) the promissory note or notes of this corporation evidencing such loan or loans or any renewals or entensions thereof; and (d) any other instruments or agreements of this corporation which may be required by Lender or SBA in connection with such loans, renewals, and/or extensions; and that said officers in their discretion may accept any such loan or loans in installments and give one or more notes of this corporation therefor, and may receive and endorse in the name of this corporation any checks or drafts representing such loan or loans or any such installments;

(2) FURTHER RESOLVED, that the aforesaid officers or any one of them, or their duly elected or appointed successors in office, be and they are hereby authorized and empowered to do any acts, including but not limited to the mortgage, pledge, or hypothecation from time to time with Lender or SBA of any or all assets of this corporation to secure such loan or loans, renewals and extensions, and to execute in the name and on behalf of this corporation and under its corporate seal or otherwise, any instruments or agreements deemed necessary or proper by Lender or SBA, in respect of the collateral securing any indebtedness of this corporation;

(3) FURTHER RESOLVED, that any indebtedness heretofore contracted and any contracts or agreements heretofore made with Lender or SBA on behalf of this corporation, and all acts of officers or agents of this corporation in connection with said indebtedness or said contracts or agreements, are hereby ratified and confirmed;

(4) FURTHER RESOLVED, that the officers referred to in the foregoing resolutions are as follows:

_____	_____	_____
(Typewrite name)	(Title)	(Signature)
_____	_____	_____
(Typewrite name)	(Title)	(Signature)
_____	_____	_____
(Typewrite name)	(Title)	(Signature)
_____	_____	_____
(Typewrite name)	(Title)	(Signature)
_____	_____	_____
(Typewrite name)	(Title)	(Signature)

(5) FURTHER RESOLVED, that Lender or SBA is authorized to rely upon the aforesaid resolutions until receipt of written notice of any change.

CERTIFICATION

I HEREBY CERTIFY that the foregoing is a true and correct copy of a resolution regularly presented to and adopted by the Board of Directors of _____

(Name of Applicant)

at _____ on the _____ day of _____ , _____ , at which a quorum was present and voted, and that such resolution is duly recorded in the minute book of this corporation; that the officers named in said resolution have been duly elected or appointed to, and are the present incumbents of, the respective offices set after their respective names; and that the signatures set opposite their respective names are their true and genuine signatures.

_____

(Seal)   Secretary

This form was electronically produced by Elite Federal Forms, Inc.

SBA FORM 160 (11-85) REF: SOP 50 10 EDITION OF 11-67 WILL BE USED UNTIL STOCK IS EXHAUSTED

ILLUSTRATION 4-E

- ✧ *Articles of Organization*—This document is used to register an LLC with the state in order to be legally registered and recognized as a legal entity.
- ✧ *LLC Agreement*—This document is adopted by its members at the time of registration and sets forth the official rules that govern the LLC.
- ✧ *List of LLC Members*—The lender will require a current list of LLC members and the managing members or other officers (those who hold any legal position of authority as defined in the LLC Agreement).
- ✧ *Certificate of good standing*—The lender will require a certificate of good standing for the LLC, which is usually issued by the secretary of state in the home state of the business, which regulates legal entities. This certificate provides confirmation that the corporation is duly recognized by the state and authorized to conduct business.

Financial Information

The lender will require complete financial disclosure from you in order to fairly evaluate the proposed loan. This information will help the lender and the SBA confirm that you are eligible for SBA participation.

Financial information is pertinent to your eligibility for SBA assistance, since it will establish how you (and any related interests) measure against the maximum SBA financial qualification limits to confirm eligibility. Financial information also informs the lender about how you have and are performing, which may have a bearing on the prospects of future success.

Personal financial statements. The lender will require a personal financial statement from every business owner and from any other party that has been proposed to personally guarantee the loan. The personal financial statement must provide the lender with an accurate summary of the individual's assets, liabilities, income, and other pertinent data.

Sometimes prospective borrowers submit inaccurate financial information that either understates or overstates their financial position. Some of these erroneous submissions are due to genuine confusion or lack of understanding of how to define the requested financial information. Others try to inflate the appearance of the financial wherewithal being disclosed so as to convince the lender that their application is more qualified than it really is. These efforts are usually easy for the lender to recognize.

It is a federal crime to knowingly submit false information in order to induce a lender to provide a loan.

While there are many financial statement forms available, the SBA's form is the required form to submit. A copy of the SBA Form 413 (the Personal Financial Statement) is found in Illustration 4-F.

To clarify questions that may arise while preparing the personal financial statement, remember the following guidelines:

✧ Establish a date of the report and describe the various asset and liability accounts at their approximate value as best known. For simplicity, round entries to the nearest $1,000.

✧ This report is not an audit, so each entry will not be scrutinized to the penny. But be assured that the lender can spot exaggerations and will question you about any entries that seem out of context or unrealistic. Credit reports are also used to compare the report liabilities to the debt disclosed by the individual.

✧ List liquid asset accounts (including cash, accounts receivable, and marketable securities) according to the most recent balance you can document. If the transaction depends on you injecting cash as part of the settlement, the lender will ask for verification of these funds at the application stage in the form of bank or brokerage statements, etc.

✧ Real estate, automobiles, and other major assets should be valued at the likely price at which they could be sold in a reasonable marketing period. The financial statement provides space for more details about real estate assets on its page 2, including the address, the title names, the purchase date, the purchase price, the present market value, and the present mortgage balance. This additional information is necessary, since real estate comprises a majority of many individuals' net worth, and lenders will assess any estimate of valuation.

✧ Remember to include the value of any closely held stock or partnership interests owned, particularly in the subject business. These assets should be valued according to the percentage of ownership, based on a reasonable assessment of the market value of the company or the company's actual book value. Be prepared to justify that valuation.

✧ Under "Other Assets," record the value of personal household assets such as furniture, art, silverware, furs, jewelry, antiques, silver, and other personal effects. The lender will not seek to use these assets to secure the loan, but inclusion of the value

OMB APPROVAL NO. 3245-0188
EXPIRATION DATE:11/30/2004

PERSONAL FINANCIAL STATEMENT

U.S. SMALL BUSINESS ADMINISTRATION

As of _____ , _____

Complete this form for: (1) each proprietor, or (2) each limited partner who owns 20% or more interest and each general partner, or (3) each stockholder owning 20% or more of voting stock, or (4) any person or entity providing a guaranty on the loan.

Name	Business Phone
Residence Address	Residence Phone
City, State, & Zip Code	

Business Name of Applicant/Borrower

ASSETS	(Omit Cents)	LIABILITIES	(Omit Cents)
Cash on hand & in Banks	$ _____	Accounts Payable...........................	$ _____
Savings Accounts.........................	$ _____	Notes Payable to Banks and Others...........	$ _____
IRA or Other Retirement Account	$ _____	(Describe in Section 2)	
Accounts & Notes Receivable	$ _____	Installment Account (Auto)	$ _____
Life Insurance-Cash Surrender Value Only	$ _____	Mo. Payments $_____	
(Complete Section 8)		Installment Account (Other)	$ _____
Stocks and Bonds	$ _____	Mo. Payments $_____	
(Describe in Section 3)		Loan on Life Insurance	$ _____
Real Estate.............................	$ _____	Mortgages on Real Estate	$ _____
(Describe in Section 4)		(Describe in Section 4)	
Automobile-Present Value.................	$ _____	Unpaid Taxes	$ _____
Other Personal Property...................	$ _____	(Describe in Section 6)	
(Describe in Section 5)		Other Liabilities	$ _____
Other Assets	$ _____	(Describe in Section 7)	
(Describe in Section 5)		Total Liabilities -	$ _____
		Net Worth -	$ _____
Total	$ _____	**Total**	$ _____

Section 1. Source of Income		Contingent Liabilities	
Salary	$ _____	As Endorser or Co-Maker	$ _____
Net Investment Income	$ _____	Legal Claims & Judgments	$ _____
Real Estate Income	$ _____	Provision for Federal Income Tax	$ _____
Other Income (Describe below)*	$ _____	Other Special Debt	$ _____

Description of Other Income in Section 1.

*Alimony or child support payments need not be disclosed in "Other Income" unless it is desired to have such payments counted toward total income.

Section 2. Notes Payable to Banks and Others. (Use attachments if necessary. Each attachment must be identified as a part of this statement and signed.)

Name and Address of Noteholder(s)	Original Balance	Current Balance	Payment Amount	Frequency (monthly,etc.)	How Secured or Endorsed Type of Collateral

SBA Form 413 (3-00) **Previous Editions Obsolete**
This form was electronically produced by Elite Federal Forms, Inc.

(tumble)

ILLUSTRATION 4-F

Section 3. Stocks and Bonds. (Use attachments if necessary. Each attachment must be identified as a part of this statement and signed).

Number of Shares	Name of Securities	Cost	Market Value Quotation/Exchange	Date of Quotation/Exchange	Total Value

Section 4. Real Estate Owned. (List each parcel separately. Use attachment if necessary. Each attachment must be identified as a part of this statement and signed.)

	Property A	Property B	Property C
Type of Property			
Address			
Date Purchased			
Original Cost			
Present Market Value			
Name & Address of Mortgage Holder			
Mortgage Account Number			
Mortgage Balance			
Amount of Payment per Month/Year			
Status of Mortgage			

Section 5. Other Personal Property and Other Assets. (Describe, and if any is pledged as security, state name and address of lien holder, amount of lien, terms of payment and if delinquent, describe delinquency)

Section 6. Unpaid Taxes. (Describe in detail, as to type, to whom payable, when due, amount, and to what property, if any, a tax lien attaches.)

Section 7. Other Liabilities. (Describe in detail.)

Section 8. Life Insurance Held. (Give face amount and cash surrender value of policies - name of insurance company and beneficiaries)

I authorize SBA/Lender to make inquiries as necessary to verify the accuracy of the statements made and to determine my creditworthiness. I certify the above and the statements contained in the attachments are true and accurate as of the stated date(s). These statements are made for the purpose of either obtaining a loan or guaranteeing a loan. I understand FALSE statements may result in forfeiture of benefits and possible prosecution by the U.S. Attorney General (Reference 18 U.S.C. 1001).

Signature: Date: Social Security Number:

Signature: Date: Social Security Number:

PLEASE NOTE: The estimated average burden hours for the completion of this form is 1.5 hours per response. If you have questions or comments concerning this estimate or any other aspect of this information, please contact Chief, Administrative Branch, U.S. Small Business Administration, Washington, D.C. 20416, and Clearance Officer, Paper Reduction Project (3245-0188), Office of Management and Budget, Washington, D.C. 20503. **PLEASE DO NOT SEND FORMS TO OMB.**

ILLUSTRATION 4-F

of these assets ensures that any assets you acquired with consumer debt are offset. Also, the net value is a relevant disclosure of your wealth accumulation.

✧ Segregate liabilities into distinct categories, including bank notes (i.e., car loans, personal notes, and student loans), credit accounts (i.e., Visa, MasterCard, Discover, and other retail credit accounts), and real estate debt (any debt that encumbers your real property, including second mortgages and HELOCs (home equity line of credit).

✧ The personal financial statement form provides a space on which you subtract the total liabilities from the total assets to calculate your net worth.

✧ Estimate total annual income and identify the primary sources, such as salaries, real estate income, investment income, interest, or other sources. These various sources should be detailed separately on an annualized basis.

✧ The personal financial statement form provides a space for the disclosure of any contingent liabilities that may include potential taxes or fines, guaranteed or cosigned obligations, or other special debts that are not direct obligations as of the date of the financial statement.

✧ Any asset or liability entry that needs explanation should be listed in specified sections on page two. In these sections you can disclose any information that will assist the lender's understanding of specific entries. In addition, there is a section for the details about life insurance you own, including the insurer, amount of coverage, beneficiaries, cash surrender value, and the name of any assignees.

✧ Be sure to sign and date the financial statement. Your social security number is usually required in order to verify identification.

Single Versus Married

It is very important to distinguish asset/liability ownership of individuals from what their financial position may be as part of a married couple. If one spouse owns an interest in a business and submits a personal financial statement to support a loan request, no jointly owned assets should be reflected at their full value. Likewise, an appropriate percentage of any joint obligation of the marital estate should be reflected on the statement to demonstrate the actual financial position of the individual.

The lender will carefully evaluate your personal financial statement to assess whether it reflects that you may have adequate personal resources to finance the business without SBA assistance. Generally, if your liquid assets (cash, nonretirement securities, cash surrender value of life insurance, and other assets immediately convertible to cash) exceed the loan request on the loan, your application will probably be declined or you'll be offered a smaller loan based on your ability to provide for your needs with existing resources. The only exceptions are those liquid assets previously pledged to another lender for other financing or other special circumstances that will have to be explained.

Copies of personal income tax returns. The lender will require you to provide copies of personal income tax returns along with all schedules for the past three years. And, in compliance with SBA rules, you will be required to execute IRS Form 4506-T to authorize the lender to obtain a transcript of each tax return from the IRS for verification. This requirement is in response to many past unscrupulous applicants who used fictitious tax returns to qualify for SBA loans. A copy of IRS Form 4506 -T(Request for Copy or Transcript of Tax Form) is found in Illustration 4-G.

Lenders will require that you certify the submitted tax returns (and financial statements) with either an attached statement of authenticity or with an original signature on the document. The latter is certainly easier, but make sure not to sign on the form's signature line when signing a copy of a tax return. It could be technically viewed as an original form if obtained by the IRS and create new tax problems. Use a colored pen such as blue or red, so that the signature is easy to find and obviously is not copied.

Business financial statements. The lender will require you to submit the past three years' business financial statements. This information permits the lender to examine your recent financial performance and evaluate results during each period. The lender will compare many components from each year to analyze a number of factors that describe the company's success.

If practical, have your financial statements prepared by an accountant or a certified public accountant (CPA). Depending on the size of the business (sales of $1 million plus) and the amount of capital financing requested ($750,000 and higher), an accountant's assistance may be absolutely necessary. Their work is going to be viewed with more credibility than internally prepared financials from the best software, because the lender is assured of their professional expertise and independence.

Form **4506-T**
(January 2004)

Department of the Treasury
Internal Revenue Service

Request for Transcript of Tax Return

▶ Do not sign this form unless all applicable parts have been completed.
Read the instructions on page 2.
▶ Request may be rejected if the form is incomplete, illegible, or any required part was blank at the time of signature.

OMB No. 1545-1872

TIP: Use new Form 4506-T to order a transcript or other return information free of charge. See the product list below. You can also call 1-800-829-1040 to order a transcript. If you need a copy of your return, use **Form 4506**, Request for Copy of Tax Return. There is a fee to get a copy of your return.

1a Name shown on tax return. If a joint return, enter the name shown first.	1b First social security number on tax return or employer identification number (see instructions)
2a If a joint return, enter spouse's name shown on tax return	2b Second social security number if joint tax return

3 Current name, address (including apt., room, or suite no.), city, state, and ZIP code

4 Address, (including apt., room, or suite no.), city, state, and ZIP code shown on the last return filed if different from line 3

5 If the transcript or tax information is to be mailed to a third party (such as a mortgage company), enter the third party's name, address, and telephone number. The IRS has no control over what the third party does with the tax information.

CAUTION: *Lines 6 and 7 must be completed if the third party requires you to complete Form 4506-T.* **Do not** *sign Form 4506-T if the third party requests that you sign Form 4506-T and lines 6 and 7 are blank.*

6 **Product requested.** Most requests will be processed within 10 business days. If the product requested relates to information from a return filed more than 4 years ago, it may take up to 30 days. Enter the return number here and check the box below. ▶

a **Return Transcript,** which includes most of the line items of a tax return as filed with the IRS. Transcripts are generally available for the following returns: Form 1040 series, Form 1065, Form 1120, Form 1120A, Form 1120H, Form 1120L, and Form 1120S. Return transcripts are available for the current year and returns processed during the prior 3 processing years . . . . ☐

b **Account Transcript,** which contains information on the financial status of the account, such as payments made on the account, penalty assessments, and adjustments made by you or the IRS after the return was filed. Return information is limited to items such as tax liability and estimated tax payments. Account transcripts are available for most returns . . . . ☐

c **Record of Account,** which is a combination of line item information and later adjustments to the account. Available for current year and 3 prior tax years . . . . ☐

d **Verification of Nonfiling,** which is proof from the IRS that you did not file a return for the year . . . . ☐

e **Form W-2, Form 1099 series, Form 1098 series, or Form 5498 series transcript.** The IRS can provide a transcript that includes data from these information returns. State or local information is not included with the Form W-2 information. The IRS may be able to provide this transcript information for up to 10 years. Information for the current year is generally not available until the year after it is filed with the IRS. For example, W-2 information for 2003, filed in 2004, will not be available from the IRS until 2005. If you need W-2 information for retirement purposes, you should contact the Social Security Administration at 1-800-772-1213 . . . . ☐

CAUTION: *If you need a copy of Form W-2 or Form 1099, you should first contact the payer. To get a copy of the Form W-2 or Form 1099 filed with your return, you must use Form 4506 and request a copy of your return, which includes all attachments.*

7 **Year or period requested.** Enter the ending date of the year or period, using the mm/dd/yyyy format. If you are requesting more than four years or periods, you must attach another Form 4506-T.

____/____/____   ____/____/____   ____/____/____   ____/____/____

Signature of taxpayer(s). I declare that I am either the taxpayer whose name is shown on line 1a or 2a, or a person authorized to obtain the tax information requested. If the request applies to a joint return, **either** husband or wife must sign. If signed by a corporate officer, partner, guardian, tax matters partner, executor, receiver, administrator, trustee, or party other than the taxpayer, I certify that I have the authority to execute Form 4506-T on behalf of the taxpayer.

Telephone number of taxpayer on line 1a or 2a
( )

Sign Here

▶ Signature (see instructions)   Date

▶ Title (if line 1a above is a corporation, partnership, estate, or trust)

▶ Spouse's signature   Date

For Privacy Act and Paperwork Reduction Act Notice, see page 2.   Cat. No. 37667N   Form **4506-T** (1-2004)

PART 2

ILLUSTRATION 4-G

There are three general levels of financial reporting:

1. *Compilation.* This financial report has the basic level of confirmation, since the accountant compiles the internally generated report of receipts and payments and creates a financial statement based on the account classifications defined by the business. The accountant will correct any blatant errors discovered but will typically depend on the client to provide most of the definition of supplied information, which is reported in a standardized format.

2. *Review.* This report is prepared by compiling the financial information after it is classified by the accountant, who also conducts several tests to assure accuracy and consistency. The CPA accepts a greater responsibility for production of this report and issues a review statement certifying the report's accuracy. The accountant is professionally obligated to report inconsistencies found in the accounting methods or in preparation of these financial statements. Further, the CPA confirms that the information has been prepared in accordance with generally accepted accounting principles (GAAP).

3. *Audit.* This report is the highest level of scrutiny of all financial reporting, where the accountant prepares the financial statement after testing every revenue, expense, asset, and liability classification and confirming the validity of hundreds of entries. The report is issued with an opinion of the CPA as to its accuracy and fairness, disclosing any exceptions or inconsistencies to generally accepted accounting principles.

There are no formal standards with which to qualify when a business should use one financial accounting report or another. This decision should be made based on the particular needs of the business and who is requiring the information. A compilation is fine for a company with $20 million in sales if there is only one shareholder who does not plan to borrow money. However, a company with sales of $53 million desiring to make a public equity offering must have three years of audited financial statements.

The lender will inform you which level of financial reporting is required or preferred by the lender. If there are several shareholders or the company's borrowing requirements are expected to exceed $750,000, it is a good idea to consider a review-level financial report. The review statement will provide sufficient credibility of the company's financial controls, without the high cost of audit.

Recognize that the financial statements are probably the most important part of the application that determines whether or not you'll qualify for financing. Therefore, the quality of preparation is germane to the company's ability to obtain a loan. Many businesses utilize an in-house bookkeeper or accountant to organize their financial records and produce a basic financial statement for operations. A capable person in this role is essential since this information is usually the basis for the work performed by the company's CPA for the annual financial and tax reports.

Companies certainly should have monthly financial statements as a management tool, but usually, depending on the size and complexity of the business, internally prepared statements suffice for these requirements. If the company's lender requires more than annual statements, it is probably going to quarterly statements. These could be compiled by an independent accountant without incurring unreasonable expense, and then producing a review-level or audit report at the end of the year. A very small business (sales less than $500,000) generally does not need independently prepared financial statements.

If your loan request is approved, expect that the lender will require you to submit annual financial reports, as of the last day of the company's fiscal year. Regardless of the type of financial statement prepared for the company, the report should be completed within ninety days after the end of the reporting period.

Interim financial statement. The lender will require the loan application to include an interim financial statement no more than ninety days old. Updated financial information is particularly important during the last half of the year, when more time will have elapsed since the previous year-end report. The need for an interim report is accentuated by an SBA requirement that the loan guaranty application include updated interim financial statements.

Reconciliation of net worth. Provide the lender with a reconciliation of net worth, if needed. Often, there are adjustments made to the retained earnings, or other equity accounts, that will render the net worth out of balance with previous reporting periods. These adjustments are not always obvious and can slow down the lender's analysis of the financial statements. Prepare a reconciliation of any such changes ahead of time and provide a detailed explanation of all adjustments.

Analysis of financial statements. It is beneficial for you to provide the lender with a detailed narrative of the business financial reports, describing the results of each reporting period. This analysis permits you to influence the lender's interpretation of the financial statements and ensure a complete understanding and perspective of the operating results.

Place emphasis on information that concisely explains any negative results and, of course, highlights the positive results. If appropriate, you can even prepare a separate restatement of the financial results with any extraordinary adjustments illustrated to demonstrate the full impact of the noted information.

Some of the financial ratios explained in Chapter 3 may also assist you in preparing an analysis for the lender's review.

Accounts receivable aging report. The lender will require an accounts receivable aging report as of the date of the latest interim or year end financial statement. The total balance of this report should be reconciled to the accounts receivable balance on the most recently submitted interim financial statement. This information provides the lender with an indication of the strength (or weakness) of the company's working capital position and intermediate liquidity outlook.

Inventory aging report. If inventory represents a significant asset of the business, it is helpful to provide the lender with an inventory aging report so that components of the company's inventory (raw materials, work-in-process, or finished goods) can be evaluated and the aging of each of these categories defined. This report should also be dated and reconciled to the inventory balance stated on the most recent interim or year-end financial statement.

If inventory is an important component of the company's assets, the lender will be interested in the valuation method used by the company to account for the value of inventory. There are two accounting methods by which a business can assess its inventory values:

1. *First In–First Out (FIFO).* This method values inventory based on the cost of the inventory unit when acquired—units are expensed out as used, based on the original price paid per unit. This method is the more aggressive of the two methods, because it permits the business to retain higher-valued units on the books while expending typically lower-cost units. This method results in a higher inventory valuation.

2. *Last In—First Out (LIFO)*. This method values inventory based on the latest cost of inventory units—units are expensed out based on the latest market price without regard to the actual price paid for the particular units. LIFO is the more conservative of the two methods because it requires the business to expense the higher-price units first as depleted, which results in a lower inventory valuation.

Accounts payable aging report. The lender will require an accounts payable aging report as of the date of the latest interim or year-end financial statement. The total balance of this report should be reconciled to the accounts payable balance on the most recently submitted interim financial statement. This information provides the lender with an indication of the strength (or weakness) of the company's working capital position and how well it is managing its trade debt.

Copies of business income tax returns. The lender will require copies of business income tax returns along with all schedules for the past three years. As with your personal income tax returns, in compliance with SBA rules, you must execute IRS form 4506-T to authorize the lender to obtain a transcript of each tax return from the IRS for verification.

It may be helpful to prepare a memorandum discussing the tax reporting methods and procedures employed by the business. Some guidance for the lender to navigate them through the differences between the business's financial statements and tax returns may be useful. Most businesses tend to reduce profits where possible on income tax reports in order to lower taxable income. Financial statements may be a better indication of the company's true economic results.

Providing information to reconcile the differences between your tax returns and financial statements will help reduce the lender's concerns.

Financial projections. The lender will be interested in your company's projections of future financial performance for at least two years following the proposed loan. The company's ability to accurately project these figures and justify the basis for these predictions is an important component of the loan application.

Provide the following financial projections to support the loan application:

✧ *Balance sheet pro forma.* Using the most recently submitted interim balance sheet, you should demonstrate the immediate

Pro Forma Balance Sheet

Company _____ Date _____

	Beginning Financial Position	Changes +/–	Ending Financial Position
ASSETS			
Current Assets			
1. Cash			
2. Accounts Receivable			
3. Inventory			
4. Other Current Assets			
5. Total Current Assets (add lines 1 + 2 + 3 +4)			
Fixed Assets			
6. Land			
7. RE Improvements			
8. Equipment			
9. Other Fixed Assets			
10. Less Depreciation			
11. Total Fixed Assets (add lines 6 + 7 + 8 + 9 minus line 10)			
Other Assets			
12. Other Assets – Intangibles			
13. Transaction/Org. Costs			
14. Total Other Assets (add lines 12 + 13)			
15. Total Assets (add lines 5 + 11 + 14)			
LIABILITIES			
Current Liabilities			
16. Accounts Payable			
17. Current Portion of LTD			
18. Taxes Payable			
19. Notes Payable			
20. Other Liabilities			
21. Total Current Liabilities (add lines 16 + 17 + 18 + 19 + 20)			
Long-Term Liabilities			
22. Notes Payable			
23. Mortgages			
24. Shareholder Notes			
25. Total Long-Term Liabilities (add lines 22 + 23 + 24)			
EQUITY			
26. Common Stock			
27. Paid In Capital			
28. Retained Earnings			
29. Current Period Earnings			
30. Distributions			
31. Total Equity (add lines 26 + 27 + 28 + 29 minus line 30)			
32. Total Liabilities and Equity (add lines 21 + 25 + 31)			

Note: Line 15 must equal Line 32 in order to balance.

ILLUSTRATION 4-H

effect the loan proceeds would have on the company's balance sheet. This projection is best demonstrated by a comparative spreadsheet showing the present (preloan) balance sheet with appropriate debits and credits detailing the effects of the loan transaction in the column to the right of each affected account; then a summation of the pro forma balance sheet in the last column to the right, reflecting the postloan financial position of the business. An example of this balance sheet projection format is found in Illustration 4-H.

✧ *Profit/loss statement projections.* Prepare a detailed income projection for the company for two years based on the existing financial trends and the changes that are expected to result directly from the proposed loan. There are additional suggestions about how to develop profit/loss projections in Chapter 3.

✧ *Cash flow projections.* Using the first year's income projections, prepare a monthly cash flow projection to demonstrate the company's cash cycle during the first year following the loan transaction. Be sure to reflect the principal and interest payments of the requested loan as scheduled.

More sophisticated borrowers will even account for the timing of revenues generated on a receivable basis, goods purchased on trade credit, and seasonal changes in sales. There is additional information about how to develop cash flow projections in Chapter 3.

Collateral Information

It is helpful to the lender—and accelerates consideration of the loan application—if you provide information in advance about the assets to be offered to the lender as collateral to secure the loan. This data helps the lender assess collateral adequacy, understand your predisposition to secure the loan, and evaluate the loan proposal with these factors. This section outlines a number of items the lender can use to evaluate the specifics of your proposed collateral.

Generally, borrowers will not have the suggested professional reports at the time of loan application, particularly for real property collateral. But any available collateral information will assist the lender's understanding of exactly how you can secure the loan.

Most of the valuation or analytical information will have to have

---

✧ **Anticipate how much collateral may be required.**
✧ **Decide which assets are off-limits in advance.**
✧ **Confer with your spouse concerning assets that are owned jointly.**

been prepared very recently if you are to use it for the present loan. Appraisals, environmental reports, and even surveys more than six months old are useful as a guideline but are stale in terms of the lender being able to rely on this information.

There may be a significant difference between the lender's impression of the valuation of collateral assets and your own assessment. Lenders discount the market or cost values of collateral assets when determining the adequacy of collateral against the requested loan. This discount is understandable, since the lender has to maintain a safety margin to hedge on possible depreciation and cover possible liquidation costs.

Sometimes lenders will seem too conservative in determining a prudent advance rate on specific collateral assets. You may be able to address this problem with more information demonstrating another way to evaluate the value of the subject asset. For example, providing the lender with recent comparable sales records, planned development that has been announced in the area, or other data that may have been overlooked can help establish the value of similar assets to those offered as collateral. This supporting information may give you the opportunity to negotiate better leverage for the collateral.

In determining liquidation or collateral value, lenders will use the lower of cost or appraised value of an asset. If you're acquiring an asset at a price significantly lower than an appraiser's opinion of the market value, the reality is that the lender will still base its credit decision on the actual sales price. You will not be allowed to leverage against "phantom" equity. Expect lenders to assert the collateral base as the lower of appraised value or sale price.

When a loan proposal is approved, lenders will offer terms based on the requirement of certain assets being encumbered as collateral. Sometimes lenders will specify their requirement that a significant amount of extra collateral be pledged against the loan as an "abundance of caution." This decision may be made "because it's there" and encumbering more collateral will provide extra protection for the lender and prevent you from obtaining another loan.

Loan commitments do not have to be the final word. You can always refuse the lender's offer and try to negotiate with the lender to amend the deal to reflect more reasonable terms. *Everything is negotiable.* Sometimes qualified borrowers can find other lenders, hungrier for business, that offer easier terms.

Resist the lender's inclination to secure too much collateral if you have alternatives. Challenge the lender to justify the quantity of collateral requested and the method used to determine the adequacy of that collateral.

Ultimately, this exercise may not change the lender's requirements, but it may cause the lender to either (1) reconsider the leverage (how much advanced) of certain assets, or (2) give you a better interest rate to reflect lower risk on the deal.

Before entering serious negotiations for a loan, decide exactly which business or personal assets that you will make available to pledge as collateral to secure the loan. In the detailed categories of assets described below, I offer some suggestions concerning their suitability as collateral and the exposure to the asset owner to use it as collateral. I also make recommendations about how to manage some of the situations you may face if certain assets are requested as collateral by the lender. But be prepared with an answer before questions are posed so as to keep priorities straight and eliminate regret as an outcome of the loan terms.

Additionally, it may be useful to note that the SBA cannot refuse to guarantee a loan due only to insufficient collateral. Conversely, in an ironic twist of the regulations, if the borrower possesses enough assets to fully secure the loan, in most 7(a) programs the lender is obligated to at least cover 100 percent of the loan amount with collateral.

Another point to remember when negotiating collateral is the lender's "golden rule." Know exactly what the company's and individual's limits are before negotiations begin.

Depending on the nature of your collateral, the following information can assist the lender in understanding these assets:

Real property collateral. If you propose to pledge a mortgage interest in a parcel of real property owned by the business or its owners to secure the loan, furnishing the following documentation to the lender will be helpful in their evaluation of this collateral:

- ✧ *Legal description*—The lender should receive a "metes and bounds" description of the property obtained from a survey, if available, or at least the district and land lot number of the property. This information may be found on the warranty deed, or other mortgage documents, or it may be attached to the property's purchase contract.
- ✧ *Appraisal*—The lender should receive a copy of any current or aged property appraisal on the subject property, if one exists. [Note—the lender cannot use this appraisal to determine its own valuation of the property; providing it as evidence of value will only serve to demonstrate its value in a study commissioned at an earlier date.]

✧ *Description of property improvements*—The lender should receive a description or list of the various improvements and features of the property that may increase its value (such as extra curb cuts, zoning classifications, and adjacent development).

✧ *Survey*—The lender should receive a copy of a survey or plat of the property. A survey was probably obtained when the property was purchased. A plat of the property can usually be obtained in the county tax assessor's office but is not as useful as a survey.

✧ *Location map*—The lender should receive a portion of a local city or county map that depicts the general area containing the property site, including an indication of the exact position of the property.

✧ *Engineering reports*—The lender should receive any available engineering studies conducted at the property, especially for older facilities. These reports will reflect the structural condition of the improvements based on inspections of the structure by qualified engineers, and a discussion of the general condition of the structure.

✧ *Environmental studies*—The lender should receive any Phase 1, Phase 2, or other environmental evaluations reports that may have been previously prepared for the property. If the property contains underground storage tanks (USTs), the lender should be given copies of any testing or inspection results of the USTs as far back as available.

✧ *Environmental questionnaire*—Prepare an Environmental Questionnaire and Disclosure Statement, which details pertinent information about real property that will secure the loan. If the property has never been used for commercial or agricultural purposes, there may be sufficient grounds for the lender to waive the requirement of a Phase 1 study, based on the responses to this questionnaire. A copy of this form can be found in Illustration 4-I.

✧ *Photographs*—The lender should receive photographs of the property and its improvements. Visualization of the property can reinforce the borrower's description of the property and enable the lender's recognition of the value of the asset.

✧ *Lease agreements*—The lender should receive copies of leases for tenants who occupy a portion (less than 50 percent) of the subject property, or income generated from other properties pledged as collateral. The lender should be willing to recognize the cash flow contributions from the income generated from renting portions of the property. While the borrower must generate sufficient income from business operations to repay its debt, the extra leasing income will strengthen the borrower's case by demonstrating a higher margin of debt service coverage.

✧ *Insurance*—Provide the lender information describing insurance coverage provided for the real property improvements. While insurers do not provide coverage for unimproved property (other than liability), all improvements should be insured against fire or other hazards to the extent of their replacement costs. Lenders will mandate such coverage as a condition of extending credit using real estate assets as collateral.

✧ *Sales contract*—If you are acquiring the subject real property as part of the total transaction, the lender should receive a copy of the executed sales contract.

Concerning personal residences. Frequently, tension will arise during the loan negotiation process between you and the lender concerning the lender's suggestion that you should encumber your personal residence. The lender may justify this requirement by citing the need to secure your personal guaranty, or that the business property value is insufficient to secure the loan. Sometimes the equity value of your residence will cover this equity shortfall needed to fully secure the loan, but sometimes the personal residence equity is not needed.

If the transaction requires the personal equity to secure the loan, you may have to choose whether to pledge the house or pass on the loan commitment. If you are married, the spouse typically is a 50 percent co-owner of the residence and will have to consent to any such encumbrance.

According to Regulation B—the Equal Credit Opportunity Act—a lender cannot request, suggest, or imply that a business owner's spouse must become either an obligor or personal guarantor on a transaction in which the spouse does not have an ownership interest in the business.

Environmental Questionnaire and Disclosure Statement

Loan # _____

The undersigned, as owner or buyer of the Property described on Exhibit "A" attached hereto, is familiar with the operations currently conducted on the property, has made a reasonably diligent inquiry into the former uses of the Property, and hereby declares and certifies that to the best of its knowledge the following information is true and correct.

A response is required for each item. Please note and continue answers on a separate sheet, if necessary.

Commercial Real Estate

Current/Former Uses of the Property

1. Provide dates for construction of current improvements and any improvements that have been demolished or removed.

_____

_____

_____

2. Description of current uses.

_____

_____

_____

3. Names of all owners since 1940.

_____

_____

_____

ILLUSTRATION 4-1

4. Names of previous occupants.

_____

_____

_____

5. Description of all previous uses since 1940.

_____

_____

_____

6. Current and past uses of adjacent property.

_____

_____

_____

7. Was the Property ever parceled differently?
   ❐ Yes   ❐ No

8. Were there ever different addresses for the site?
   ❐ Yes   ❐ No   If yes, please give full details.

_____

_____

_____

9. Are there or have there ever been any disposal facilities, dump sites, or facilities involving hazardous waste within 2,000 feet of the site?
   ❐ Yes   ❐ No   If yes, describe.

ILLUSTRATION 4-1

_____

_____

_____

Asbestos

1. Is there asbestos currently in any of the construction materials contained in the building?
   ❐ Yes   ❐ No   If so, where?

_____

_____

_____

2. If so, has a survey been conducted to assess the type, amount, location, and condition of asbestos on the site?
   ❐ Yes   ❐ No   If so, please attach a copy of any survey report.

3. Have asbestos air samples been taken?
   ❐ Yes   ❐ No   If so, what were the results?

_____

_____

_____

Polychlorinated Biphenyls ("PCBs")

1. Have PCBs been used in electrical transformers, capacitors, or other equipment at the Property?
   ❐ Yes   ❐ No   If so, please describe the use and quantity of PCBs used on the Property.

_____

_____

_____

ILLUSTRATION 4-1

Fuel/Chemical Storage Tanks, Drums, and Pipelines

1. Are there any aboveground or underground gasoline, diesel, fuel oil, chemical storage tanks, or other hazardous materials on the Property?
   ❒ Yes   ❒ No   If so, please describe substances stored and capacity of tank(s).

   _____

   _____

   _____

2. Are any of the tanks known to leak now or to have leaked in the past?
   ❒ Yes   ❒ No   When was the most recent test? _____
   Results?

   _____

   _____

   _____

3. Provide an inventory of materials, quantity, age, construction material, and leak protection systems on each tank.

   _____

   _____

   _____

4. Are any other chemicals stored on the Property in drums or other containers?
   ❒ Yes   ❒ No   If so, please describe the substances, quantities stored, and types and conditions of container.

   _____

   _____

   _____

ILLUSTRATION 4-1

5. Have there been any spills, leaks, or other releases of chemicals on the Property?
❒ Yes   ❒ No   If so, please describe the chemicals and quantities released, any cleanup measures taken, and any results of any soil or groundwater samples performed to detect the presence of the chemicals spilled, leaked, or released on the Property.

_____

_____

_____

6. Please attach copies of any permits or licenses pertaining to the use, storage, handling, or disposal of chemicals on the Property.

7. Are any of the tanks known to leak now or to have leaked in the past?
❒ Yes   ❒ No

Water Discharges

1. List all sources of wastewater discharges to surface waters, groundwaters, septic systems, or holding ponds.

_____

_____

_____

2. List all sources of wastewater discharges to public sewer systems and storm collection systems.

_____

_____

_____

3. Please attach copies of any water discharge permits, licenses, or registration pertaining to operations on the Property.

ILLUSTRATION 4-1

Air Emissions

1. Describe air emissions from each source of air pollutants, including fuel-burning equipment. Describe type of fuel burned.

_____

_____

_____

2. Describe air pollution control equipment used to reduce emissions for each source of air emissions.

_____

_____

_____

3. Are air emissions monitored?
   ❐ Yes   ❐ No   If so, please indicate frequency of monitoring and attach results.

_____

_____

4. Please attach copies of any air permits, licenses, or registrations pertaining to operations on the Property.

Waste Disposal

1. Describe the types of liquid wastes, other than wastewater described above, and solid wastes generated at the Property.

_____

_____

_____

ILLUSTRATION 4-I

2. Describe how the liquid and solid wastes generated at the Property are disposed of.

_____

_____

_____

_____

3. Please attach copies of any waste disposal permits or licenses pertaining to operations on the Property.

Soil Contamination

1. Have there been any spills, leaks, or other releases of hazardous materials on the Property?
   ❏ Yes ❏ No If so, describe the materials and quantities released, any mitigation measures, and the results of soil or groundwater samples performed.

_____

_____

_____

_____

2. Are there any known spills, leaks, or other releases on adjacent sites?
   ❏ Yes ❏ No

3. Is there evidence of contamination plumes moving onto the site from adjacent sites?
   ❏ Yes ❏ No

Agricultural Property

If the property has been or is used for agricultural purposes, the following additional information should be provided.

ILLUSTRATION 4-1

1. Have pesticides, herbicides, or other agricultural chemicals been applied to the Property? ❏ Yes ❏ No If so, please describe the locations where such pesticides or chemicals were applied, the types of pesticides or chemicals applied in each area, and the results of any soil or groundwater analyses performed to detect pesticides or chemicals used at the site.

_____

_____

_____

2. Have pesticides, herbicides, or other agricultural chemicals been mixed, formulated, rinsed, or disposed of on the Property? ❏ Yes ❏ No If so, please describe the locations where such pesticides were mixed, formulated, rinsed, or disposed, the type of pesticides or chemicals mixed, formulated, rinsed, or disposed of at each location, and the results of any soil or groundwater analyses performed to detect pesticides or chemicals mixed, formulated, rinsed, or disposed of at the site.

_____

_____

_____

Industrial Property

If the Property has been or is used for industrial purposes, the following additional information should be provided:

1. Has the Property been used for disposal of any liquid or solid waste? ❏ Yes ❏ No If so, describe the location of all disposal sites, the type of wastes disposed at each site, the results of any soil or groundwater samples taken in the vicinity of each site, and the manner in which each site not currently in use was closed.

_____

_____

_____

ILLUSTRATION 4-1

2. Have evaporation or storage ponds been located on the Property?
❒ Yes ❒ No If so, describe the location of all ponds, the type of wastes placed in each pond, the results of any soil or groundwater samples taken in the vicinity of each pond, and the manner in which each pond not currently in use was closed.

_____

_____

_____

3. Have wastewater treatment facilities, such as acid neutralization vaults, been located on the Property?
❒ Yes ❒ No If so, please describe the location of all facilities, the types of wastes treated in each facility, the results of any soil or groundwater samples taken in the vicinity of each facility, and the manner in which each facility not currently in use was closed.

_____

_____

_____

4. Are there raw chemicals or waste chemical storage areas on the Property?
❒ Yes ❒ No If so, please describe the location of all such areas, the type of products or wastes stored in each area, the amount of products or wastes stored in each area, the results of any soil or groundwater samples taken in the vicinity of each area, and the manner in which each not currently in use was closed.

_____

_____

_____

Studies, Reports, Citations, Enforcement

1. Attach a copy of each environmental study, report, or assessment which has been performed on the Property's soil, air, or water conditions.

ILLUSTRATION 4-I

2. Have any federal, state, or local agencies ever investigated, cited, or been involved on the Property for violations of any environmental law?

❒ Yes ❒ No   If so, describe in full.

_____

_____

3. Has any public agency listed the Property as a site requiring or qualifying for cleanup under any environmental law?

❒ Yes ❒ No   If so, describe in full.

_____

_____

_____

Adjoining Property

1. Are there any of the above-referenced hazardous substances or pollutants present on adjoining properties or properties in the immediate area of the Property?

❒ Yes ❒ No

Date: _____   _____

_____

_____

Buyer(s) Signature

_____

_____

_____

Owner(s)/Seller(s) Signature

Attachment: Exhibit "A" Legal Description

ILLUSTRATION 4-1

If the transaction does not necessarily require your residential equity in order to provide sufficient collateral for the loan, then the lender is seeking "an abundance of caution" by requesting extra collateral coverage. This extra collateral either reflects the lender's very conservative loan policy or is intended to remind you of your very personal commitment to ensure that the lender will be repaid. While lenders do not foreclose on personal residences securing business loans as often, that is the ultimate risk of allowing the lender to place a lien on it.

However, in defense of the lender and the SBA, they want the borrowers to provide assurance that repayment of the loan will be a high priority, regardless of the success of the business operations. This extra lien also protects their interest position in line to the individual's net worth. A personal guaranty can be worthless if unsecured and the individual has obtained additional financing after the subject SBA loan.

The requirement to encumber a personal residence has killed many transactions, because some borrowers are simply not willing to meet this condition. But it is a business decision that you may well have to face when obtaining small business financing.

There are some strategies to employ in attempting to convince the lender to waive or modify the requirement of using your personal residence as collateral. These suggestions may or may not be applicable, depending on your situation or even state of residence.

✧ You can offer to substitute other assets not previously requested by the lender to replace the personal residence collateral requirement.

✧ You can explain to the lender that your spouse will absolutely not agree to such an encumbrance. This position may prove to be an effective negotiating ploy if the equity is not needed to fully secure the loan—and the lender cannot require the spouse to do anything.

✧ You can offer to pledge a 50 percent undivided interest in the personal residence. This scenario reduces the individual's exposure to losing the property to foreclosure, but still gives the lender a lot of leverage. This option assumes that a spouse owns a 50 percent interest.

✧ Long before the loan application begins, you can execute a quit claim deed of the property to your spouse for the 50 percent interest in the personal residence. With this maneuver, you will not legally own the residence and would not include it on your personal financial statement. Accordingly the lender cannot request it as collateral. This tactic carries a number of potential risks: if there is mortgage financing on the property, one party transferring it might trigger a "due on sale clause"; there might be tax consequences related to the "sale" of the property; and transferring it to a spouse may affect the tax deductions related to the residence, depending on the household. Before using this strategy, seek counsel from your attorney and CPA.

✧ If the residential equity is truly not needed to fully secure the loan, you can sometimes get the lender to agree that, upon successful completion of three or four years of consistent loan payments, the lender will release the mortgage against the personal residence. This compromise will demonstrate a good faith effort by both parties to accommodate this sensitive requirement.

Sometimes borrowers will not be given any other alternative than to agree to the requirement of pledging a subordinated lien on their home in order to obtain the business loan. In fact, it is probably accurate to say that a majority of small business owners at one time or another have pledged their residences to get business financing. One consolation is that if the house has a large first mortgage, it is not likely that the business lender would ever foreclose on it and have to pay out more money to satisfy another large loan in order to turn around and sell the house. That is too risky for the lender.

Also, borrowers generally do not need to worry about trapping a high interest rate on their first mortgage by adding a second lien on the residence. When interest rates are falling, most bankers will be very accommodating to allow the owner to refinance their residence if it will save money and lower payments. As long as there is no new money being advanced by the first mortgage holder, the lender will usually agree to subordinate to the new lender so long as the second lien holder can remain in the same value position after the new mortgage is obtained.

Personal property collateral. If you propose to pledge a lien interest in personal property to secure the loan, you should plan to provide the following documentation in order to help the lender evaluate these assets:

✦ *Description*—The lender should receive a schedule of the personal property assets that includes the following information:
- Asset description
- Name of manufacturer
- Date acquired
- Cost
- Model and serial numbers
- Location (if the borrower has more than one location)

✦ *Appraisal*—The lender should receive a copy of a current or old appraisal of the subject assets, if one exists. Or, you should research current quotes of what the assets are currently being marketed for, as a point at which to start discussions about the current values.

✦ *Photographs*—If these assets comprise a major portion of the collateral value you intend to use, the lender should receive photographs of the personal property assets. Visualization of the personal property will reinforce your assertion of the value of these assets.

✦ *Price quotes*—If you plan to acquire personal property assets as part of the total transaction, the lender should receive a price quotation that details the description and costs of the assets being acquired.

Automotive collateral. If you propose to pledge a security interest in automotive assets to secure the loan, the following documentation is helpful to evaluate and assess these assets:

✦ *Description*—The lender should receive a schedule of the automotive assets that includes the following information:
- Asset description
- Name of manufacturer
- Date acquired
- Cost
- Model and serial numbers
- Mileage (or log hours)
- State of registration and license number

✦ *Title*—The lender should receive copies of the title of the vehicles, if available.

✧ *Appraisal*—The lender should receive a copy of a current or old appraisal of the subject assets, if one exists. Or, you should assemble relevant quotes of what the assets are currently being marketed for if this information will demonstrate their relative value.

✧ *Photographs*—If these assets comprise a major portion of the collateral value you intend to use, the lender should receive photographs of the automotive assets. Visualization of the vehicles can reinforce your assertion of the value of these assets.

Securities collateral. If you propose to pledge a security interest in listed securities to secure the loan, the following documentation is helpful to evaluate these assets:

✧ *Brokerage statements*—The lender should receive copies of recent brokerage account statements or a schedule of the securities portfolio with updated market price quotes if the securities are not held by a brokerage firm. (It is a federal crime to make copies of the share certificates or bonds.)

✧ *Schedule of closely held securities*—If using closely held securities as collateral, you should prepare a memorandum describing the securities. This information should include your valuation and method of valuation, the relative stake of the entity represented by your securities, and a recent financial statement of the entity. You will be required to deliver the actual securities to the lender at loan closing for safekeeping during the loan term.

The use of listed securities as collateral for a commercial loan is discouraged. The lender will be restricted by Regulation U to value any listed security used as collateral at only 50 percent of its current market value. Securities priced under $5 per share are generally not accepted by most lenders. And since the lender cannot always be assured of control of your brokerage account, the lender may require that it hold your bonds or share certificates for safekeeping during the term of the loan.

These securities cannot be pledged or assigned to another entity or person per se. You are required to actually execute a blank sales receipt to the secured party that is relying on these securities as collateral. Language in most collateral agreements permits the lender to actually initiate a trade of these securities if there is a change in the valuation of the securities that diminishes the lender's collateral position below a required minimum.

That is, the lender can sell the securities and liquidate the loan with your collateral at any time—regardless of whether you are actually in default for the length of the remaining term. Obviously, such a sale could ensure an investment loss for you or have significant tax implications, depending on your basis in the securities.

The requirement of the lender holding the securities can also be very risky if sudden market changes create the desirability or need to trade the securities quickly. The lender would then become part of that decision if you decide to pledge these securities as collateral.

Even if the lender is amenable to working with you in such a scenario, the time required to get the lender's consent or to actually obtain possession of the securities can be delayed. You risk that the lender's decision period can lead to additional market losses (or missed opportunities for you to profit).

Delays in getting possession of the securities can also interfere with your ability to meet the delivery requirements of the rigid securities market. You should not risk your portfolio assets in this manner unless there is a written agreement as to how these situations will be handled.

An alternative is to approach your brokerage firm for a loan on your portfolio and to substitute these funds for the portion of the loan that would have been obtained using the securities as collateral. Most major brokerage firms make loans on very reasonable terms against listed securities because they are better positioned to monitor the market changes than other lenders.

The individual security holder should be comfortable with the brokerage firm's ability to make a short-notice margin call. You must understand that these loans are subject to being liquidated quickly if the value of the portfolio falls suddenly.

Notes receivable collateral. If you propose to pledge any notes held in order to secure the loan, the following documentation is helpful to evaluate these assets:

✦ *Description*—The lender should receive a schedule of any notes you or your co-owners hold, including the following information:
  • Name of debtor
  • Principal amount of the note
  • Interest rate

- Terms of repayment
- Collateral
- Current status of the account (current, past due, etc.)

✧ *Collateral values*—The lender should receive any information available to identify and justify the value of the collateral.

✧ *Copy of notes*—The lender should receive a copy of each note.

Depository account collateral. If you propose to pledge a security interest in a depository account or certificate(s) of deposit to secure the loan, the following documentation is helpful to evaluate these assets:

✧ *Description*—The lender should receive a schedule of all such accounts, including the following information:
- Name of depository and name in which the account is identified
- Type of account
- Account balances
- Current interest rate paid on account
- Maturity of each account

✧ *Depository account statements*—The lender should receive a copy of recent account statements that confirm the balances listed in the schedule.

You should be aware that IRA, Roth IRA, Keogh, 401(k), and any other type of retirement account are all prohibited by law from being used as collateral to secure a loan for any business purpose.

Accounts receivable/Inventory collateral. If you intend to pledge a security interest in the business's accounts receivable or inventory to secure the loan, the following documentation is helpful to evaluate these assets:

✧ *Accounts receivable aging*—The lender should receive a detailed report as of the date of the most recent financial statement showing the current aging of the accounts.

✧ *Bad debt schedule*—The lender should receive an up-to-date schedule of bad debts, with an explanation of each account and your efforts to recover any sums outstanding.

✧ *Inventory report*—The lender should receive a current detailed report of your business's inventory, segregating raw materials, work-in-process, and finished goods.

✧ *Obsolete inventory*—The lender should receive a schedule of your obsolete inventory and disclosure of your current book value of those assets.

✧ *Inventory valuation*—The lender should receive a narrative report detailing how you value the inventory and whether any particular components of the inventory may be subject to volatile price risks or obsolescence.

✧ *Borrowing base certificate*—The lender will require you to prepare and submit a borrowing base certificate at regular intervals. This form is used to define the periodic balances and changes in your eligible collateral for asset-based loans. This form is usually updated on a daily or weekly basis, depending on the specific arrangement between the lender and borrower.

✧ *Customer lists*—The lender should receive a list of the names, addresses, and telephone numbers of the regular customers of the business. The lender needs this information in the event it is ever necessary to attempt to collect the accounts directly from the customers.

Cash surrender value. If you want to pledge a security interest in the cash surrender value of a life insurance policy held to secure the loan, the following documentation is helpful to evaluate these assets:

✧ *Copy of insurance policy*—The lender should receive a copy of the insurance policy that has accrued the cash surrender value being offered as collateral. (Note—upon approval, the lender should require that you surrender the original policy, which will be held by the lender until the loan terms are satisfied.)

✧ *Policy declaration*—The lender should receive the most recent statement or policy declaration from the insurance carrier, affirming the balance of the policy's cash surrender value.

✧ *Assignment form*—Determine whether the insurance carrier requires a specific document to be executed in order to pledge the proceeds of the cash surrender value of the particular policy. If so, the borrower should obtain it from the insurance company.

Marketing Information

You should give the lender a marketing plan, information, and marketing collateral to ensure that they understand exactly what the business of the borrower is, and how you communicate with existing and prospective customers. In this information category, define the business, describe how it is marketed, and provide details about its future plans for expanding its revenue base

What are the products or services of the business? Define exactly what products or services are provided by the business and how they are delivered. It is easy to understand a company that sells radios, but it takes a greater study to relate to a company that manufactures digitized, variable overdrive power systems.

Fully explain what your clients do with those products or services. Do you manufacture, distribute, retail, resell, liquidate, remodel, recover, research, or remanufacture the products? If your company sells services, is it providing research, information, analysis, advice, or solutions?

The lender should be able to completely understand what specific niche you serve and the particular market the business addresses. And if you can distinguish your business as unique, the lender should be able to understand why the business is discernibly different from its market competition.

How does the business operate? Explain to the lender exactly how the business operates. After defining the products or services, explain how the business uses them, sells them, manufactures them, or installs them. In addition, detail the logical sequence of events that defines the normal course of the business operation. Again, the purpose is to educate the lender about what you do, so that the lender can be more responsive to what you want to do.

For example, if you can sell fifteen dozen doughnuts in twelve minutes, and it takes twenty minutes to prepare, fry, and glaze ten dozen doughnuts, the lender's understanding those facts would help them justify the need for more capacity to meet profitable sales demand.

Who is the typical customer for your products or services? Two of the most important management skills a business owner can have are knowing who the customer is and projecting who the customer could be. This information is crucial in the design of the product or service, pricing, business location, capability to perform, and strategic planning to determine and achieve its business goals.

By sharing this information with the lender, you communicate your marketing management strength. This information supports the financing request because it will give the lender confidence that you understand your market and are clearly focused on its revenues.

How does the business market or advertise itself? Included in the loan application package should be a description of the ways in which you market and advertise the business. There is not necessarily a right or wrong way to raise awareness about the business, but explaining the activities and media through which you promote the business lends more credibility for sales efforts.

Lenders should receive copies of any print ads, flyers, brochures, specialty products, or other tangible items that have been distributed to advertise and raise awareness of the business. You can also produce a detailed report about media advertising buys such as radio, television, cable, Internet, printed brochures, yellow pages, billboards, or signage. Also important are the civic organizations, trade associations, community activities, contributions, sponsorships, youth sports leagues, fund-raising events, and other community involvement through which you have promoted the business.

Who is the competition? Identify the other businesses that provide the same products or services and that are trying to attract the same customers. Be honest in assessing the competitors' strengths, weaknesses, and advantages and be specific about the position of each competitor in the market. In explaining where you stand in comparison, describe the plan to maintain or increase market share. The lender needs to know the unique features of the market you're operating within and the opportunities you see there.

How will you increase revenues? Some of the most important information you can give to the lender is a marketing plan to describe how the business will increase its revenues. If the loan proposal is to provide additional assets or capital to directly increase revenues, you have to support that proposal with a plan detailing exactly how such sales increases will be accomplished.

The financial projections will provide a numerical measure of the revenue increases you predict, but the marketing plan has to define the basis for those predictions. In other words, you have to relate to specific numerical increases by describing what causes them. If the loan enables you to make twenty more dozen doughnuts per hour and you can sell these doughnuts for eight hours at $3 per dozen, it stands to reason that the revenues will increase by $480 per day, or $14,400 per month.

This detailed explanation and reasoning lends credibility and rationality to your financial projections. The process of dissecting and describing the correlation between the marketing efforts and financial results also communicates to the lender that you understand the operational capabilities and limitations of the business.

Miscellaneous Information

Many categories of information are going to relate specifically to your particular situation, depending on the nature of the business or purpose of the loan. Several of these categories of information are included in this section. Listed here in alphabetical order, they should be used if your business situation applies to them.

Affiliates. Affiliated companies affect your participation in the SBA loan guaranty programs. Affiliates are defined as another business entity in which you, or any owner of at least 20 percent of your company, owns a minimum of 20 percent. The revenues and/or number of employees of any affiliated company are measured collectively with the subject enterprise that is seeking the SBA loan for purposes of determining eligibility under the SBA loan guaranty program.

That is, any and all business interests in which you and any of your partners or shareholders, individually or collectively, own at least a 20 percent stake, are counted along with the entity seeking to borrow money. The purpose is to determine the total sales, number of employees, net income, or net worth to compare to the eligibility limitations for obtaining a loan guaranty.

The lender will be required to confirm your eligibility if affiliated companies exist, so you should be prepared to provide the lender with the following information, which will be shared with the SBA:

✧ *Year-end financial statement*—The most recent year-end financial statement of each affiliated company.
✧ *Interim financial statement*—The most recent interim financial statement, if the year-end statement provided is more than ninety days old at the time this information is forwarded to the SBA.

If eligibility is subjected to close scrutiny due to the relative size of any affiliate, it may be necessary to provide the past three years of financial statements in order to enable the lender to average the statements, as provided for in the regulations.

Construction loans. If you're seeking to obtain financing for the construction of improvements to real property, you will be required to have an additional layer of documentation strictly concerning the construction itself. These documents are specifically intended to satisfy the lender that the expected business risks are not compounded by any other risks associated with the construction aspect of the transaction.

The format of a normal construction loan often requires the lender to make an initial advance of loan proceeds for the purchase of real property and then make additional draws to finance construction progress on an "as completed" basis. In other words, the lender will provide you with enough funds to pay for 20 percent of the construction costs after 20 percent of the construction is completed.

This type of lending carries additional risks due to the involvement of a third party that is responsible for the management of the construction project. The building contractor has to get the project started and keep the project moving between the draws of borrowed funds. Contractors use either their own working capital or the borrower's equity, which is initially advanced through the lender's fund control.

In addition, the contractor has to be able to complete the project for the predetermined amount, or you could run short of funds without having a completed building. With constantly changing building codes, zoning regulations, and multiple layers of building inspectors, the lender must be diligent in ensuring that the proposed structure will be constructed in compliance with all applicable laws.

Most lenders wisely use a construction consultant who specializes in monitoring projects on their behalf and supervises the contractor during the term of project. This consultant will review the pertinent information before the loan closes in order to assure the lender that the project is: (1) feasible according to plans, specifications, and contract; (2) is in compliance with applicable local building and zoning regulations; and (3) can be completed with the approved financing budget.

After loan closing, the consultant will monitor the progress of the project and inspect the project site each time the contractor requests a loan draw. This inspection will determine whether the contractor has made sufficient progress on the structure to justify their requested loan advance, in accordance with the agreed-upon terms governing the lender's construction loan. By working strictly for the lender, the consultant protects the lender's interest on the project site and ensures that the money will not get ahead of construction progress.

The extraordinary risk faced by you and the lender is that the financial condition of the contractor can create serious problems if the contractor cannot keep the project going between loan draws. A stalemate occurs if the contractor draws all of the loan funds available but cannot pay for labor or materials necessary to get to the next stage of the project.

More experienced lenders will often require a modest financial review of the proposed contractor that you intend to use. They will request nominal financial data and request to see a Dunn & Bradstreet or credit report. Additionally, they will ask for trade references (subcontractors such as electricians, plumbers, etc.), suppliers, previous clients, and even the contractor's bank. Lenders will be very hesitant to finance a construction project with a shaky contractor who cannot provide solid references. You should be thankful—serious problems arise when there is a cash-strapped contractor on the job.

If you're seeking construction financing, the lender will likely require that the following documentation be produced in order to close the loan. (References below to the lender may be applicable to the lender's construction consultant, who will supervise the project on behalf of the lender. References to the borrower may be applicable to the contractor, who will likely interface directly with the construction consultant for the transmission of much of this information.

- ✧ *Performance and material bonds*—On larger projects, lenders often require that the borrower's building contractor provide some form of financial guaranty in order to assure the lender that the contractor's financial condition will not pose a threat to completing the project. This bond, basically an insurance policy, is given to the lender on behalf of the contractor, and ensures that funds will be available to complete the project should the contractor's financial condition interrupt the job.
- ✧ *Executed AIA construction contract*—This widely accepted standard contract is used to define the project agreement between the contractor and the building owner. It should be submitted with any and all attachments, amendments, or addenda in order to provide the lender with the complete agreement between the two parties. Most lenders will require that the borrower enter into these contracts with at least a 10 percent retainage provision. Retainage is a term that refers to earned

funds that are held back from payment until the very end to ensure that the balance of the contract is performed as agreed. Ten percent is fairly typical because it coincides with the standard profit built into most contracts for the builder. These funds are held until the final inspection of the project has been approved by the lender and the certificate of occupancy ("CO") is issued by the local building authority.

✧ *Cost breakdown*—The lender will require a schedule of values, which defines each component of cost assigned by the contractor for the project. This information is relevant on either a fixed-price or cost-plus contract. It permits the lender to evaluate the reliability of the contractor's cost estimates to complete the project, and will become the allocation limit for the lender when they start responding to draw requests.

✧ *Boundary survey*—The lender will require a boundary survey to establish the parameters of the subject property and will want to get bearings on exactly where the building will be built on the site. This survey will also document that the site plans are compliant with local zoning guidelines (so far as required setback lines) and alert the lender to all easements on the property and any boundary encroachments.

✧ *Complete set of sealed construction plans*—Before loan closing, the lender will require the borrower to provide a full set of blueprints signed by the architect and stamped by the local authorities that must approve plans (building, zoning, fire, etc., departments). In evaluating the project, the lender and project consultant will compare these plans with the budget, contract, and other information that has been submitted to ensure project feasibility within the financing being committed.

✧ *Complete set of construction specifications*—The lender will require the borrower to provide a full schedule of project specifications, which will include complete details about every component and system in the project.

✧ *Soil reports*—The lender will require the borrower to provide copies of any soil tests completed on the site for the purpose of evaluating the percolation, compression, contamination, or other metrics required by local regulations.

✧ *Construction schedule*—The lender will require the borrower to provide the construction schedule agreed upon between the contractor and borrower. The construction schedule will need to conform to the term of the proposed loan schedule, and the lender will continue to monitor progress after construction begins.

✧ *Curb cut permits*—Where applicable, the lender will require the borrower to provide copies of any curb cut or other disturbance permits that have been obtained from the appropriate local government subdivision for the site.

✧ *Building permit*—The lender will require the borrower to provide a copy of the building permit that has been obtained from the appropriate local government subdivision for the project.

✧ *Proof of insurance*—The lender will require the borrower to provide declarations of insurance confirming that the contractor has adequate liability, workers' compensation, and builder's risk insurance on the project. This insurance has to name the lender as the additionally insured, and provide for written notice to be given to the lender prior to policy cancellation.

✧ *Utility letters*—The lender will require the borrower to provide copies of letters obtained from various utility companies, confirming to the borrower that these utilities have agreed to furnish their services to the subject property. At a minimum, these letters should be obtained from the providers of electricity, natural gas, telephone service, cable, and water and sewer.

✧ *Zoning letter*—The lender will require the borrower to provide a copy of a letter from the appropriate local government subdivision responsible for zoning, confirming the zoning code of the subject property and defining the specific use permitted on the site.

Franchise businesses. Many small business owners choose to affiliate with franchised businesses. There are many advantages to this strategy, such as the access to proprietary products, methods, and services for the business to sell. Also, name recognition in the public marketplace is easier to promote with the backing of a national organization. Although all of these advantages come with a price, franchised businesses generally have a lower failure rate than nonfranchised businesses.

If you plan to finance a franchised business, the lender will need the following information in order to proceed with the loan request:

✧ *Information on franchisor*—The lender will want to be familiar with the franchisor, particularly with lesser-known ones that may not yet have national recognition. The lender should be provided with the informational brochures and marketing materials that you received in selecting the particular franchisor. It may also be helpful to provide contact information with the franchisor and another franchisee.

✧ *Franchise agreement*—The lender will require a copy of your executed franchise agreement, including all attachments and exhibits. The lender needs to know how the franchisor's agreement is structured in the event of the need to dispose of your franchised operation. Determining which party would control the local use of the trade name, proprietary equipment, and methods directly affects the franchise's value to the lender as collateral and defines the lender's risk in dealing with the specific franchisor.

✧ *Franchise disclosure statement*—The Federal Trade Commission requires a franchisor to publish a disclosure report to provide the franchisee with specific operational and financial information about the franchisor and its management. This report is intended to protect prospective buyers from receiving dishonest or fraudulent information from unscrupulous franchise operators or sales representatives. A copy of this report should be submitted to the lender for review.

Special assets. Some borrowers possess certain assets that require extraordinary consideration when offered as collateral for a proposed loan. Although there is no asset that assures the borrower of loan approval, some assets definitely strengthen the chances of loan approval. Lenders relish the opportunity of lending money that is obtainable even if not readily accessible.

These special assets might include any of the following categories detailed below. Included here are suggestions about how you might use such assets to obtain business loans. For any of these options, insist that the lender provide financing at a lower interest rate, since the nature of the asset will virtually assure the lender's repayment.

Seek advice from an attorney before executing any documents pledging these kinds of assets to a lender. With more common assets, such as real property or equipment, the Uniform Commercial Code provides the lender with standard language, forms, and precedent to perfect the lender's interest in the borrower's assets. When pledging these special assets, a custom agreement will be written to provide for the lender's security. Your attorney must be involved to protect your interests in a situation where lenders and their attorneys probably have very little experience. Failure to evaluate such an agreement adequately could lead you to grant rights to the lender that could end in disastrous results.

You must ensure that the lender's liquidation of the loan would be conducted in a specified manner. Liquidation should not threaten the future value of these special assets or create unnecessary conflicts that damage the residual value of the asset after the loan has been satisfied.

- ✧ *Contracts*—One special asset is the long-term payout provisions of a deferred contract to which you have satisfied the obligation. Common for former entertainment or sports professionals, this type of asset is also being seen as the settlement for a job buyout from many *Fortune* 1000 companies. The contracts often guarantee the recipient a fixed sum to be paid out over a specified term, ensuring an income stream over that period.
- ✧ *Lottery awards*—As more states run lotteries to generate revenues, there are more winners. Most of the major awards provided in these contests are paid out over a twenty-year period and can be assigned to a third party.
- ✧ *Trusts*—Many persons have the benefit of a trust that has been established to administer either an inheritance or a large financial settlement. These trusts specify to whom, under what conditions, and when the proceeds are to be distributed to the beneficiary. Unless specifically prohibited by the trust, the income stream can generally be assigned to a third party. The lender will need assurances that there are no special conditions that could alter or stop the income stream. Usually, the corpus assets of the trust cannot be pledged to a third party. This situation may not be true for smaller trusts or for those with a limited number of beneficiaries.
- ✧ *Tax exempt bonds*—Many tax-exempt securities cannot be used as collateral because they are restricted from third-party assignment by the issuer. However, the income stream and final proceeds of the matured securities sometimes can be pledged by the holder. The trustee of the bond issuer can be directed

to send interest payments and principal proceeds to any party designated by the beneficiary. This arrangement effectively allows the beneficiary to use the corpus of these investments to secure a commercial loan.

SBA Documents

Depending on how active your lender is in the SBA program, you may be as familiar with SBA documents as the lender. The application for a loan guaranty is typically prepared by the lender or sometimes by a consultant engaged either by the lender or the borrower. Although the SBA loan applications have a bad reputation for being onerous, it is not really very complicated.

Lenders who process a regular volume of SBA-guaranteed loans usually rely on software that produces SBA-approved application documents. Lenders who do not handle many SBA loans may be struggling to manually prepare these documents, which now for the most part are available on Adobe documents that can be completed and saved on a computer—a long way from the manual forms prepared on a typewriter that were used when this book was originally published!

The application consists of a variety of SBA-mandated forms intended to gather information required by law or regulation. It is really the additional information required to accompany the SBA forms that create the most work for the borrower and lender. The challenge for the lender is to ensure that it collects all of the specific information needed for a specific transaction before approving the deal and submitting the guaranty request to the SBA. No two loans are ever alike.

There is a possible advantage to your drafting and providing the 7(a) SBA guaranty application documents to the lender together with the loan proposal. You benefit by providing the requested information in the format that the lender will have to use. Optional but recommended, this presentation can save the lender some work and will hopefully decrease the time required to process the application. (*Note*: SBA forms required for a 504 program debenture will always be prepared by the CDC, which would be less inclined to borrower assistance. Still, downloading and reviewing them can be educational for 504 borrowers.)

If the lender does not process many SBA applications, your assistance can be particularly helpful. The lender may actually utilize the documents you prepare if typed neatly. Whether or not you choose to complete these documents, it is helpful to understand the purpose of each document and the information being requested.

The following list includes the documentation needed to prepare an SBA 7(a) Loan Guaranty Program application. (All SBA forms required to process the lender's application for 7(a) guaranty can be found on the SBA website at *www.sba.gov/tools/Forms/smallbusinessforms/fsforms/ index.html.*)

Form 4: Application for Business Loan

This SBA form contains most of the basic information requested about the business, including a proposed allocation of the loan proceeds, a detailed schedule of the existing business liabilities, and covenants binding the borrower to specific SBA rules and regulations. A copy of this form can be found in Illustration 4-J.

Most of the additional information requested to support the loan proposal is defined as an exhibit to this document and is intended to accompany the application when submitted to the SBA. Detailed earlier in this chapter these items include:

- ✧ *Exhibit A*—Schedule of collateral
- ✧ *Exhibit B*—Personal financial statement (Form 413, see Illustration 4-F)
- ✧ *Exhibit C*—Business financial statements for the past three years, including balance sheet, profit and loss statement, and reconciliation of net worth; also an interim financial statement no more than ninety days old, with a current aging of accounts receivable and accounts payable; also earnings projections for at least two years
- ✧ *Exhibit D*—Statement of history of the business
- ✧ *Exhibit E*—Resumes of the business managers and owners
- ✧ *Exhibit F*—Names, social security numbers, and personal financial statements of any identified guarantors
- ✧ *Exhibit G*—List of any equipment to be acquired with loan proceeds, and name and address of seller
- ✧ *Exhibit H*—Details of any bankruptcy proceedings of any company officers
- ✧ *Exhibit I*—Details of any pending lawsuits involving the business

✧ *Exhibit J*—Names and addresses of any related parties employed by the SBA, a federal agency, or the lender
✧ *Exhibit K*—Details of any affiliated interests (20 percent or more) of the owners of the business applicant, along with recent financial statements on their affiliated entities
✧ *Exhibit L*—Details of any related party from which the business applicant regularly buys products or services, or to which the business applicant regularly sells products or services
✧ *Exhibit M*—For franchised business applicants, a copy of the franchise agreement and the FTC disclosure statement
✧ *Exhibit N*—Estimated construction costs and a statement of the source of any additional funds
✧ *Exhibit O*—Preliminary construction plans and specifications

Statement Required by Law and Executive Order

This statement is an attachment to Form 4 and requires applicants to acknowledge their intention to comply with several federal laws and executive orders. This acknowledgment is documented with the applicant's signature on an attached form.

These particular laws and executive orders include the Freedom of Information Act (5 U.S.C. 552), Privacy Act (5 U.S.C. 552a), Right to Financial Privacy Act of 1978 (12 U.S.C. 3401), Flood Disaster Protection Act (42 U.S.C. 4011), Executive Orders—Floodplain Management & Wetland Protection (42 F.R. 26951 & 42 F.R. 26961), Occupational Safety and Health Act (15 U.S.C. 651 et seq.), Civil Rights Legislation, the Equal Credit Opportunity Act (15 U.S.C. 1691), Executive Order 11738—Environmental Protection (38 F.R. 25161), Debt Collection Act of 1982, Deficit Reduction Act of 1984 (31 U.S.C. 3701 et seq. and other titles), Immigration Reform and Control Act of 1986 (Pub. L. 99-603), Lead-Based Paint Poisoning Prevention Act (42 U.S.C. 4821 et seq.), and Executive Order 12549, Debarment and Suspension (13 C.F.R. 145).

This list contains references to several laws with which the average citizens may not be familiar. A summary of each executive order and law is provided on the form so that the borrower can get a general understanding of each law and regulation before executing the form. And, of course each law, regulation, and executive order is available in its entirety through the web to anyone who wants to really learn more.

PART 2

U.S. Small Business Administration	OMB Approval No: 3245-0016
APPLICATION FOR BUSINESS LOAN	Expiration Date: 11/30/04

Individual	Full Address

Name of Applicant Business	Tax I.D. No. or SSN

Full Street Address of Business	Tel. No. (inc. A/C)

City	County	State	Zip	Number of Employees (Including subsidiaries and affiliates)
Type of Business		Date Business Established		At Time of Application _____
Bank of Business Account and Address				If Loan is Approved _____
				Subsidiaries or Affiliates (Separate for above) _____

Use of Proceeds: (Enter Gross Dollar Amounts Rounded to the Nearest Hundreds)	Loan Requested		Loan Request
Land Acquisition		Payoff SBA Loan	
New Construction/ Expansion Repair		Payoff Bank Loan (Non SBA Associated	
Acquisition and/or Repair of Machinery and Equipment		Other Debt Payment (Non SBA Associated)	
Inventory Purchase		All Other	
Working Capital (including Accounts Payable)		Total Loan Requested	
Acquisition of Existing Business		Term of Loan - (Requested Mat.)	_____ Yrs.

PREVIOUS SBA OR OTHER FEDERAL GOVERNMENT DEBT: If you or any principals or affiliates have 1) ever requested Government Financing or 2) are delinquent on the repayment of any Federal Debt complete the following:

Name of Agency	Original Amount of Loan	Date of Request	Approved or Declined	Balance	Current or Past Due
	$			$	
	$			$	

ASSISTANCE List the name(s) and occupation of anyone who assisted in the preparation of this form, other than applicant.

Name and Occupation	Address	Total Fees Paid	Fees Due
Name and Occupation	Address	Total Fees Paid	Fees Due

Note: The estimated burden completing this form is 12.0 hours per response. You will not be required to respond to any collection of information unless it displays a currently valid OMB approval number. Comments on the burden should be sent to U.S. Small Business Administration, Chief, AIB, 409 3rd St., S.W., Washington, D.C. 20416 and Desk Office for Small Business Administration, Office of Management and Budget, New Executive Office Building, room 10202 Washington, D.C. 20503. OMB Approval (3245-0016). **PLEASE DO NOT SEND FORMS TO OMB. SUBMIT COMPLETED APPLICATION TO LENDER OF CHOICE**

SBA Form 4 (8-01) Use Previous Edition Until Exhausted   Federal Recycling Program   Printed on Recycled Paper   Page 1

This form was electronically produced by Elite Federal Forms, Inc.

ILLUSTRATION 4-J

ALL EXHIBITS MUST BE SIGNED AND DATED BY PERSON SIGNING THIS FORM

BUSINESS INDEBTEDNESS: Furnish the following information on all installment debts, contracts, notes, and mortgages payable. Indicate by an asterisk (*) items to be paid by loan proceeds and reason for paying them (present balance should agree with the latest balance sheet submitted).

To Whom Payable	Original Amount	Original Date	Present Balance	Rate of Interest	Maturity Date	Monthly Payment	Security	Current or Past Due
Acct. #	$		$			$		
Acct. #	$		$			$		
Acct. #	$		$			$		
Acct. #	$		$			$		
Acct. #	$		$			$		

MANAGEMENT (Proprietor, partners, officers, directors, all holders of outstanding stock – 100% of ownership must be shown). Use separate sheet if necessary.

Name and Social Security Number and Position Title	Complete Address	%Owned	*Military Service From To	*Sex
Race*: American Indian/Alaska Native ☐ Black/African-Amer. ☐ Asian ☐ Native Hawaiian/Pacific Islander ☐ White ☐			Ethnicity* Hisp./Latino ☐ Not Hisp./Latino ☐	
Race*: American Indian/Alaska Native ☐ Black/African-Amer. ☐ Asian ☐ Native Hawaiian/Pacific Islander ☐ White ☐			Ethnicity* Hisp./Latino ☐ Not Hisp./Latino ☐	
Race*: American Indian/Alaska Native ☐ Black/African-Amer. ☐ Asian ☐ Native Hawaiian/Pacific Islander ☐ White ☐			Ethnicity* Hisp./Latino ☐ Not Hisp./Latino ☐	
Race*: American Indian/Alaska Native ☐ Black/African-Amer. ☐ Asian ☐ Native Hawaiian/Pacific Islander ☐ White ☐			Ethnicity* Hisp./Latino ☐ Not Hisp./Latino ☐	

*This data is collected for statistical purpose only. It has no bearing on the credit decision to approve or decline this application. One or more boxes may be selected.

THE FOLLOWING EXHIBITS MUST BE COMPLETED WHERE APPLICABLE. ALL QUESTIONS ANSWERED ARE MADE A PART OF THE APPLICATION.

For Guarantee Loans please provide an original and one copy (Photocopy is Acceptable) of the Application Form, and all Exhibits to the participating lender. For Direct Loans submit one original copy of the application and Exhibits to SBA.

1. Submit SBA Form 912 (Statement of Personal History) for each type of individual that the Form 912 requires.

2. If your collateral consists of (A) Land and Building, (B) Machinery and Equipment, (C) Furniture and Fixtures, (D) Accounts *Receivable*, (E) Inventory, (F) Other, please provide an itemized list (labeled Exhibit A) that contains serial and identification numbers for all articles that had an Original value of greater than $500. Include a legal description of Real Estate Offered as collateral.

3. Furnish a signed current personal balance sheet (SBA Form 413 may be used for this purpose) for each stockholder (with 20% or greater ownership), partner, officer, and owner. Include the assets and liabilities of the spouse and any close relatives living in the household. Also, include your Social Security Number. The date should be the same as the most recent business financial statement. Label it Exhibit B.

4. Include the financial statements listed below: a,b,c for the last three years; also a,b,c, and d as of the same date, - current within 90 days of filing the application; and statement e, if applicable. Label it Exhibit C (Contact SBA for referral if assistance with preparation is wanted.) **All** information must be signed and dated.

a. Balance Sheet
b. Profit and Loss Statement (if not available, explain why and substitute Federal income tax forms)
c. Reconciliation of Net Worth
d. Aging of Accounts Receivable and Payable (summary not
e. detailed)
   Projection of earnings for at least one year where financial statements for the last three years are unavailable or when SBA requests them.

5. Provide a brief history of your company and a paragraph describing the expected benefits it will receive from the loan. Label it Exhibit D.

6. Provide a brief description similar to a resume of the education, technical and business background for all the people listed under Management. Label it Exhibit E.

ILLUSTRATION 4-J

ALL EXHIBITS MUST BE SIGNED AND DATED BY PERSON SIGNING THIS FORM

7. Submit the names, addresses, tax I.D. number(EIN or SSN), and current personal balance sheet(s) of any co-signers and/or guarantors for the loan who are not otherwise affiliated with the business as Exhibit F.

8. Include a list of any machinery or equipment or other non-real estate assets to be purchased with loan proceeds and the cost of each item as quoted by the seller as Exhibit G. Include the seller's name and address.

9. Have you or any officers of your company ever been involved in bankruptcy or insolvency proceedings? If so, please provide the details as Exhibit H. If none, check here:
                  Yes   No

10. Are you or your business involved in any pending lawsuits? If yes, provide the details as Exhibit I. If none, check here: Yes | No

11. Do you or your spouse or any member of your household, or anyone who owns, manages or directs your business or their spouses or members of their households work for the Small Business Administration, Small Business Advisory Council, SCORE or ACE, any Federal Agency, or the participating lender? If so, please provide the name and address of the person and the office where employed. Label this Exhibit J. If none, check here:

12. Does your business, its owners or majority stockholders own or have a controlling interest in other businesses? If yes, please provide their names and the relationship with your company along with a current balance sheet and operating statement for each. This should be Exhibit K.

13. Do you buy from, sell to, or use the services of any concern in which someone in your company has a significant financial interest? If yes, provide details on a separate sheet of paper labeled Exhibit L.

14. If your business is a franchise, include a copy of the franchise agreement and a copy of the FTC disclosure statement supplied to you by the Franchisor. Please include it as Exhibit M.

CONSTRUCTION LOANS ONLY

15. Include as a separate exhibit (Exhibit N) the estimated cost of the project and a statement of the source of any additional funds.

16. Provide copies of preliminary construction plans and specifications. Include them as Exhibit O. Final plans will be required prior to disbursement.

EXPORT LOANS

17. Does your business presently engage in Export Trade? Check here: Yes | No

18. Will you be using proceeds from this loan to support your company's exports? Check here: Yes | No

19. Would you like information on Exporting? Check here: Yes   No

AGREEMENTS AND CERTIFICATIONS

Agreements of non-employment of SBA Personnel: I agree that if SBA approves this loan application I will not, for at least two years, hire as an employee or consultant anyone that was employed by SBA during the one year period prior to the disbursement of the loan.

Certification: I certify: (a) I have not paid anyone connected with the Federal Government for help in getting this loan. I also agree to report to the SBA office of the Inspector General, Washington, DC 20416 any Federal Government employee who offers, in return for any type of compensation, to help get this loan approved.

(b) All information in this application and the Exhibits are true and complete to the best of my knowledge and are submitted to SBA so SBA can decide whether to grant a loan or participate with a lending institution in a loan to me. I agree to pay for or reimburse SBA for the cost of any surveys, title or mortgage examinations, appraisals, credit reports, etc., performed by non-SBA personnel provided I have given my consent-

(c) I understand that I need not pay anybody to deal with SBA. I have read and understand SBA Form 159, which explains SBA policy on representatives and their fees.

(d) As consideration for any Management, Technical, and Business Development Assistance that may be provided, I waive all claims against SBA and its consultants.

If you knowingly make a false statement or overvalue a security to obtain a guaranteed loan from SBA, you can be fined up to $10,000 and/or imprisoned for not more than five years under 18 usc 1001; if submitted to a Federally insured institution, under 18 USC 1014 by Imprisonment of not more than twenty years and/or a fine of not more than $1,000,000. I authorize the SBA's Office of Inspector General to request criminal record information about me from criminal justice agencies for the purpose of determining my eligibility for programs authorized by the Small Business Act, as amended.

If Applicant is a proprietor or general partner, sign below:

By: _____

If Applicant is a Corporation, sign below:

_____

Corporate Name and Seal   Date

By: _____
                  Signature of President

Attested by: _____
                Signature of Corporate Secretary

SUBMIT COMPLETED APPLICATION TO LENDER OF CHOICE

ILLUSTRATION 4-J

PART 2

APPLICANT'S CERTIFICATION

By my signature, I certify that I have read and received a copy of the "STATEMENTS REQUIRED BY LAW AND EXECUTIVE ORDER" which was attached to this application. My signature represents my agreement to comply with the approval of my loan request and to comply, whenever applicable, with the hazard insurance, lead-based paint, civil rights or other limitations in this notice.

Each proprietor, each General Partner, each Limited Partner or Stockholder owning 20% or more, each Guarantor and the spouse of each of these must sign. Each person should sign only once.

Business Name: _____

By: _____   _____
      Signature and Title   Date

Guarantors:

_____   _____
Signature and Title   Date

_____   _____
Signature and Title   Date

_____   _____
Signature and Title   Date

_____   _____
Signature and Title   Date

_____   _____
Signature and Title   Date

_____   _____
Signature and Title   Date

_____   _____
Signature and Title   Date

SBA Form 4 (8-01) Use Previous Edition Until Exhausted   Page 4

ILLUSTRATION 4-J

Statement of Financial Need

This document describes the proposed financial transaction, defines the entire costs or expenses involved, and identifies the source of funds to cover each cost or expense. A copy of this form can be found in Illustration 4-K.

Other SBA Documents

Other documents and statements that form part of the loan application include the following:

- ✧ *Form 413:* Personal Financial Statement—This document was described earlier in this chapter in the section discussing personal financial information. It is usually included as Exhibit B to the business loan application.
- ✧ *Form 912:* Statement of Personal History—This document is described earlier in this chapter in the section discussing personal administrative information. A copy of this form can be found in Illustration 4-L.
- ✧ *Form 159:* Compensation Agreement—This document is needed to disclose to the SBA any professional fees that you have paid or will pay in connection with the application, qualification, or closing of an SBA loan. This form is to be used for any packagers, consultants, accountants, attorneys, engineers, lenders, or other parties who have provided specific services or supporting documents to you in preparing the SBA application, providing due diligence related to the SBA loan, or closing the loan. A copy of this form can be found in Illustration 4-M.
- ✧ *Form 1624:* Certification Regarding Debarment—This document is required to attest that the borrower—the individual and the business entity—has not been debarred from doing business with the federal government due to any administrative, disciplinary, or other action specifically restricting the respective party. A copy of this form can be found in Illustration 4-N.
- ✧ *Form 1846:* Statement Regarding Lobbying—This document is required to attest that you—both the individual and the business entity—have not paid or promised to pay an elected federal official, their employees, or other federal employees for any influence in connection with this transaction. A copy of this form can be found in Illustration 4-O.

Statement of Financial Need

	Funds Provided by Owners	Use of Loan Proceeds	Total Funds Required
A. Fixed Assets Acquisition/Repair			
Automotive	_____	_____	_____
Furniture and Fixtures	_____	_____	_____
Land	_____	_____	_____
Building Construction / Purchase	_____	_____	_____
Building Improvements	_____	_____	_____
Leasehold Improvements	_____	_____	_____
1. Other: _____	_____	_____	_____
2. Other: _____	_____	_____	_____
Total Fixed Asset Acquisition	_____	_____	_____
B. Debt Repayment			
Accounts Payable (Attach List)	_____	_____	_____
Notes Payable (Complete "Indebtedness" SBA Form 4)	_____	_____	_____
Total Debt Payment	_____	_____	_____
C. Working Capital			
Operating Cash	_____	_____	_____
Inventory	_____	_____	_____
Prepaid Expenses (Attach List)	_____	_____	_____
Advertising	_____	_____	_____
Deposits (Attach List)	_____	_____	_____
Training	_____	_____	_____
Accounts Receivable Financing	_____	_____	_____
Organizational Costs (Attach List)	_____	_____	_____
Other (Specify) Transaction Costs	_____	_____	_____
1. Other: _____	_____	_____	_____
2. Other: _____	_____	_____	_____
3. Other: _____	_____	_____	_____
Total Working Capital	_____	_____	_____
TOTAL FUNDS	_____	_____	_____

Source of funds provided by owners:

1.

2.

3.

Signature _____ Date _____

ILLUSTRATION 4-K

✧ *IRS Form 4506-T:* Request for Transcript of Tax Return—This document permits the lender to obtain a transcript of your income tax return for verification comparison to the income tax returns you submitted in the loan application. A copy of this form can be found in Illustration 4-G.

✧ *Justification*—The lender (and therefore you as the borrower) has to provide justification for why the SBA guaranty should be provided for the proposed transaction. There is no regulation form on which to submit this information.

There are several reasons why SBA-guaranteed loans are superior to conventional financing in the lending marketplace. These reasons include:

Terms—The SBA term limits allow the small business concern to borrow money for longer terms, which mean lower debt service and better cash flow for companies, which is particularly important in their earlier years.

Interest rates—In some instances, the interest rate caps on SBA-guaranteed loans represent a lower rate than many that small businesses would otherwise qualify for.

Qualification—Traditional lending sources avoid certain industries because of the inherent risks of lending money on special-use assets, such as bowling alleys or day care centers. The guaranty provides incentives for lenders to extend funds into these industries by absorbing some of the inherent risk.

In addition, the SBA is sensitive to two particular uses of loan proceeds, both of which must be explained in order to justify the loan:

1. *Change of ownership.* The lender must demonstrate that the borrower is purchasing an entity not as a passive investment, but rather as a business to be personally operated by the borrower. Further, the lender has to prove that the buyer and seller are not related in a business sense, and that there is no better alternative financing available.

2. *Refinancing debt.* The lender must demonstrate that there is a clear advantage to the borrower to refinance any debt with an SBA loan and that the previous loans have performed as agreed. The SBA will examine transcripts of the lender's previous loan to confirm that the lender is not unloading a bad loan on the agency.

Return Executed Copies 1, 2, and 3 to SBA

OMB APPROVAL NO.3245-0178
Expiration Date:9/30/2006

United States of America
SMALL BUSINESS ADMINISTRATION
STATEMENT OF PERSONAL HISTORY

Please Read Carefully - Print or Type

Each member of the small business or the development company requesting assistance must submit this form in TRIPLICATE for filing with the SBA application. This form must be filled out and submitted by:

1. By the proprietor, if a sole proprietorship.
2. By each partner, if a partnership.
3. By each officer, director, and additionally by each holder of 20% or more of the ownership stock, if a corporation, limited liability company, or a development company.

Name and Address of Applicant (Firm Name)(Street, City, State, and ZIP Code)

SBA District/Disaster Area Office

Amount Applied for (when applicable) | File No. (if known)

1. Personal Statement of: (State name in full, if no middle name, state (NMN), or if initial only, indicate initial.) List all former names used, and dates each name was used. Use separate sheet if necessary.

First | Middle | Last

2. Give the percentage of ownership or stocked owned or to be owned in the small business or the development company

Social Security No.

3. Date of Birth (Month, day, and year)

4. Place of Birth: (City & State or Foreign Country)

Name and Address of participating lender or surety co. (when applicable and known)

5. U.S. Citizen? ☐ YES ☐ NO
If No, are you a Lawful Permanent resident alien: ☐ YES ☐ NO
If non- U.S. citizen provide alien registration number:

6. Present residence address:
From:
To:
Address:

Most recent prior address (omit if over 10 years ago):
From:
To:
Address:

Home Telephone No. (Include A/C):
Business Telephone No. (Include A/C):

PLEASE SEE REVERSE SIDE FOR EXPLANATION REGARDING DISCLOSURE OF INFORMATION AND THE USES OF SUCH INFORMATION.

IT IS IMPORTANT THAT THE NEXT THREE QUESTIONS BE ANSWERED COMPLETELY. AN ARREST OR CONVICTION RECORD WILL NOT NECESSARILY DISQUALIFY YOU; HOWEVER, AN UNTRUTHFUL ANSWER WILL CAUSE YOUR APPLICATION TO BE DENIED.

IF YOU ANSWER "YES" TO 7, 8, OR 9, FURNISH DETAILS ON A SEPARATE SHEET. INCLUDE DATES, LOCATION, FINES, SENTENCES, WHETHER MISDEMEANOR OR FELONY, DATES OF PAROLE/PROBATION, UNPAID FINES OR PENALTIES, NAME(S) UNDER WHICH CHARGED, AND ANY OTHER PERTINENT INFORMATION.

7. Are you presently under indictment, on parole or probation?
☐ Yes   ☐ No   (If yes, indicate date parole or probation is to expire.)

8. Have you ever been charged with and or arrested for any criminal offense other than a minor motor vehicle violation? Include offenses which have been dismissed, discharged, or not prosecuted (All arrests and charges must be disclosed and explained on an attached sheet.)
☐ Yes   ☐ No

9. Have you ever been convicted, placed on pretrial diversion, or placed on any form of probation, including adjudication withheld pending probation, for any criminal offense other than a minor vehicle violation?
☐ Yes   ☐ No

10. I authorize the Small Business Administration Office of Inspector General to request criminal record information about me from criminal justice agencies for the purpose of determining my eligibility for programs authorized by the Small Business Act, and the Small Business Investment Act.

CAUTION: Knowingly making a false statement on this form is a violation of Federal law and could result in criminal prosecution, significant civil penalties, and a denial of your loan, surety bond, or other program participation. A false statement is punishable under 18 USC 1001 by imprisonment of not more than five years and/or a fine of not more than $10,000; under 15 USC 645 by imprisonment of not more than two years and/or a fine of not more than $5,000; and, if submitted to a Federally insured institution, under 18 USC 1014 by imprisonment of not more than thirty years and/or a fine of not more than $1,000,000.

Signature | Title | Date

Agency Use Only

11. ☐ Fingerprints Waived
Date | Approving Authority

☐ Fingerprints Required
Date | Approving Authority

Date Sent to OIG

12. ☐ Cleared for Processing
Date | Approving Authority

13. ☐ Request a Character Evaluation
Date | Approving Authority

(Required whenever 7, 8 or 9 are answered "yes" even if cleared for processing.)

PLEASE NOTE: The estimated burden for completing this form is 15 minutes per response. You are not required to respond to any collection of information unless it displays a currently valid OMB approval number. Comments on the burden should be sent to U.S. Small Business Administration, Chief, AIB, 409 3rd St., S.W., Washington D.C. 20416 and Desk Officer for the Small Business Administration, Office of Management and Budget, New Executive Office Building, Room 10202, Washington, D.C. 20503. OMB Approval 3245-0178. **PLEASE DO NOT SEND FORMS TO OMB.**

SBA 912 (10-03) SOP 5010.4 Previous Edition Obsolete

This form was electronically produced by Elite Federal Forms, Inc.

ILLUSTRATION 4-L

SBA LOAN NO.

COMPENSATION AGREEMENT FOR SERVICES IN CONNECTION WITH APPLICATION AND LOAN FROM (OR IN PARTICIPATION WITH) SMALL BUSINESS ADMINISTRATION

The undersigned representative (attorney, accountant, engineer, appraiser, etc.) hereby agrees that the undersigned has not and will not, directly or indirectly, charge or receive any payment in connection with the application for or the making of the loan except for services actually performed on behalf of the Applicant. The undersigned further agrees that the amount of payment for such services shall not exceed an amount deemed reasonable by SBA (and, if it is a participation loan, by the participating lending institution), and to refund any amount in excess of that deemed reasonable by SBA (and the participating institution). This agreement shall supersede any other agreement covering payment for such services.

A general description of the services performed, or to be performed, by the undersigned and the compensation paid or to be paid are set forth below. If the total compensation in any case exceeds $1,000 (or $300 for: (1) regular business loans of $15,000 or less; or (2) all disaster home loans) or if SBA should otherwise require, the services must be itemized on a schedule attached showing each date services were performed, time spent each day, and description of service rendered on each day listed.

The undersigned Applicant and representative hereby certify that no other fees have been charged or will be charged by the representative in connection with this loan, unless provided for in the loan authorization specifically approved by SBA.

GENERAL DESCRIPTION OF SERVICES

Paid Previously $ _____
Additional Amount to be Paid $ _____
Total Compensation $ _____

(Section 13 of the Small Business Act (15 USC 642) requires disclosures concerning fees. Parts 103, 108, and 120 of Title 13 of the Code of Federal Regulations contain provisions covering appearances and compensation of persons representing SBA applicants. Section 103.13-5 authorizes the suspension or revocation of the privilege of any such person to appear before SBA for charging a fee deemed unreasonable by SBA for services actually performed, charging of unreasonable expenses, or violation of this agreement. Whoever commits any fraud, by false or misleading statement or representation, or by conspiracy, shall be subject to the penalty of any applicable Federal or State statute.)

Dated _____, _____

_____
(Representative)

By _____

The Applicant hereby certifies to SBA that the above representations, description of services and amounts are correct and satisfactory to the Applicant

Dated _____, _____

_____
(Applicant)

By _____

The participating lending institution hereby certifies that the above representations of service rendered and amounts charged are reasonable and satisfactory to it.

Dated _____, _____

_____
(Lender)

By _____

NOTE: Foregoing certification must be executed, if by a corporation, in corporate name by duly authorized officer and duly attested; if by a partnership, in the firm name, together with signature of a general partner.

PLEASE NOTE: The estimated burden hours for the completion of this form of SBA Form 147, 148, 159, 160, 160A, 529B, 928, and 1059 is 6 hours per response. You will not be required to respond to this information collection if a valid OMB approval number is not displayed. If you have any questions or comments concerning this estimate or other aspects of this information collection, please contact the U.S. Small Business Administration, Chief, Administrative Information Branch, Washington D.C. 20416 and/or Office of Management and Budget, Clearance Officer, Paperwork Reduction Project (3245-0201), Washington, D.C. 20503.

This form

SBA FORM 159 (2-93) REF SOP 70 50 Use 7-89 edition until exhausted

ILLUSTRATION 4-M

**Certification Regarding
Debarment, Suspension, Ineligibility and Voluntary Exclusion
Lower Tier Covered Transactions**

This certification is required by the regulations implementing Executive Order 12549, Debarment and Suspension, 13 CFR Part 145. The regulations were published as Part VII of the May 26, 1988 *Federal Register* (pages 19160-19211). Copies of the regulations may be obtained by contacting the person to which this proposal is submitted.

(BEFORE COMPLETING CERTIFICATION, READ INSTRUCTIONS ON REVERSE)

(1) The prospective lower tier participant certifies, by submission of this proposal, that neither it nor its principals are presently debarred, suspended, proposed for disbarment, declared ineligible, or voluntarily excluded from participation in this transaction by any Federal department or agency.

(2) Where the prospective lower tier participant is unable to certify to any of the statements in this certification, such prospective participant shall attach an explanation to this proposal.

Business Name _____

Date _____   By _____
                                         Name and Title of Authorized Representative

                                         _____
                                         Signature of Authorized Representative

SBA Form 1624 (12/92)
This form was electronically produced by Elite Federal Forms, Inc.

Federal Recycling Program   Printed on Recycled Paper

ILLUSTRATION 4-N

STATEMENT REGARDING LOBBYING

Statement for Loan Guarantees and Loan Insurance

The undersigned states, to the best of his or her knowledge and belief, that:

(1)　　If any funds have been paid or will be paid to any person for influencing or attempting to influence an officer or employee of any agency, a Member of Congress, an officer or employee of Congress, or an employee of a Member of Congress in connection with this commitment providing for the United States to insure or guarantee a loan, the undersigned shall complete and submit Standard Form LLL, "Disclosure of Lobbying Activities," in accordance with its instructions.

(2)　　Submission of this statement is a prerequisite for making or entering into this transaction imposed by Section 1352, Title 31, U.S. Code. Any person who fails to file the required statement shall be subject to a civil penalty of not less than $10,000 and not more than $100,000 for each such failure.

Signature: _____

Date: _____

Name and Title: _____

Federal Recycling Program　Printed on Recycled Paper

SBA Form 1846 (8-92)

*U.S. Government Printing Office: 1993

ILLUSTRATION 4-O

There are a few additional SBA documents required with the loan application that must be prepared by the lender. These include Form 4-I (the Lender's Application for Guaranty) containing the Lender's Analysis, and Form 1846, the Statement Regarding Lobbying.

All documentation required by the lender to render a credit decision and to qualify for the SBA guaranty must be compiled by the lender and then submitted to the SBA (unless lender has attained Preferred Lender Program (PLP) status). The lender must have approved the loan and be prepared to make it subject to the SBA guaranty before the SBA will review it.

While the list of data contained in this chapter may seem complicated, it is mostly information that is routinely available to and used by business owners. New government regulations will sometimes increase the number of items on this list by adding new forms to submit to comply with legislation. Neither the lender nor the SBA can change federal rules but must find ways to ensure compliance without interfering with transactions.

The SBA and the lender have a responsibility to administer and abide by the law. While some regulations and documents may seem frivolous, there is usually a history behind them that made it necessary to inconvenience many people to prevent the future misdeeds of a few people. Lawmakers rarely look in the rearview mirror though, and it is usually hard to revisit and repair unintended consequences.

To modify some of the more irrelevant, burdensome requirements of this process will require business owners to seek congressional reform to alleviate some of the regulatory roadblocks and costs of borrowing capital for small businesses.

Another important assertion needed in the borrower's justification statement is confirmation that the borrower cannot locate reasonable financing elsewhere. Lack of funds available on similar repayment terms or a lower interest rate permits the borrower to offer this statement to assure the SBA that government funds are not unnecessarily supplementing the borrower's financing when alternatives are available.

CHAPTER **5**

Explaining the
Worst Circumstances

Sometimes bad things happen to good people. More than ever before, lenders seem to be open to work with borrowers who have suffered through events in the past that harmed them financially for a period and devastated their credit records. In this chapter, you'll learn:

- ✧ How to deal with past personal imperfections
- ✧ How to provide an explanation that will be heard
- ✧ Getting past the difficult times
- ✧ Adversity happens to many people

Explaining Those Special Situations

Many people face extraordinary or sometimes tragic situations that ripple through their lives, including their financial well-being. Some of these people are or decide to become small business owners, and they need to get investors or lenders to support their businesses.

Borrowers who have faced special circumstances will learn that it does generally weaken their stature when seeking a loan or at least dampen the lender's enthusiasm for considering the request. Because these situations require greater preparation, the borrower's determination may be tested to get business financing.

These circumstances can vary, ranging from the indiscretions of youth to medical catastrophes. Often these circumstances have nothing to do with the borrower's past business performance, moral obligation to repay debts, or prospects for succeeding in the future, but the results have included a disruptive effect on credit scores, profitability, or even home ownership, which are metrics all lenders use when evaluating credit decisions.

It is very important for the borrower to be completely and even meticulously honest with the lender in disclosing and discussing these situations. Was the borrower at fault? Was the borrower a victim? Can the borrower rehabilitate this financial condition? Whatever the answer to either question, borrowers should be straightforward and transparent so as to not make a past problem a larger problem today.

The lender will have to evaluate whether, based on the borrower's disclosures, the borrower presents an excessive risk and cannot be approved for financing. This question will be automatically answered affirmatively if the borrower attempts to hide or avoid their past problems, or fails to convince the lender to investigate these previous problems in their proper context.

The following suggestions are intended to assist you in overcoming these conditions where your personal track record was tarnished but you still have merit to go forward. Such events need not always prevent you from advancing to the next opportunity in life. This discussion is not intended to instruct anyone how to develop excuses to perpetuate a record of failure, deceit, or fraud. By following these steps to explain particular situations, you can begin down the road to recovery and moving on to your next chapter in life, hopefully with a well-financed business.

Bankruptcy

Bankruptcy is a provision of federal law for individuals or businesses to resolve the difficult financial position of being insolvent or over-leveraged. From a business viewpoint, bankruptcy can be a strategy to manage the devastating impact of business or economic disruption. Though sometimes abused, bankruptcy can be the debtor's best logical decision in many circumstances.

The decision to seek protection in bankruptcy should not be made lightly, and will definitely carry a steep price. Many businesses have filed for protection prematurely on poor or no advice without recognition of the consequences or preparation to face them. Once the decision is made, the debtor will generally live with it for many years.

Often bankers, particularly those dealing with consumers and small businesses, will have a knee-jerk reaction to those who have previously sought protection under bankruptcy, which is generally negative. Some lenders treat bankruptcy as the ultimate violation of the borrower's moral code. Legitimate bankruptcy cases do not involve morals—they

---

Skeleton in the closet?

✧ Be forthright with all the facts.
✧ Present a comprehensive explanation.
✧ Be prepared for tough examination of the facts.

are about money. Bankruptcy is usually not about an unwillingness to repay money, but rather the inability. Out of lack of understanding or perhaps an intolerant attitude, sometimes lenders will present a difficult challenge to obtain financing once bankruptcy is part of your past.

Bankruptcy cases are under the jurisdiction of federal courts to protect individuals or companies from creditors when their existing or potential liabilities exceed their assets. This protection is intended to prevent a particular creditor from unfairly collecting a debt at the expense of other creditors. It also protects debtors' legal rights while giving them safe haven to reorganize or liquidate assets to repay their obligations. Bankruptcy can provide debtors a second chance without undue interference from creditors.

There are three classes of bankruptcy:

1. *Chapter 7*—This class of bankruptcy is for liquidation of the debtor's estate to settle claims against it. A trustee is appointed by the court to sell all of the assets, and the proceeds are distributed according to a mandated priority of claims. Debtors can generally retain their essential property, such as personal residence, vehicle, etc.
2. *Chapter 11*—This class of bankruptcy is generally for the reorganization of a business, although individuals can qualify for this chapter. In Chapter 11, debtors are permitted to retain most of their assets, but have to restructure their financial affairs in a manner approved by the court that reflects that they will be able to pay their debts back from future earnings while containing the operation of the business.
3. *Chapter 13*—This class of bankruptcy is for individuals to restructure or renegotiate the repayment terms of all liabilities with creditors. Regular payments are usually made through a court-appointed trustee until all debts are repaid.

There are countless circumstances, reasonable and otherwise, that lead parties to seek protection in bankruptcy court. Without doubt, most parties are forced to choose this strategy due to events beyond anyone's control. In some cases, borrowers will have the chance to overcome the stigma of bankruptcy and start over. Chances are probably better for that if the bankruptcy was an individual case rather than a business case.

Consider a few of the following true-life examples of bankruptcies:

The first example involved a mother who delivered a baby that was eight weeks premature. The child required intensive care for almost six months. Thirty days after the child was released from the hospital, the parents received a $300,000 invoice from their hospital with thirty days to pay it.

During the pregnancy term, the father was laid off from an international airline that had filed for bankruptcy protection. The airline abruptly converted its case to Chapter 7 and was liquidated. The insurance benefits were cancelled, and the laid-off dad could not pay for COBRA. With neither insurance coverage nor a job, the father could not produce $300,000 on short notice.

Filing bankruptcy was the only way for this family to protect its house from seizure to satisfy the claims made by the hospital. It was not indicative of how well these people had previously managed financial affairs, they had a sterling credit history. But had they not taken this extreme step, an unavoidable catastrophic event would have cast hardworking, productive people into financial purgatory for the rest of their lives.

How could anyone recreate a positive financial record without additional credit being extended? Fortunately an understanding banker listened, worked a little harder, and provided financing for a new business that put this family on its way to rebuilding their lives.

A second example involves an ambitious chiropractor who started a practice six weeks after graduation, initially without a single patient. After obtaining an easy short-term, high-interest loan to buy equipment, he tried to build the business. But the patient list did not grow fast enough to earn money for the payments.

Bankruptcy was the only way to keep creditors from walking out with the medical equipment that the chiropractor needed to see patients and try to make payments. Should the misjudgment of an aggressive young person be a lifelong impediment to success?

This chiropractor stayed at it and finally built the practice up to a very profitable level. The equipment was eventually paid off with interest, and later he secured another loan to finance the purchase of a building to house the growing practice. Now the practice employs eight people and pays a lot of taxes because a practical banker listened and took the entire story into account.

The third example is one of the most widely studied corporate bankruptcy cases ever in the United States involving a publicly owned manufacturing company known as Johns-Manville Corporation. This company was formed in 1858 and was the world's leading manufacturer of a number of fiberglass and asbestos building materials. Asbestos was used for many years for insulation, but was later determined to be a carcinogen that led to cancer in many people who handled it or were in close proximity to it over time. Johns-Manville was targeted with a flood of lawsuits from thousands of persons who had in fact developed cancer attributable to the asbestos. Johns-Manville was faced with a catastrophic liability that would have continued to grow until it consumed the company.

In 1982 the company filed a pre-emptive bankruptcy case that enabled it to develop a manageable structure to provide for payment of these undefined liabilities while continuing to operate. This action ensured its ability to survive and pay all eventual claims, which were filed through a trust established in 1988 for victims of its products.

This strategy was a bold move that changed how bankruptcy is viewed. Using bankruptcy as an offensive strategy permitted the company to settle its liabilities, which would have never been accomplished without court protection. And it permitted the company to survive and pay later claimants, who would not even know of future losses at the time that the company was under attack. Today they continue to enjoy over $2 billion in annual revenue and are owned by Berkshire Hathaway, the investment holding company controlled by Warren Buffet.

Obviously, bankruptcy is susceptible to being abused by those who file, but it must be stressed that bankruptcy can also be a legitimate, strategic tool available to make better a bad situation that threatens individuals and businesses. Some lenders bristle at the notion of negotiating with borrowers who have had a bankruptcy case in their past, but each case must be evaluated according to its own particular circumstances.

The lender should not assume that a borrower who has been involved in a bankruptcy case has a character flaw. There are plenty of cases where overzealous or unreasonable creditors have forced bankruptcies rather than seeking more prudent and viable remedies to deal with problem situations. And lenders must recognize that another lender's inflexibility can sometimes only make situations worse and leave borrowers cornered with very limited options that unjustly penalize them over a longer term.

Lenders must consider the circumstances surrounding any borrower who has been involved in a bankruptcy case. Sometimes a better test of character is watching how the borrower manages to re-emerge and start over after bankruptcy.

Borrowers involved in a prior bankruptcy may actually become a lower risk for lenders. These borrowers have a wealth of experience in dealing with difficult situations, better preparing them for the economic risks associated with operating a small business. Surviving these tough circumstances adds to the borrower's management and financial education.

Federal law restricts how soon parties can file for bankruptcy protection a second time. This limitation protects subsequent lenders who deal with these borrowers.

If you or your company have been involved in a bankruptcy case (personal or business), the lender will usually discover this fact very early in the application process. It is better for you to disclose the facts before the lender reads this information in a credit report.

But before disclosing the bankruptcy, make sure the loan officer is interested in the transaction. If the loan officer is not comfortable with the attributes of the deal before learning about the bankruptcy, you'll never get her full attention on the application.

Credit reports include information about prior connections with any bankruptcy. In addition to personal bankruptcy cases, the credit report records any business in which the borrower was on record as an owner, executive officer, or partner. Even if the individual had no control over the events leading to a business bankruptcy, he or she must be prepared to explain the circumstances of the case.

Because the proceedings of a bankruptcy case are a matter of public record, the lender will be able to obtain a copy of your entire case file via the Internet to verify everything—the dates, creditors, debts, and final disposition of the case. In other words, a less-than-honest account of the bankruptcy case could permanently destroy your credibility with the lender.

In addition to telling the loan officer the bankruptcy story, provide a written explanation and accompanying documentation for the lender's study and review. Because the loan officer will probably have to relay the information in writing, it is better for you to transcribe a detailed account as the basis for the lender's report.

Document the circumstances thoroughly with a timeline and substantiate any difficulties that led to seeking bankruptcy protection. If you were truly a victim of circumstances, document the facts and back up your story with affidavits from other parties, accident reports, medical records, pictures, newspaper articles, and any other information available to support these claims.

You should prepare a detailed summary of how the case was resolved and remember to discuss what they did after the case was dismissed. This brief needs to be supported with documents verifying your personal involvement in the situation, court filings, financial reports, and trustee's report. How have your affairs changed since the bankruptcy? What has been accomplished to put your financial affairs in order?

If the bankruptcy experience was due to imprudent management rather than tragic circumstances, this truth is equally important. Depending on how much time has elapsed, how much money was lost by the creditors, and how you have managed in the post-petition period, the lender may still consider the loan application.

Litigation

Living in the most litigious society in the world can give a new meaning to the term "liability." Because over 75 percent of the world's lawyers are in the United States, American citizens have higher odds than anywhere else of being sued over a dispute of any nature. This exposure is increased for small business owners. Defendants can spend considerable sums of money and sometimes suffer severe financial consequences even when it is proven that they did nothing wrong.

When your financial statement is scarred with the extraordinary costs of defending a suit, or when you've settled a suit to limit these costs, the loan officer is entitled to a detailed explanation. By putting the matter in context and perspective, you can help the loan officer understand the impact of the litigation to the company's finances. This explanation helps you move the application process beyond the legal situation, allowing the positive aspects of the loan proposal to be considered and emphasized.

Offer the lender copies of the lawsuit, your answer, and the final resolution of the case. In justifying the effects of defending the case, provide the lender with copies of invoices, receipts, and other documents to show how the business was affected. If your attorney has a detailed opinion of your case, give copies of this correspondence to the lender. At least the loan officer will understand your situation after this disclosure and not fear the risk of being misled. But even if sympathetic, the loan officer retains the responsibility of underwriting the loan request according to the resulting risk to the business. The loan officer will have to take the results of the litigation on the business into account, regardless of whether or not you were at fault.

Most lenders will not proceed with a loan request if there is a material lawsuit pending at the time of the application. Routine matters that occur in the normal course of business and that do not threaten your overall financial condition should not interfere with the loan application. But if there is a matter of any substance against the company that is unresolved or on appeal, the lender will probably wait until final judgment has been rendered before proceeding.

Any significant judgment against you could significantly change the financial condition. If you were forced into a large settlement, or if the other party was enabled to lien your assets, the lender could suddenly have a problem loan. The collateral assets securing the loan could possibly have more claims outstanding than value.

If the situation has already cleared the judicial process and you're faced with a judgment, the lender will be interested in how the matter is handled. If you lose in court, the judgment must be honored. The lender will be interested in how you react, because it may be indicative of how you would react in a similar dispute with the lender at some future date.

Divorce

Divorce can be disastrous for a small business owner. Because the process can be emotionally strenuous for all the individuals involved, months of underperformance in business responsibilities may elapse. In addition, the financial settlement can be disruptive if you're forced to buy out or share the business ownership interests with your spouse.

If the business owner has recently completed the divorce process, it is important to provide an explanation to the lender about any impact the divorce had on the business or the owner's personal financial condition. Document this explanation with copies of bank records, financial statements, and a copy of the final divorce settlement. Disclosing personal (that is, emotional rather than financial) aspects of the divorce should be avoided, as they are not only irrelevant but also potentially distracting and therefore detrimental to the loan application.

Because of the stressful issues in divorce cases, the vengeful actions of one party may create liabilities for the other party. Alternatively, one party may refuse to pay legitimately allocated liabilities that are in the joint names of both parties. Divorce can become a disaster to your credit history and future ability to borrow money.

You need to carefully document these circumstances in order to demonstrate your circumstances in such a situation. Divorce is probably the most abused excuse used by persons with bad credit. To earn credibility, you have to show how the negative credit performance was created through the irresponsible actions of others.

The best defense is to make payments or pay off any unpaid accounts whether individually or jointly held, regardless of who was supposed to pay them. Try to protect a good credit history when possible, and pursue the other party later for recovery of these sums. To limit their future exposure, immediately close the joint credit accounts when the divorce process first begins and notify creditors that you will not be responsible for future liabilities created on any account by your ex. While you can't escape joint and several liability on existing balances, a notice can prevent a creditor from holding you liable for subsequent charges.

After discovering negative credit report information as a result of the divorce, you should contact the three major credit bureaus, Experian, Transunion, and Equifax, and provide a short, concise statement detailing the situation. The credit bureaus are obligated to include this explanation in all future inquiries.

If the divorce is not yet finalized, consider waiting until the process is over before making a business loan application. When you're resolving the complicated and emotional issues of divorce, your anxiety will be compounded by the pressures of seeking credit. You'll benefit by focusing on the business at hand—one major negotiation at a time.

Bad Decisions

To err is human, but some mistakes are more costly than others. In a dynamic economy, strategic decisions must be made on a regular basis. Because small business owners are constantly making decisions with long-term implications, they will sometimes make costly mistakes.

In a changing world, small business owners often perform as the chief executive officer, chief financial officer, chief operating officer, advertising agent, transportation specialist, tax expert, and computer prodigy; then they go home to be a compassionate parent, loving spouse, and supportive partner. These roles are defined by a constant stream of ideas from newspapers, magazines, sitcoms, talk shows, books, videos, movies, talk radio, social networking, blogs, and billions of Internet sites. So how can anyone make mistakes?

It is an age overrun with ideas and communication. Today's eighth wonder of the world is tomorrow's dinosaur. More decisions are demanded than ever before, but humans are still limited to one brain.

I give this explanation in order to offer universal forgiveness for making occasional bad business decisions. As long as the decision is based on the best option at the time, it should not be reconsidered. When you document an error for the lender, this page should be submitted with the loan request to provide some perspective to the loan officer.

When the loan officer is told about errors, your candor is factored into an assessment of the actions taken to overcome the mistake. If you qualify under the other criteria necessary to obtain financing, previous errors should not prevent you from getting a loan.

Bad Health

Consider what would happen to the economic status of a borrower who becomes ill for an extended period. There are many possible consequences and most of them include serious financial damage. Should that mean that the borrower can never qualify for business credit? What if the borrower had a spotless track record before the illness? It hardly seems equitable that after battling to survive, the borrower should also have to battle for the survival of the business. Once the borrower recovers, there remains the hard work of helping the business to recover.

The answer is to provide written proof to communicate and confirm the medical circumstances to the lender. The loan officer wants to know how the illness affected you personally and how that impacted the operation of the business. You can expect compassion for these situations but should accept the burden of proof. Rather than telling the loan officer all of the details of the medical treatment and procedures, a generic description of the medical condition will provide enough personal information. After satisfying the general situation questions, emphasize economic health and focus on the financial details.

How much time did you have to spend away from the business? Who replaced you and at what cost (both salary and lost revenue or productivity)? Is the illness behind you and the financial damage contained? Providing answers to these questions will be the starting point to evaluating whether a new loan can be part of resuming normal business going forward.

Bad Credit

Compounding several of the problems mentioned above is the trickle-down effect each has on your personal credit history. If your cash flow is interrupted for any reason and cash reserves are exhausted, payments to creditors will slow down accordingly. You must eventually deal with this problem, since slow credit payments are one of the most troublesome problems in the eyes of the lender.

It is important to manage personal credit closely to keep your payment history clean and avoid perpetuating negative entries into a credit record. Lenders focus on a number of aspects in the credit report, including the total amount of credit outstanding, payment history, and any public records that indicate the unsatisfactory conduct of personal affairs.

Most lenders today rely on a "credit score" to assess a prospective borrower's creditworthiness, which is a complex index determined by a number of factors such as:

✧ Length of current and prior employment
✧ Length of residency
✧ The amount of total debt
✧ The amount of credit outstanding versus the credit available
✧ Presence of any legal filings, proceedings, judgments, or bankruptcy
✧ Payment history on existing and previous debt
✧ Number of inquiries from prospective lenders

As recently as 2009, the national average score was around 700, with about 58 percent of our population having scores of 700 or greater. Historical evaluation has concluded that someone with a score of 599 has a 51 percent probability of a serious default (60+ days) on a mortgage loan.

Understanding how to manage this process cannot change one's previous poor credit record, nor is there a magical way to "repair" bad credit. Be wary of people promising to repair your credit and improve your score overnight. You can do whatever they can do for free. All they can do is root out the errors and mistakes on your report and possibly improve its accuracy. And even attempting to do that for someone else may be illegal in some states.

A poor credit history can result from many causes other than an irresponsible borrower. To clean up a tarnished track record:

✧ Pay off debts as quickly as possible, eliminating any numerous small debts first.
✧ Be sure to also repay every creditor that lists the debt as charged off.
✧ After reducing the remaining liability to those with higher balances, target the ones with higher interest rates to be paid off next.
✧ Talk to creditors about the situation and try to get a payment holiday that may upgrade past due payments to current status.
✧ Work out a realistic, but aggressive payment schedule in good faith. If the loan performs as agreed, ask the creditor for a written commendation for working out of a negative position.

But improving current and future credit performance can always improve your situation and end the poor performance record that may be reflected in the recent credit report. Begin by using the following strategies:

✧ Pay off as much credit as possible by using savings, having a yard sale, taking back recently purchased merchandise, liquidating assets, borrowing money from the business, collecting outstanding debts, or even drawing down the cash surrender value of a life insurance policy. Obtain cash (without borrowing more) to pay off these accounts as fast as possible. Rather than reducing all the accounts, pay off the ones with the lower balances. It is better to have five past due accounts than ten past due accounts.

✧ After the small debts are cleared, prioritize by paying off debt with higher payments or higher interest rates first. Paying off these accounts first gives you more flexibility in the future.

✧ Manage your payments so as not to exceed thirty days past due if possible, even if it means hand delivering the payment. Payments less than thirty days late are not reported to the credit bureau.

✧ If cash shortage is temporary, arrange to limit the number of creditors who will receive late payments. Rather than making one $500 payment on time and being late on four payments of $125, it is better to pay the four accounts on time and be late only on the one $500 payment.

✧ The credit bureau does not receive reports of late payments from such liabilities as public utilities, telephone companies, long distance suppliers, cable operators, merchandise buying clubs, and private note holders. Slowing payments to these accounts will not affect a public credit record and may help keep it cleaner. Getting too far behind on utility bills, however, will risk disconnection of that service, resulting in a deposit to be paid on restoration of service.

If you have bad credit, the lender should be told why. Often bad credit is not the result of poor management or lack of responsibility, but rather circumstances that affect your ability to meet those responsibilities consistently. To earn the lender's confidence, you must demonstrate that those circumstances have been improved to a degree that

Contact the credit bureau to ensure all information on the credit report is accurate. If there are any errors, be persistent in following up to get them corrected—it takes time but the credit bureau is obligated by law to correct any errors and eliminate stale information.

will not interfere with your ability to make payments on the loan being requested.

Federal law requires all credit reporting agencies to provide a free credit report to any consumer who requests it annually. These free reports will not include the credit score, but do reveal all of the data used to calculate it. Understanding the report and the level of accuracy reflected on it is the first step to improving the credit record.

Always go to the credit reporting agencies directly to ensure that your information is managed by the fewest number of parties possible. You can get more information about your credit report from any of the three major credit reporting bureaus:

www.equifax.com/home/en_us
www.experian.com/lp/credit-report-r.html
www.transunion.com/

Don't pay for sham credit repair operations—no one can legally provide anyone else with a new credit history, and trying to create one is illegal. If there are serious errors on the credit report that can't be fixed, contact an attorney.

CHAPTER **6**

Increasing the Chances of Loan Approval

There are many subtle ways to improve the chances of loan approval and to nibble further and get a better deal. Entrepreneurs are creative, persistent people who will do whatever it takes to get the deal done. In this chapter, you'll learn:

⬦ The effectiveness of an organized, positive approach
⬦ Dealing directly with the whole story
⬦ How to finesse the finer points of the transaction

Complete and Organized Information

The easiest, most basic strategy to increase chances of getting a loan proposal approved is to provide the lender with all of the necessary information in a professional, organized manner. Too many borrowers are rejected or needlessly delayed because they do not take the time to provide the required documentation in a coherent manner.

Now more than ever, lenders have to completely understand the borrower's operation, past and future, and how the loan request fits into that story. All of this information has to be documented in order to provide a tangible picture of the business, including the facts and figures necessary to approve the proposed loan. Without sufficient data to answer all of the questions, the lender will either have to ask for more information or take the easy way out by saying *no* to the proposal.

Often, you will have the lender's complete attention at the first meeting when the loan proposal is submitted. The lender may be ready to get started on the request immediately after this meeting. If the process is delayed by your failure to provide sufficient information or promptly respond to the lender's inquiries, the lender may get distracted with other deals and lose any momentum that had been created for yours.

Be on the offensive with information and answers about the business while the lender is interested and attentive to the loan proposal. If you passively let the application period stretch out over weeks, it will soon become months, and that will make the loan more difficult to approve. The lender will either lose focus on it or forget why there was any enthusiasm about assisting you in the first place.

Anticipating what data will be needed and which questions will be asked should not be difficult for thoughtful businesspersons. Consider the loan approval process like a sales campaign. Preparing this information in advance will make a positive impression about your management capabilities and competence.

Based on the information listed in Chapter 4, assemble any data that might possibly be relevant to the loan request. By providing this information in the initial meeting, you increase the lender's responsibility to respond without delay, while the deal is very fresh on their mind. Because each borrower's situation is unique, it is impossible to anticipate every item the lender will need to evaluate the loan request. But listen carefully and be prepared to respond quickly and thoroughly.

Positive Thinking

Regardless of the strengths or weaknesses of your proposal, it will sound better if you present it in a confident, enthusiastic tone. Your positive demeanor can be effective in developing the lender's excitement and favorable impression of the proposal. Enthusiasm is important to demonstrate that you are committed to the business and confident about the purpose and goals of the financing. This confidence will carry over into the lender's review, assisting the lender in selling the deal internally for approval of the transaction.

By accentuating the positive, you concentrate on the successes and not on the failures. Even if the business has suffered its share of losses, the emphasis should be on the wins—the upbeat stories that reinforce the reasons for lending money to this company.

Increase the odds of hearing "YES!"

✧ Organize a thorough set of information before applying for a loan.
✧ Be prepared to respond quickly to any and all information requests.
✧ Dedicate the time required in advance rather than allowing the process to drag over several weeks or months.

The Only Way to Get an Answer Is to Ask

Business people often hear horror stories from other small businesses about the condition of the lending market. Innuendoes, rumors, and negative tales convince many borrowers that there are no funds available. And at this writing in the summer of 2010, conditions may have never been worse for small business loans. But that is only one side of the story. Just because someone else got turned down for a loan does not mean it's a bad time to apply, or that there aren't banks aggressively seeking loans. As described throughout this book, there are many parameters on which a loan request is judged, any one of which can lead a lender to deny someone's request for financing.

Concentrate on getting the loan approved on its own merits, without being discouraged by the failures of others. Even if there are flaws that will concern the lender, the worst thing that can happen is that the lender will say *no*. If you don't ask, the lender cannot say yes.

Convincing the lender to provide financing is much like selling your services or products. You have to identify prospects, qualify them, make the pitch, and close the deal. Getting the lender to make a loan requires the same steps. Sometimes, like in any sales situations, there are curves, objections, questions, and delays. But like pursuing a good client, lenders have to be sold just as thoughtfully.

After researching the market, determine which lenders are prospects to handle the transaction. Which lender is best suited to provide the services to you? Which lender is interested in the market in which this business is conducted? Which lender wants your business? Which lender is willing to invest the time, confidence, and funding to help you succeed?

Does this lender understand your business? Is the lender interested in what you are trying to accomplish? Does the lender feel comfortable with small businesses at your stage of growth? Is the lender qualified and experienced in lending with the SBA loan guaranty programs? Can the lender feel comfortable with your strategy? Does the lender recognize how you address the risks involved?

If the lender passes these qualifications, lay out the proposal and ask for the loan. Presenting the loan request confidently, you should have an organized, complete package of information—concise, clearly stated, convincing, and supported by your assumptions.

In addition, prepare for the lender's objections. You need to answer questions with direct, documented information that satisfies the lender's concern. Rather than assuming that the reply is sufficient, ask the lender if the question has been fully answered.

It is easier to answer a question before it is asked. By anticipating questions, you can include the answers in the loan application. In that manner, you benefit by controlling the slant and specifics of the information.

If you're not sure how to answer a specific question, it is best to call the lender back as soon as practical to provide the response. Follow up the phone call with a letter or e-mail to reiterate the answer and ensure a mutual understanding on the point.

In concluding the meeting, summarize the business strategy, restate the deal, and review the answered objections. The goal is to make it easy and logical for the lender to give a positive reply to the loan request.

Dealing Directly with Negative Information

If part of your history includes a horror tale, such as one of the situations described in Chapter 5, it should never be hidden or dealt with in any way other than in complete candor and transparency. As suggested in other sections of the book, make sure the lender is really interested in the positive attributes of the proposition before venturing into life's tragedies. But after becoming serious about the proposal, lead the lender gently through the negative part of the story or the special circumstances.

In Chapter 5 there are suggestions about how to discuss several sensitive situations that you may have experienced. By not apologizing for these events, you acknowledge that they are inescapably an integral part of past experiences. It is unlikely that you purposely intended to encounter these situations.

The lender is not likely to be particularly sympathetic or concerned. Don't expect the lender to be forgiving. What you need is for the lender to concede to an open-minded recognition that these past events do not necessarily predict your future and that they have been finally resolved without any additional impact on the business. Accordingly, this history should not preclude you getting a business loan today.

Understanding the lender's perspective on these circumstances will help you predict the lender's reaction and will therefore help you prepare for this disclosure. The key objectives are to not alarm the lender and to provide plenty of evidence that you don't have a pertinent character flaw, that you have a bright future, and that you represent an acceptable business risk to the bank.

✦ Think positive!

✦ Unasked questions won't be answered.

✦ Carefully select lenders more likely to be interested in the business.

✦ Fully inform the lender about the business proposal in concise terms.

Documentation about these events is important. How have these events affected you? How have you tried to minimize these effects for the benefit of family and creditors (in that order of importance)? What has transpired since the event and how have you diligently and capably recovered? Complete honesty is the only policy, even when it hurts. The more direct the information from you, the better positioned you are to get another chance.

Meeting at Your Office

As simple as it sounds, meeting on your turf can provide an advantage when presenting a loan proposal. When lenders are away from their desks, they are more likely to listen to borrowers without the defenses normally provided to them in their own office space.

The lender cannot be distracted or interrupted in your office. There are no phone calls, letters to sign, memos of review, or checks to approve. Meeting at your place of business makes any additional information the lender may request accessible, and permits the lender to view your management and leadership firsthand.

The most important advantage is that the lender can see, hear, smell, and touch your business: customers, the store, busy employees, and the loading docks accepting and shipping inventory. Because the level of activity (if relevant) can also create a positive impression for the lender, their visit should be scheduled during busier hours, when there are a lot of customers, employees, machines, or other business activity involved. Translating the vision of the operation from the loan proposal to other decision makers will be easier for the lender if it can be described from a first-person visual recollection.

> Be straightforward, candid, and transparent about any negative history after the lender is interested in the deal.

Not Enough Collateral?

Most denied loan proposals are due to insufficient collateral. You cannot always reduce the amount of funds needed, and the lender is usually not able or willing to extend beyond the normal collateral coverage requirements. Sometimes there are minor ways to enhance or stretch the values of collateral assets to provide the lender with sufficient coverage, or at least to get close enough to convince the lender to give consideration to a portion of the deal being unsecured.

Examining the Lender's Valuation Method

Make sure the lender is using accurate, reliable information when determining the value of your collateral. This suggestion may require you to invest in a second opinion with another appraiser. If that second opinion convinces the lender to increase the loan, it is worth the time and cost.

If the collateral includes real estate, be aware that increased scrutiny of real estate lending in the past several years has resulted in myriad new regulations and requirements of appraisers. The effect of these changes has been a general depression of real estate valuations, due to the appraisal industry's fear of future challenges of its assessments.

The 1989 Financial Institutions Reform, Recovery and Enforcement Act (FIRREA) established firmer rules about the relationship between lenders and appraisers, including the qualifications of the appraiser, which became more stringent as loans became larger. Many of these rules have even become tighter following the real estate bubble of 2008–2009. Now banks are encouraged to use a third party to engage the appraiser and review the report for its compliance with professional standards before the lender sees it. While an understandable answer to many abuses that did occur, these procedures also bring on added challenges for borrower and lender alike.

An appraisal is simply an estimate of value, based on three distinct valuation approaches: market, replacement cost, and income approach. Most full appraisals assess a valuation using each of the three approaches to determine a final statement of value based on a weighted average of the three, depending on the specifics of the property and context of the assignment. In general terms, the three approaches are defined as follows:

1. *Market value.* This approach measures the likely value of a property based on recent, comparable sales ("comps") of properties of similar size and use in the particular area of the subject. The appraiser attempts to find other nearby sales of properties that share as many features as possible so that the opinion is created from an "apples to apples" comparison.

2. *Replacement cost.* This approach measures the likely cost of rebuilding the improvements on a particular property, plus the current value of the land based on comparable sales.

3. *Income approach.* When applicable, the appraiser examines the income being generated by a property, or the likely income that is projected to be generated from the property, based

on prevailing market rents or other use of the property, and projects a valuation based on an average capitalization, or "cap" rate. The cap rate is a generally agreed on rate of return that would be required from that particular use of capital if invested by a reasonable investor.

Be aware that appraisers have varying degrees of familiarity with the immediate geographic area and the type of improvement you own. Cooperate fully with the appraiser when the property is examined. It is a good idea to be on hand, if possible, and to be prepared to provide any information the appraiser might request. The more information the appraiser has, the more accurate valuation the property should get.

If the collateral includes furniture, fixtures, and equipment (FF&E), you should understand the method under which the lender values this collateral. Most lenders will routinely discount these assets 50 percent, but you should notice whether that valuation is based on the book value or the cost value. Encourage the lender to use the cost of the asset, since depreciation on many of these assets often will not affect their liquidation value.

If fixtures and equipment are affixed to the real property improvement, they should be assessed in the context of the real property value. Major equipment items also should be viewed in the perspective of what they contribute to your enterprise onsite.

If the FF&E is a major portion of the collateral assets, you may even decide to request an appraisal. In doing so, you can reduce the risk of undervaluation if you provide the lender's appraiser with relevant information about the assets.

Too often, lenders use liquidation companies and auctioneers for appraisals of FF&E assets. The liquidation value is based on a quick-sale approach and is therefore going to be substantially less than the true economic value of the asset. Liquidation value assumes that the asset is sold on a distressed basis to the highest bidder on one random date. If sold over a reasonable time period, the asset generally would yield a much higher value.

Many lenders have a knee-jerk reaction to collateral liquidation, due to an unpleasant past experience or just not wanting to deal with the messiness of repossessing such assets. You have to counteract that attitude with assurance about how the lender could reasonably expect to recover the loan when collateral is liquidated correctly. Lenders are apt to want to liquidate the collateral too fast, which always depresses sale prices.

It's no secret that buyers scent blood when they watch a nervous banker pacing around an equipment auction, wondering how much of a loss is going to be taken. A better sale method would be to place the FF&E on consignment with a dealer of used equipment or furniture, letting the assets be sold over a reasonable period when market demand will pay a higher price. These might be the same dealers who are only too glad to buy the FF&E for ten cents on the dollar at the lender's auction.

You should know the value of the assets on a liquidation basis, after understanding how to liquidate those assets on a reasonable basis. This information may permit you to negotiate stronger collateral valuations with the lender and ensure that the lender gives you adequate credit for the collateral assets.

Offering the Lender Other Assets

If collateral assets are short, you can offer to pledge other assets to the lender so that the loan will meet the lender's requirements. Other assets can sometimes cover a small margin needed by the lender as an alternative to lowering the loan amount.

When using this strategy, be prepared to be generous in supplying whatever is available. If lenders do not ask for a particular asset in the beginning, then they probably do not place much value on it.

These other assets may have marginal value, but if totaled, could provide the lender with a substantial contribution toward eliminating any existing collateral shortfall. These assets may include your FF&E, automobiles, rolling stock, accounts receivable, inventory, cash surrender value of insurance policies, notes receivable, and other miscellaneous assets on your business or personal balance sheet.

Maximizing the Valuation of Current Assets

Small business lenders usually do not attach much value to your accounts receivable and inventory assets. This failure to recognize the value of these assets is prudent, since both can disappear in days unless the lender controls them.

Borrowers are often frustrated at the difficulty of leveraging their current asset strength, unless they are willing to pay 25 percent to 30 percent interest to a factoring company or asset-based lender. The margin of adequate financing is sometimes tied up in the current assets of a business, and is seemingly untouchable at a reasonable cost to the borrower.

One method to increase the leverage of these current assets is to request that the lender include them in the borrower's collateral pool as a contribution toward the collateral requirements of the borrower's term loan. The borrower can enhance the value of these assets by offering to permit the lender to monitor the assets and by being willing to pay the related service fees to the lender for the cost of such monitoring.

In other words, if the lender would give the borrower credit for a lower-than-average advance percentage on current assets (for example, a 50 percent advance on sixty-day receivables and a 35 percent advance on inventory), this credit would provide the borrower with the margin of collateral needed to get the loan proposal approved. In exchange for the lender approving a long-term loan with short-term collateral, the borrower would allow the lender to monitor these assets to ensure adequate coverage continues.

The borrower would be required to provide the lender with a regular statement of its accounts and inventory balances on perhaps a weekly or monthly basis. This statement would detail the changes of accounts receivable and inventory, along with account and inventory details that comprise the totals and would enable the lender to liquidate them. The borrower would also have to be willing to pay the lender the extra cost of reviewing these statements each period, recognizing the legitimate effort required over the term of the loan. These fees may equate to 1 percent to 2 percent of the loan balance each year.

This option is infrequently employed and is suited only for established businesses with a long track record of successful operations and good management reporting systems. As a creative option, it may make the difference in qualifying for a loan. After the loan has been serviced for a couple of years, and the principal balance has been paid down below the normal margin required of the main collateral assets, the borrower may negotiate a release of the current asset collateral in order to lower costs and reporting requirements.

The Rope of Hope—Projecting Performance

You are always required to provide the lender with projections of the company's financial performance for at least two years. These estimates are intended to give the lender confidence that you can service the debt with cash flow from operations.

These projections are more difficult to estimate for start-up businesses or for businesses that intend to use the loan proceeds for making major changes in their operations. It is incumbent on you to use caution and salesmanship when developing these projections, since these numbers are a very important component of ultimate loan approval.

Financial projections can be described as a "Rope of Hope." You have the opportunity to *swing* or *hang*, depending on the success and accuracy of the projections.

You can swing by using the projections persuasively, convincing the lender that the loan proceeds will enable you either to increase profitable revenues or reduce specific costs in order to provide the monies to make future loan payments. The "rope" enables you to obtain the funds needed to accomplish this success.

But if the projections do not come to fruition, then you will hang. Loan default is certain, caused by an inadequate cash flow available to service the debt. This situation could lead to liquidation of the collateral assets, as well as a possible lawsuit against you and any loan guarantors.

Any persuasive presentation to promote your ability to perform has to be reinforced with actual performance. In this sense, financial projections can be a powerful tool for you to use in convincing the lender of the prudence of the proposed loan. But these same projections can smother you with an untenable situation that could lead to the company's demise.

Start-Up Businesses

Regardless of your industry or business, the toughest loan for a lender to consider is one to a start-up business. In almost all circumstances, this phase of a business is the most difficult for the borrower, and certainly the most risky for the lender.

In focusing on the risks faced by the lender in this situation, you need to overcome the skepticism that accompanies the lender's desire to help. You must assure the lender that you can effectively marshal available resources to generate profitable revenues quickly enough to survive and repay the loan as scheduled. For a start-up business loan, there is greater emphasis on equity capital, because the lender wants you to have enough cash reserve to meet unexpected expenses or unanticipated slowness in sales, as well as practically have some "skin in the game." Without sufficient funds at risk, borrowers might not work as hard to make the business work, particularly if the going gets tough.

If the borrower is a start-up business, the following items required in the loan application (discussed in Chapter 4) need special emphasis to overcome the lender's aversion to this stage of business lending:

Inadequate collateral?

✦ **Question the lender's valuation method of collateral assets and offer additional supporting information.**
✦ **Supplement collateral with other business or personal assets to make up for any shortfall.**
✦ **Offer monitored receivables and inventory assets to shore up weak coverage and gap the insufficient margin of full collateral coverage.**

Borrower's equity. The lender will be adamant about requiring a strong capital contribution from you in the form of operating cash and contribution toward major assets purchased. There is no substitute for operating funds to ensure that you can weather the start-up phase of the business, which always produces many unforeseen expenses.

Your revenue expectations, if over- or underestimated, can also play havoc with the cash requirements of the start-up period. You should have an independent readily available source of short-term working capital to manage these requirements in the event that the financial projections are inaccurate.

Financial projections. Your financial projections are going to be scrutinized very carefully, because start-up borrowers usually do not have a previous track record against which to compare the reasonableness of these numbers. Every figure will be questioned when you present the projections to the lender.

Construct your income and expense projections realistically. You cannot research these figures too much. What kind of marketing efforts are required to produce sales? What fixed expenses are involved in opening the business? What variable costs are incurred at the level of sales projected?

Consult with noncompetitors in similar markets to determine whether or not the projections are attainable. Experienced business owners who will not be affected can quickly evaluate the forecasts to ensure that you haven't missed something significant that could lead to disaster.

Feasibility. Make an effort to demonstrate to the lender that the new business idea is feasible and that you can, in fact, succeed with the plan. In identifying the demand for the product or service, show your experience or ability to meet that demand.

The country is littered with the skeletons of great business ideas that were not thought out far enough. One former professional football player started a local chain of necktie stores to capitalize on his popularity and the attention his personal stylish and colorful neckties had received. Unfortunately, he lived in Miami, Florida, where most of the local business community does not frequently wear neckties because of the tropical climate. He may have had a better prayer as an anonymous tie reseller in New York, but obviously didn't sufficiently evaluate the feasibility of his plan in Miami.

For 7(a) loans, at publication date these loans are limited to $2 million with a maximum guaranty of the lower of either 75 percent of the loan balance or the prevailing guaranty dollar limit as determined by the agency's funding leverage in that year. Industry advocates continue to press Congress to raise these limits to $5 million in reflection of the need to serve more businesses.

Marketing plan. Demonstrate to the lender that you have identified a viable target audience and have ascertained the most effective method of directing that audience to the business. Good businesses must have a lot of paying customers to become great businesses.

Consider a marketing and advertising plan that will provide a means to communicate with your targeted consumers, that group most likely to buy your products or services. Most start-up businesses do not have enough money to determine marketing through trial and error. Consulting with an experienced advisor in this field is a good idea if you can afford it.

If you own a franchised company, much of this information will be provided as part of the franchise package of benefits. Even so, it is wise to consult with a specialist in the market area to test the franchiser's assumptions about how to advertise the business locally.

Start-up businesses should expect to have a more difficult job getting a loan approved. But emphasis on these items will help give the lender more confidence in the most important factors of the business: cash flow and revenue generation.

CHAPTER 7

Getting the Loan Funded:
The Closing Process

Some loans can be easy to get committed, but the devil to contend with in really getting any money. Getting approval is only the halfway mark—it's never a real deal until the money is in hand. In this chapter you'll learn:

- ✧ The due diligence required to close the deal
- ✧ How to make the process go smoother and faster
- ✧ Where to slow down the expensive closing fees

So the Loan Is Approved—Now What Happens?

Once the loan has been approved by the lender and the SBA guaranty is granted, the lender is responsible for setting the activities in motion to have the loan transaction executed (commonly referred to as "closed") and funded. This process is involved in itself, despite all the work that has been expended getting the application assembled and the loan approved.

During the loan closing phase you may be required to produce additional documentation, specific to the collateral assets. The lender or its attorney is charged with preparing the loan and security documents in accordance with provisions of the SBA Loan Authorization and Agreement. The lender may or may not take an active role in the process.

Borrowers sometimes get frustrated at the time required to move from SBA approval to actually funding the loan. It is typical that at this stage of the loan myriad professional consultants become involved—

appraisers, engineers, surveyors, and attorneys—because understandably neither the borrower nor lender wants to spend money on the required due diligence before having the loan formally approved. There is much work to be done, and usually, the borrower has to get in line behind other transactions for these professional services that are needed.

The first activity required is for the lender and the lender's attorney to review the SBA Loan Authorization and Agreement, ensuring that it accurately reflects the lender's understanding of and intent for the transaction. If not, changes have to be addressed with the SBA in writing, which may delay further closing activity. Once the lender has confirmed this information, the parties are ready to start working toward a closing.

Next, the lender or closing attorney will engage in a series of activities for which you will be obligated to pay—whether or not the loan is ever funded. Depending on your collateral, the lender will order a title search, an appraisal, an environmental report, and a survey for the real property, as well as a lien search on the FF&E assets. These reports will validate the identity of title holder and determine whether there are other liens, encumbrances, or claims on the property (or assets); the market value; whether the environment condition is acceptable; and whether there are any zoning violations or encroachments on the property. This information is needed to assure the lender that the collateral can provide the protection assumed with the terms of the loan approval.

Should any of these reports come back with different results than expected, or with other problems identified, there will probably be additional time delays to resolve them, a modification of the loan terms, or even withdrawal of the lender's commitment. It is important that you recognize the gravity of this stage of the funding process, manage the lender's response to any unexpected results, and get the issues resolved quickly. This information is discussed further in this chapter.

Remember that the closing attorney is not an arbitrary participant in the closing process. The closing attorney represents only the lender. One attorney cannot represent two parties in the same transaction. Whether you should be represented by an attorney is a different question and is addressed in Chapter 8.

There is a growing trend among major SBA-participating lenders to prepare their own closing documents for SBA loans. Closing costs have become a new competitive tool in recent years with lenders utilizing software to produce the legal documents and forms used for loan transactions, which are customized for every state.

Some lenders prepare their own loan closing documents from a variety of widely used banking software, customized for each state. Attorneys' participation with these lenders is generally reduced to title searches, document reviews, and escrow responsibilities, which drastically reduces the fees paid by borrowers. If there is a choice of more than one lender, ask about whether they offer this service before committing to a loan.

This chapter will describe the activities that are common for loan closings, why these activities are needed, and what the associated costs are likely to be. Further, this chapter explains how you can shorten the time necessary to get the loan closed, and maybe even reduce some of the associated costs.

The SBA Authorization and Loan Agreement

The first step toward closing the loan is when the lender obtains the SBA Authorization and Loan Agreement ("Authorization") from the SBA. This document contains the terms and conditions under which the SBA will provide the loan guaranty to the lender. The lender must comply with the provisions of this document to the letter or risk having the SBA guaranty canceled or "repaired," which is SBA's term for a reduction in the amount they will reimburse the lender for a defaulted loan.

The Authorization will describe the loan transaction, its term, collateral required, guarantors, and the other negotiated conditions. The lender or its attorney uses the Authorization as a guide to develop the specific set of closing documents needed to comply with the loan agreement.

The form of the SBA Authorization along with the promissory note, security agreement, guaranty agreements, and settlement sheets are required to be in a format specified by the SBA to document the loan on most loans (some Express Loan programs permit lenders to use their own forms). Presented in a standard boilerplate template, the Authorization is organized electronically so to be customized for every transaction. Some prominent sections of the authorization include:

Declarations. This portion of the document declares the SBA's authorization and agreement to guarantee the lender's loan as specified, identifying the borrower, the amount of the loan, and the extent of the guaranty. Also, the guaranty fee will be spelled out in this area.

Documentation. The next portion of the Authorization defines which SBA documents are required by the agency to enact this guaranteed transaction. Among the most common are:

- ✧ *SBA note: Form 147*—The SBA requires the lender to use this form as the promissory note governing the transaction.
- ✧ *SBA settlement sheet: Form 1050*—The SBA requires the lender to report each disbursement of loan proceeds on this form, which identifies to whom the loan proceeds are paid. This requirement ensures that the loan is disbursed in a manner consistent with the SBA approval of the loan.

✧ *Compensation agreements: Form 159*—The SBA requires the lender to submit this form for each party who received a professional fee for work related to the subject loan.

✧ *Authorization*—The SBA requires the lender to obtain the borrower's signature on the Authorization and retain the original in the loan file.

Precedents. This portion of the Authorization usually defines four conditions that the lender must affirm and comply with in order to ensure the SBA participation:

1. The lender must acknowledge that the guaranty is subject to the provisions of the Guaranty Agreement between the SBA and the lender.

2. The lender must acknowledge and agree to disburse the loan within a specified time frame, unless the SBA consents to extending that period.

3. The lender must affirm that it has not received any evidence of unsatisfied adverse changes in the borrower's financial condition or status since the loan approval that would warrant withholding further disbursement of the loan.

4. The lender affirms that the Authorization is subject to the representations made by the borrower, representations made by the lender, conditions set forth by the lender in its application for the guaranty, and conditions set forth in the Authorization.

Terms. The last portion of the Authorization defines the specific terms under which the contemplated loan is to be enacted in order to qualify for the guaranty.

✧ *Repayment terms*—The Authorization defines the exact repayment terms under which the loan is extended, including the following information:

✧ *Repayment period*—The repayment term of the loan is defined, including the number of years in which repayment is to occur and the number of installments expected in that period. The first payment date is also specified.

✧ *Interest rate*—The interest rate of the loan is defined. If the rate is variable, the index by which the rate may be adjusted is explained, along with the time period in which such an adjustment may occur. Disclosure is made that, if the SBA repurchases its guaranteed portion of the loan in the event of default, the interest rate will be permanently fixed at the then current interest rate.

✧ *Maturity*—The maturity of the loan is defined as the length of time it takes for the loan to be paid in full. There are several variables that determine the maturity. For example, the lender is permitted to apply installment payments first to any outstanding interest and then to the principal. This provision can significantly impact the repayment of the loan in a situation where the borrower is frequently late in submitting payments.

The Authorization states that any unpaid principal and interest will be due at the date of the last scheduled installment, regardless of the amount of a normal installment. The borrower will also be liable for reimbursing the lender for any extraordinary costs incurred in administrating, collecting, or liquidating the loan at the time of the final payment.

A "due on sale" provision is contained in this section; it states that if the borrower transfers or encumbers any asset used as collateral for the loan without permission from the lender and the SBA, the maturity of the loan may be accelerated.

The lender is permitted to assess the borrower with a late penalty of 5 percent of the payment amount for any installment received more than ten days after that payment was due.

✧ *Use of proceeds limitations*—The Authorization specifies the exact allocation of loan proceeds as approved by the lender and the SBA, with the following provisions governing these distributions:

1. The lender is to distribute the funds whenever possible with joint payee checks issued to the borrower and the ultimate recipient of the proceeds.

2. The borrower must usually present documentation to substantiate the allocations, such as a contract, bill of sale, price quote, or invoice. If the borrower has been approved for working capital financing, the lender will expect an updated budget of where the proceeds will be allocated. These funds will be distributed directly to the borrower. If the borrower is refinancing another loan, the other lender will have to furnish a written payoff as of the date of closing.

PART 3

3. Up to 10 percent of the loan amount, to a maximum of $10,000, may be disbursed directly to the borrower as working capital if the final budgeted allocation of loan proceeds and closing costs do not use the entire loan.

✧ *Collateral requirements*—The Authorization will specify the exact assets that are to be used to secure the loan, and will detail the conditions under which their encumbrance is expected. A variety of SBA security documents may be referred to, depending on the specific collateral offered by the borrower:

✧ *Form 1059: Security Agreement*—The borrower is required to execute this form to encumber personal property assets, and the Authorization should specify in which lien position the lender should be. If the lender is to be subordinated to a senior lender, the Authorization will note the name of the lender and the amount of the outstanding senior loan.

The Authorization will also refer to use of the UCC-1 Financing Statement, which is a standard document for recording public notice of the lender's lien on the borrower's personal property assets. The lender will attach a detailed list of these assets (with serial numbers, if available) to the UCC-1 and will record this statement in the county where the property is located.

✧ *RO IV 147: Mortgage, Deed in Trust, or Deed to Secure Debt*—The borrower is required to execute a form to encumber real property assets, and the Authorization should specify in which lien position the lender should be. If the lender is to be subordinated to a senior lender, the Authorization will note the name of the lender and the amount of the outstanding senior loan. The exact form used will be according to the state in which the real property is situated.

✧ *Form 148: Guaranty*—The borrower (or the individuals who own the borrowing entity) are required to execute this form, which provides for a joint and several personal guaranty of the loan. Provisions describing this requirement may or may not describe collateral, depending on the agreement the borrower has reached with the lender during negotiations.

- ✧ *RO IV Form 82: Assignment of Life Insurance*—The borrower (or the individuals who own the borrowing entity) are required to execute this form if there is a requirement to provide life insurance to secure the loan. A comparable form provided by the insurer may be substituted.
- ✧ *Lease Agreement*—The borrower is required to submit a copy of the Lease Agreement (if the borrower occupied leased premises) to confirm that the remaining term of the lease is extended to a minimum of the length of the loan repayment period.
- ✧ *RO IV Form 77: Lessor's Agreement*—The borrower is required to obtain the execution of this agreement with the lessor. The Lessor's Agreement protects the lender from a landlord attempting to assert any interest in the borrower's personal assets or other assets that the lender encumbers to secure the loan and that may be situated in the landlord's premises.
- ✧ *RO IV Form 79: Collateral Assignment of Lease*—If the borrower has been approved for financing using an Eligible Passive Borrower ("EPB"), this form is required to provide the lender with an assignment of the lease on the business premises to the EPB. An EPB is employed when assets are purchased in the name of one entity and leased to the operating business concern ("Operating Company or OC"), which also guarantees the loan.
- ✧ *Additional real estate requirements*—There is an additional set of covenants and documents required if the lender is encumbering real estate collateral. These include:
- ✧ *Single property mortgage, deed in trust, or deed to secure debt*—The lender is required to file a separate mortgage, deed in trust, or deed to secure debt (depending on the state in which real property is situated) for each parcel of real property taken as collateral.
- ✧ *RO IV Form 26: Agreement as to Additional Advances*—When the lender is taking a subordinate position on the borrower's real property, the lender will require the senior lender to execute this document. This form protects the lender from losing collateral coverage if a senior lender were to advance additional proceeds to the borrower under the senior loan agreement.
- ✧ *Title insurance*—The lender is required to obtain title insurance without any survey exceptions on real property parcels where the lender is to have a first priority lien. This requirement

includes a current survey of the subject property to ensure that there are no property encroachments or boundary errors.

✧ *RO IV Form 37: Attorney's Certificate of Title*—The lender is permitted to use a guaranteed title search for parcels where the lender is to be in a subordinated lien position.

✧ *Separate guaranty*—Each owner of title on a particular parcel of real property will be required to execute a separate guaranty, even if the title holder does not have a direct interest in the borrower.

✧ *Appraisal*—The borrower is required to provide the lender with an appraisal that is not more than six months old that supports the specific valuation used to obtain approval of the loan. If the appraisal determines that the property has a lower value, the borrower will have to provide additional equity or additional collateral, or the lender may reduce the loan.

✧ *Survey*—The borrower is required to provide the lender with a current survey that shows the existing boundaries and improvements.

✧ *Minimum occupancy*—For existing buildings, the borrower is required to occupy at least 51 percent of the premises.

✧ *Additional personal property requirements*—There is an additional set of covenants and documents required if the lender is encumbering personal property collateral. These include:

✧ *Schedule A*—The lender will require that the borrower provide a detailed list of the personal property assets securing the loan. This list will be attached to the UCC-1 and the Security Agreement, both of which will contain language specifying that the property pledged will include but will not be limited to the items on Schedule A. Where applicable, all assets on Schedule A should be described with the manufacturer's name and the model and serial numbers.

✧ *Lien search*—The lender is required to conduct a lien search to evidence that the requisite lien position is acquired.

✧ *On-site inspection*—The lender must certify to the SBA that an on-site inspection of the personal property asset was conducted prior to the first disbursements of the loan proceeds.

There may be other documentation required to perfect the borrower's collateral, depending on the exact nature, ownership, and location of the collateral assets.

Conditions and covenants. The fifth section of the Authorization sets forth several conditions that the borrower must agree to comply with during the term of the loan.

- ✧ *Execution*—The borrower must agree to execute all of the documents required, which are mentioned previously in this chapter.
- ✧ *Reimbursable expenses*—The borrower agrees to reimburse the lender on demand for all expenses incurred for the borrower's application and the making and administration of the loan. Most of these expenses will be charged to the borrower at the loan closing.
- ✧ *Books, records, and reports*—The borrower agrees to maintain records of business activities (including financial reports) and to provide them to the lender upon request. Further, the borrower agrees that the lender may inspect the financial records or appraise any asset of the business at any time. The borrower also authorizes any municipal, state, or federal government authority to provide the lender or SBA with copies of information that may be on file about the borrower.
- ✧ *Management consultants*—The borrower agrees not to engage the services of a management consultant without prior approval of the lender and the SBA.
- ✧ *Distributions and compensation*—The borrower agrees to not make distributions of capital or assets, retire stock or partnership interests, consolidate or merge with another company, or make preferential arrangements with affiliated companies during the term of the loan. Further, the borrower will not provide any bonuses, distributions, gifts, or loans to any owner, director, officer, or employee in any manner other than reasonable compensation for services during the term of the loan.
- ✧ *Hazard insurance*—The borrower agrees to maintain hazard insurance on the fixed assets that are used to secure the loan. All insurance policies will name the lender as loss payee and/ or mortgagor, as appropriate. The borrower's furniture, fixtures, and equipment must be insured to at least 90 percent of replacement cost.

PART 3

Policies insuring buildings must include a mortgagor's clause indicating that the interest of the mortgagor shall not be invalidated by the neglect of the owner, and that the mortgagor will be given thirty days notice prior to cancellation. This clause is commonly referred to as the New York Standard Mortgage Clause.

✧ *Federal taxes*—The borrower must ensure that all federal withholding taxes are paid up to date and that there are no outstanding tax liens against the borrower.

✧ *Change of ownership*—The borrower must agree not to change the ownership, control of the business, the business name, or the form of business organization, without the approval of the lender and the SBA.

✧ *Receipt of SBA forms*—The borrower must execute the following SBA forms in compliance with federal regulations governing guaranteed loans:

✧ *Form 1624: Certification Regarding Debarment*—This document is required to attest that the borrower—the individual and the business entity—have not been debarred from doing business with the federal government due to any administrative, disciplinary, or other action specifically restricting the respective parties.

✧ *Form 652: Assurance of Compliance for Nondiscrimination*—This document is required to attest that the borrower and any subsequent recipients of the SBA-guaranteed loan proceeds agree to comply with SBA regulations pertaining to discrimination. These regulations require that no person be excluded from participation in, or be denied the benefits of, any federal financial assistance from the SBA based on age, color, handicap, marital status, national origin, race, religion, or sex.

✧ *Business licenses*—The borrower is required to provide the lender with a copy of business licenses and any special operating permits or licenses required by the state.

✧ *Negative pledge covenant*—The borrower agrees not to encumber or convey any asset or ownership of the business without prior approval of the lender and the SBA.

✧ *ADO Form 20: Opinion of Counsel*—The lender's attorney is required to provide an opinion regarding the loan transaction.

✧ *Other insurance*—Depending on the nature of the collateral provided by the borrower, additional insurance may be required:

✧ *Flood insurance*—If the business or collateral is located in a special hazard area subject to flooding, mud slides, or erosion, the borrower must agree to maintain Federal Flood Insurance in the maximum amount available.

✧ *Automobile insurance*—If motor vehicles are used as collateral, the borrower must agree to maintain collision and liability in an amount satisfactory to the lender, with the lender named as the loss payee.

✧ *Borrower's equity*—Prior to the first disbursement of the loan, the borrower must provide satisfactory evidence of the requisite equity injection, as represented in the loan application.

✧ *Form 155: Standby Agreement*—Any subordinate creditors of the borrower must execute a Standby Agreement to subordinate the lien rights and other general rights in favor of the SBA lender.

✧ *Organizational authority*—The borrower must substantiate its authority to enter into the loan by producing organizational documents providing such information:

If the borrower is a corporation, it must provide:

✧ Corporate Resolution—Form 160
✧ Certificate of Good Standing
✧ Articles of Incorporation
✧ Qualification of foreign corporation to do business in the resident state, if applicable

If the borrower is a partnership, it must provide:

✧ Partnership Agreement
✧ Certificate as to Partners—Form 160A
✧ Certificate of Limited Partnership, if applicable
✧ Certificate of Existence

✧ *Bulk-sales notice*—If applicable, the borrower must provide the lender with evidence of compliance with any applicable state or federal bulk-sales laws.

PART 3

✧ *Building compliance*—The borrower must provide evidence that any commercial buildings used as collateral conform to all applicable building, zoning, and sanitation codes, as well as the Americans with Disabilities Act of 1990, as amended.

✧ *Fixed asset limit*—If included, the borrower may agree to limit the acquisition of fixed assets to a particular level, subject to approval from the lender and the SBA.

✧ *Franchise agreement*—The borrower must provide the lender with a copy of any franchise agreement to which it is a party.

✧ *Alien registration*—If applicable, the borrower must provide the lender with a copy of the alien registration verification (green card) of any owners who are not U.S. citizens. Noncitizens are required to authorize the lender to submit Form G-845 to the Immigration and Naturalization Service (INS) for verification of the permanent resident status or naturalization. Legal Permanent Residents (LPR), also known as "Permanent Resident Aliens," are eligible for unrestricted participation in SBA financing, but Non-LPR are eligible only when they own less than 50 percent of the enterprise and the loan is fully secured for the life of the loan.

✧ *Environmental assessment conditions*—If the borrower is securing the loan with commercial property, the lender and the SBA will require that an environmental assessment of the property be obtained. The following conditions will be included in the Authorization:

✧ *Option to modify or cancel.* The lender and SBA reserve the right to modify or cancel the loan if environmental contamination is discovered on the property.

✧ *Environmental assessment.* The lender and the SBA will require an Environmental Disclosure Form, an Environmental Questionnaire (ADO Form 001), Transaction Screen Analysis, Phase 1 Environmental Audit, or a Phase 2 Environmental Audit. The determination of which assessment is required is based on the historic use of the property and development in the immediate area.

✧ *UST requirements.* If the property contains underground storage tanks (USTs), the borrower is required to comply with all federal and state regulations for USTs. The borrower must also provide the lender with evidence on an annual basis of compliance with these regulations, including the EPA financial responsibility regulations.

✧ *Eligible Passive Borrower*—The SBA permits borrowers to acquire capital assets (real estate or large equipment components) in separate entities in order to take advantage of various business strategies that provide unique financial, liability, or tax advantages. In such situations, the borrower is defined as an "Eligible Passive Borrower" (EPB), since the entity that acquires the assets will be a passive owner and merely lease the asset to the active business concern, or the "Operating Company" (OC). Financing passive ownership is typically ineligible for SBA assistance.

In order to qualify for this financing structure, at least 50 percent of the ownership of the EPB must identically match the ownership of the OC. Further, the OC must guarantee the entire debt, since the OC is the ultimate source of the repayment.

If using an EPB loan structure, the borrower must agree that the respective ownership in collateral assets and in the business entity will remain in the same proportion until the loan is repaid, unless the lender and the SBA consent to any change.

✧ *Construction loan conditions*—If the borrower is using any portion of the loan proceeds to build a new structure or make improvements on an existing structure, the following provisions shall be in the Authorization:

Construction documentation. The borrower will be required to provide the lender with the following documentation related to construction:
Building plans and specifications
Evidence of builder's risk insurance and workers' compensation insurance carried by the contractor
Evidence that the contractor has furnished a performance bond for 100 percent of labor and materials, with the borrower and lender named as the obligees
Agreement of Compliance: Form 601
Construction contract

Borrower's equity. Evidence of the borrower's equity contribution toward the construction project must be provided, since the borrower's funds will be used before any loan proceeds will be advanced.

Survey. The borrower must furnish an as-built survey prior to any advances of the construction funds in order to show existing boundaries and improvements.

Earthquake standards. For new buildings, the borrower must provide evidence that the project will meet the requirements of the "National Earthquake Hazards Reduction Program Recommended Provisions for the Development of Seismic Regulations for New Buildings." A certificate may be obtained from the project architect to fulfill this requirement.

Interim inspections. As the borrower requests loan advances, the lender will conduct interim inspections of the project to verify that construction conforms to plans and specifications.

Retainage. The lender will withhold 10 percent of the construction contract proceeds until the project is completed.

Lien waivers. The lender will require all contractors, subcontractors, and suppliers to sign a lien waiver prior to each loan disbursement.

Cost overruns. If the borrower's project experiences cost overruns, the borrower or the lender must provide additional funds to complete the project.

Minimum occupancy. For newly constructed buildings, the borrower is required to occupy at least 67 percent of the premises.

American-made products. To the extent possible, the borrower agrees to purchase American-made equipment and products with the proceeds of the loan.

Lottery income restriction. The borrower must acknowledge that the Authorization restricts the borrower to no more than 33 percent of annual gross revenue being generated from commissions on official state lottery sales.

Execution. The sixth section confirms the general legal conditions of the Authorization that the SBA and lender acknowledge and execute in this section.

How Can the Borrower Close the Loan Faster?

Most borrowers are ready to close the loan within a week of the final loan approval, but it is rare that the lender can be prepared in this time frame. There is a lot of work that cannot be avoided to prepare for a loan closing.

Rather than sit frustrated on the sidelines, you can be proactive and assist the lender and closing attorney with many tasks. This help will make a difference in the time required to complete the process and fund the transaction.

Start Closing Before the Loan Is Approved

Much of the due diligence required before closing, such as appraisals, surveys, and environmental assessments, is typically not conducted until after final approval of the loan. This delay is due to the unwillingness of most borrowers to risk spending thousands of dollars on these studies without having the assurance that the loan will be approved.

One method to guarantee that the time gap between SBA loan approval and loan closing is shortened is to initiate these time-consuming activities earlier in the process. While this does put some of your funds at risk, in many situations the risk is very low due to your unquestioned financial qualification for the transaction and SBA eligibility. The lender should be able to express some degree of confidence, without commitment, as to whether you should take this risk.

If your willingness to authorize the appraisal, survey, environmental assessment, life insurance, and even a title opinion and lien search get started or are completed in advance, when the loan is approved, closing could occur in a matter of days.

Review the Authorization

Obtain a copy of the Authorization from the lender or the SBA as soon as possible and carefully review it. You need to also make a determination that the document accurately reflects the transaction negotiated between you and the lender. Additionally, your review will alert you to other requirements that the lender may not be working on yet, so you can press the lender for prompt action.

Make sure that you're capable of complying with the terms of the Authorization and inquire up front about any items that you don't understand. If any modifications are needed, bring these items to the attention of the lender immediately, since changes may require several days or weeks for SBA approval.

PART 3

Get Life Insurance!

If the lender or Authorization requires you to furnish life insurance on any of the individual owners or managers, application for these insurance policies should begin immediately. A $1 million (or $100,000) life insurance policy can no longer be obtained over the telephone.

Life insurers are much more selective about issuing large policies, and most will require a blood test for even a $100,000 policy. Blood work requires time, and the underwriting of the insurer may also include financial qualification in order to justify the policy. It is not so much that insurers won't write the coverage as it is the underwriting to assess their risk and your price for the coverage.

To evidence compliance with the insurance requirement, you may be required to furnish an actual policy at the loan closing. The life insurance policy may take four to six weeks to issue. It is wise to apply for life insurance coverage as soon as possible during the loan application process if it is likely to be required.

Get the Lender's Attention

You can help the lender and closing attorney by providing additional information or performing some assigned tasks. A borrower who communicates directly, regularly, and constructively can shorten the time required to close.

Supply Additional Documentation

You may be required to produce additional material for the lender's attorney, primarily to document specific conditions and to provide further information about the collateral.

Even though some of this information may be redundant and you may have provided it previously to the lender, it is easier to reproduce it for the closing attorney than to rely on the lender. The attorney will be particularly concerned about preparation of the security documents and ensuring compliance with the terms of the Authorization. The Authorization may involve documentation that was not required during the application stage. You will need to produce this additional information for the closing attorney.

Monitor the Professionals

If you're using real estate as collateral, you will be required to have assistance from professionals for preparation of an appraisal, survey,

---

To close the loan faster:

✧ If confident of approval, prompt the lender to order independent reports ahead of loan commitment from their consultants.

✧ Study and understand an SBA authorization and loan agreement to ensure compliance.

✧ If life insurance is likely to be required, start the application process early. New insurance policies can take up to eight weeks to approve.

environmental assessment, and other information required by the lender's due diligence. These professionals may be efficient in producing their reports, or they may hold up the entire closing. Try to get connected to this part of the process to ensure that it moves as swiftly as possible.

With the offer to coordinate visits and provide additional information, track the work with these professionals as closely as possible. After determining whom the lender has engaged for these matters, establish contact in the most courteous manner possible and work to schedule an appointment.

Make an effort to be present when the professional inspects the property, although they may resist at times. Often, the professional will have questions about the site or structure and, if no one is available, assumptions may be substituted for facts. Your presence can enhance the report by supplying updated information that is usually more accurate and more detailed than would otherwise be available to the professional. The cordial coordination can sometime knock days or weeks off the process.

Put Out the Fires

Problems frequently arise during the due diligence performed in preparation for loan closing. Maybe your appraisal came in too low, or some environmental issue was discovered on the real property. Maybe an old, unsatisfied mortgage is found to be outstanding from a lender paid off ten years ago, and the property has been subsequently sold three times.

Sometimes the lender or their attorney will react to these problems as if the deal is as good as dead, and that you're simply out of luck. But, most of these kinds of problems can usually be resolved and the transaction is far from dead. Of greater concern is getting the parties focused on identifying the resolution to the problem with a minimal delay in closing the loan.

It is important to determine as quickly as possible the exact nature of the problem and the remedy for solving it. Don't rely strictly on the lender's attorney to define the resolution, because the lender's best solution is not always optimum for you. Sometimes you should obtain the appropriate professional assistance in assessing the problem and managing the resolution of it.

No one will make solving the problem a greater priority than you. Instead of waiting for someone else to initiate the resolution, stay

✧ **Manage the lender and attorney effectively by staying in contact regularly and being accessible and responsive.**

✧ **Be ready to produce any additional information upon request without complaint.**

✧ **Allow time for unexpected problems to arise and be resolved.**

PART 3

involved in the situation personally to make sure the loan closing is not postponed any longer than necessary.

If the problem is minor, you may be able to continue with the closing on schedule by setting aside enough money in escrow to cover the maximum exposure to the problem. For example, if there is an outstanding lien for $3,000 that the seller asserts has been satisfied but the holder cannot be located immediately, the seller (or borrower) can put $3,000 in escrow at closing to assure the lender that the mortgage will be satisfied.

How Can the Closing Costs Be Reduced?

One of the most frequent complaints about SBA loans is the total cost involved to close the loan. Borrowers obtaining long-term real estate financing can expect to pay as much as 6 percent(!) of the total loan to close. In reality, many of these costs are simply inherent to the deal and cannot be avoided.

The best response to these closing expenses is a combination of putting the costs in perspective with the benefits and working a little harder to determine which, if any, of these costs can be reduced or eliminated. You can influence these costs in certain circumstances. The following paragraphs describe some of the common costs associated with closing an SBA loan and how the borrower might lower them in certain instances.

SBA Guaranty Fee

The lender must pay and usually requires you to reimburse a fee to the SBA for the loan guaranty. Although the American Recovery and Reinvestment Act of 2009, and several extensions, temporarily waived guaranty fees, the present published fee schedule is as follows:

Guaranteed Portion of Loan	Guaranty Fee
$0–$150,000	2%
$150,001–$700,000	3%
$700,001–$1,000,000	3.5%
$1,000,000+	3.5% on first million; 3.75% on remainder

The fee can be calculated by determining the loan guaranty portion (as discussed earlier) and multiplying it by the appropriate fee level. This fee is essentially the insurance premium that funds the agency's loan losses from its collective portfolio of guaranteed loans.

The guaranty fee is subject to annual review when Congress establishes a new budget for the agency. There are proponents for no fees, lower fees, and higher fees, so where they are set is generally based on which political party is in control of the federal budget each year. These fees can change annually, so it may be a good idea to check *www.SBA.gov* when developing a budget for the financing cost, so as to ensure that all of the assumptions concerning these fees are accurate.

The only way to reduce this fee is to be fortunate enough to be in a competitive situation between two lenders. In good times, if both lenders really want to make the loan, you might negotiate to have one of the lenders absorb all or part of the SBA guaranty fee. This option is available only to the strongest borrowers who are highly qualified financially.

Attorney's Fees

The SBA loan is always closed by an attorney due to the complexities involved in complying with the Authorization. Lenders would simply invite too much exposure not to involve a professional for this task. And, of course, the cost of the attorneys will be passed on to you.

Depending on the dynamics of the transaction, attorneys will have varying degrees of involvement. If there is real property included, the attorneys will have more responsibilities in the closing and the costs will be proportionately greater.

Attorney's fees will vary greatly depending on the locale, the local market, the size of the firm, and the firm's familiarity with SBA loans. These fees may range from a flat fee up to roughly 1 percent of the transaction plus the cost of title insurance.

You can reduce the attorney's fees in several ways:

✧ Ask the lender to select a firm with lower costs. Understanding that you are sensitive to the closing costs, the lender may have some latitude to influence the firm selection and guide the closing to a firm with lower fees, particularly on smaller or less complicated transactions.

✧ Ask the lender to select an attorney who has previously worked for you. If the attorney does not have a conflict of interest, the familiarity with you may reduce the costs of the transaction, even though the attorney will now represent the lender.

✧ Ask the lender to obtain a written fee estimate from the attorney. In this manner, you can discuss the level of the estimate with the lender and the attorney before any work begins

Ideas to reduce closing costs:

✧ Find lender that prepares its own closing documents.

✧ If lender uses attorneys, encourage lender to negotiate for more reasonable fees, particularly on smaller or less complicated transactions.

✧ Discuss fees directly with the consultants ahead of their being given the due diligence assignments. All of these fees are subject to reasonableness, according to SBA regulations.

✧ Close the loan as near as possible to the end of the month to avoid having to advance prepaid interest charges.

and determine if it can be modified. Some attorneys, like other professionals, find it easier to charge higher fees once the work has been performed without prior fee disclosure. When seeking the business, they seem to be a little more reasonable on fees, particularly when required to provide a quote up front.

✧ If certain legal work has been done in the past couple of years that relates to the loan or the collateral, such as title examinations, you can supply this information to the attorney. If your real property has title insurance, the attorney may be able to renew the old title policy and conduct a shorter title search. This combination should significantly reduce a portion of the search and insurance fees involved.

Other Professional Fees

You will have to bear the costs of several professionals involved in the due diligence phase of closing the loan. Such specialists as an appraiser, environmental engineer, surveyor, and construction inspector may be involved to provide independent opinions for the specific transaction.

Fees for these specialists may range from $1,000 upward to $5,000 each, depending on the situation, the specific nature of their engagement, and the local market in which they work. Some of the best ways to manage these fees are as follows:

✧ Ask the lender to select a professional with lower costs. Understanding that you're sensitive to these costs, the lender may have some latitude to influence firm selection and to request that the professional negotiate a lower fee, particularly on smaller or less complicated transactions.

✧ Ask the lender to select a professional who has previously worked for you. If these professionals are familiar with you or your assets, this fact may reduce the costs of the transaction, even though they are now representing the lender. In the case of a surveyor or environmental engineer, the lender should be willing to accept an update of the previous work performed.

✧ Ask the professional for a written fee estimate. This way, you can discuss the level of the estimate with the lender and the professional before any work begins. Specialists find it easier to charge higher fees once the work has been performed. When seeking the engagement, they seem to be a little more reasonable on fees, particularly when required to provide a quote up front.

- ✧ If certain work has been done in the past couple of years for you that relates to the collateral, such as surveys or environmental reports, you can provide this information to the specialist. This information could significantly reduce the professional fees involved.
- ✧ If appropriate, ask the lender to limit the scope of the professional's engagement to the exact information required by the Authorization. Sometimes the professional's report might include information not requested or required, which can result in higher fees for you.

Recording Costs and Taxes

Many counties and states assess fees for the recording of certain documents required to perfect the lender's lien on the borrower's collateral assets, such as mortgages and UCC-1s. These fees vary greatly from state to state, but usually must be considered the cost of doing business. They are certainly not negotiable, and the lender will typically not absorb them.

Sometimes lenders err when there is more than one parcel of real property securing a loan, however, and that increases the taxes assessed to the transaction. Think about a $1 million loan that is being made secured by two parcels of property, one valued at $900,000 and the second valued at $300,000. If the lender indicates on both mortgages that there is a $1 million loan secured by each property, you will pay far more recording taxes than necessary. The lender should record the more valuable property at its value, $900,000, and the small value at its value, $300,000. In this way, appropriate taxes are paid and the lender is protected.

Prepaid Interest

As a matter of practice to conformity among lenders and the investors that purchase SBA loans, most SBA loans are placed on a standardized repayment schedule that calls for the first loan payment to be due on the first day of the second month after the loan closes.

Therefore, depending on the day of the month the loan is closed, you are responsible for paying a varying sum of prepaid interest to bridge the gap between the closing day and the first of the month, since the first payment will always collect one month's interest. For example, if a loan closes on the fifteenth day of January, the first payment will be due on March 1. However, since interest is billed in arrears (payable for the period preceding the payment), the interest collected on the March 1 payment would be for the period February 1 through March 1. Therefore, at the loan closing, the lender would collect a prepaid interest charge for the period from January 15 through January 31. This prepaid interest is in lieu of a payment being due on February 1. On larger loans, the prepaid interest can significantly alter the cash disbursed at the loan closing. You can lower this sum by closing the loan as close as possible to the last day of the month.

It is important to put the costs of closing a loan in perspective. In reality, these costs are a necessary part of borrowing money and simply cannot be avoided. You should view the costs over the life of the loan, rather than simply in the period in which they are incurred. If you're obtaining a $1 million real estate loan for twenty-five years, the $40,000 in closing costs equate to only $1,600 per year.

CHAPTER 8

Other Issues You Need to Consider

There are many other considerations to evaluate and decide before applying for an SBA loan. How much help is wanted? Is there a good investment that will ensure the best deal? In this chapter, you'll learn:

- ✦ Professional assistance: cost and benefit
- ✦ Don't be worried about the SBA
- ✦ How affiliated businesses can impact the deal

Should You Use a Loan Packager?

Many small business owners seeking financing have recognized the value of using a professional lending intermediary. But just as many business people have become victims of unscrupulous or inept loan brokers— loan brokers who either waste valuable time conducting a hopeless search for capital that never appears or who collect fees that they never earned through reasonable performance.

Loan consultants can play an important role in today's banking environment. With the consolidation of or failure of hundreds of banks and the continuing changing of the financing landscape, entrepreneurs cannot be expected to keep track of the constantly changing marketplace for money.

Fortunately, there are many consultants whose primary efforts are focused on the SBA loan market. These consultants, often referred to as "packagers," are positioned to provide small businesses with the expertise of how and where to access SBA financing. The value of these services is generally in proportion to what they cost, and the services often will be paid for by the lender if successful.

Any consultants who are willing to work on your behalf for several months without a retainer, purely on a contingency basis, are usually worth everything paid to them—nothing. Because borrowers can be fickle, seasoned consultants will not make large time investments without tangible commitments on the part of clients in form of monetary deposits. Many of these consultants have successfully raised many millions of dollars in loans for borrowers who changed their minds, resulting in no compensation for their considerable effort.

Before writing a check to engage these consultants, take the time to validate their capabilities in successfully obtaining loans. Does their track record match their confidence about how well they will accomplish their mission? This short exercise could save you from an expensive and frustrating exercise in futility.

First, request a list of references from the consultant. In contacting the businesses that engaged the services of this consultant, you can determine how well the consultant performed. Did the business obtain the financing it needed? If not, why? If so, was the time frame reasonable? Did the consultant communicate with the business on a regular and informed basis? Did the consultant have a firm grasp of the company's objectives, and were those objectives met due to the efforts of the consultant?

Then ask the consultant for references in the lending community. Obviously, the consultant will not permit you to contact any potential lender that may be the target of the loan proposal. But you can speak with other lenders, outside the scope of the proposed deal, to which the consultant has referred transactions.

What was the lender's attitude toward the consultant? Does the lender rely on the consultant merely for referrals, or does the lender express confidence in the consultant's ability to analyze potential deals? In other words, does the consultant's opinion count, or is the consultant only throwing darts at the wall with the borrower's deal.

Finally, determine whether the consultant is a member of any trade associations such as the chamber of commerce, the National Federation of Independent Businesses (NFIB), the National Association of Government Guaranteed Lenders (NAGGL), National Association of Development Companies (NADCO), or other groups that support small businesses. These memberships are not necessarily a qualification, but they can be indicative of the success and standing of the consultant in the industry. These groups rarely provide references, but you can verify the claimed membership status of the consultant.

Remember that the consultant is not the decision maker for the loan request. Rather the consultant prepares the application and helps structure the transaction. But after selecting the lender and presenting the case, the consultant loses control of the timing and decision involved.

Many lenders seem to disregard the time constraints of their customers. If the loan needs to be reviewed by a government guarantor, such as the SBA, the lender also loses control of the deal. Everyone is in a hurry. As long as the consultant demonstrates diligence in performing specific responsibilities, the consultant should not be blamed for the actions of others.

These consultants are businesspeople, too. It is not unreasonable, therefore, for consultants to request that you engage their services with a written agreement and to require a retainer as an expression of commitment on your part. Services and advice cannot be repossessed, and the consultant should not be penalized for changes in your situation or strategy that render those services and advice useless.

To be cautious, you should understand and agree to the compensation expectations of the consultant before work begins on your behalf. The consultant's willingness to work on a contingency may sound like a good arrangement for you, but it also may indicate that you're employing an inexperienced party to work on the loan application. Borrowers should beware of people who make a living collecting $250 application fees.

A reasonable consultant will not ask for a retainer unless confident about successfully completing your deal. The prospects of obtaining a loan cannot be reliably predicted without a thorough review of your financial statements and other pertinent data.

Loan consultants can easily create value for a business; they allow the borrower to concentrate on the company rather than hopping through twenty banks, leaving a track record on the owner's credit report for every lender that turned down the deal. But borrowers should be willing to pay for quality services and should know who is engaged for this important assignment.

Some banks are also starting to assess fees for packaging SBA loans. It is a valid cost of doing business because there is real labor required to prepare the information and specialized software to prepare it.

Selecting a packager:

✧ **Get borrower and lender references and check them out!**
✧ **Determine any trade association memberships and call them.**
✧ **Get fee arrangements in writing. Ensure that packager is only paid from one source: if compensated by the lender, they should not be charging the borrower directly.**
✧ **Insist on getting packager to sign a Form 159, which will be submitted to the SBA after loan closing, which protects the borrower from exorbitant fees.**

Read Before Signing

A word of caution concerning loan consultants and packagers—never, NEVER sign any documentation they prepare without reading it thoroughly and ensuring the accuracy of everything. If any information is incorrect, through error or intentional act, it is you who could be held criminally and civilly liable to the bank and the U.S. government. Make sure the information representing your financial condition and the company financial condition is completely accurate or don't sign it.

How Should You Use an Attorney?

Many borrowers utilize legal counsel for a variety of business affairs, and naturally want them involved in closing the SBA loan. Although there is nothing wrong with this procedure, it may prove to be an expensive duplication of efforts.

What your attorney can provide to the process is to review the documents you're required to execute in order to obtain the loan and to fulfill the requirements of the lender and the SBA. That review can ensure that someone representing your interest interprets these documents and understands the obligations.

What your attorney has very little chance of doing is to make many meaningful changes in the documentation for your benefit. The principal documentation used for SBA-guaranteed loans is provided by the SBA and cannot be altered. These guaranteed loans are similar to federally insured housing loans. The standardization of documentation is necessary since these loans are eligible to be sold in a secondary market by the lender.

These points are not intended to discourage anyone from engaging their own counsel, which is ultimately a good idea. Your attorney can be a welcome ally in the closing process by reviewing the Loan Authorization and Agreement along with the related closing documents to provide you with a thorough, unbiased opinion as to your obligations and responsibilities.

Dispelling Common Myths about the SBA

Some businesses have avoided seeking assistance from the SBA due to a number of misconceptions about the agency and its role among other agencies in the federal government. Professionals serving the market often have to spend time convincing qualified borrowers that participation is worth the effort and that nothing terrible would happen to the business if the SBA guaranteed the debt. Of course, the paperwork is at times a large commitment of time, but so is the paperwork for most conventional loans today. This section addresses some of the most common and misleading myths about the agency:

SBA regulations governing independent loan agents or "packagers" specify that no one can charge fees determined solely as a percentage of the loan amount, or "points" in connection with an SBA-guaranteed loan. Any third-party assistance can only be provided with charges detailed on an invoice itemizing hours spent on various tasks and the hourly rate charged. Further, all such fees must be disclosed to the lender and the SBA on SBA Form 159 (found in Illustration 4-L).

The SBA program favors women and minorities. This is not true. The SBA guaranty programs are available for participation by all persons, regardless of gender, race, color, creed, age, or ethnicity. In every fiscal year, white males have been the recipients of a plurality of all SBA loan guaranties.

The agency has employed various initiatives over the years to encourage women and minority borrowers to utilize the program, since historically both were underrepresented in the pool of business owners seeking financial assistance. However, the agency does not provide any different approval standards, special funding allocations, or other allowances for borrowers in these categories. Nor do women or minority participants receive any advantages or consideration that would provide agency assistance in a situation in which other borrowers would be denied.

Anybody can get an SBA loan. There are limits on who can qualify for SBA assistance, and it is more difficult than some people assume. Participation with the SBA guaranty program is restricted to borrowers who qualify under certain conditions relating to the size of the small business concern (in terms of revenues, net income, net worth, or number of employees; depending on the type of loan guaranty and the industry involved) and the nature of the business activity. Additionally, they have to be financially and professionally fit, with the demonstrated ability to operate a business and an established reputation of good character.

Borrowers seeking to benefit under the 7(a) guaranty program are restricted by either gross revenues of $7 million (with some exceptions based on the industry of the borrower) or limited by 500 employees in some specific industries that are labor intensive, such as manufacturing. Questions of eligibility can be directed to the agency for clarification about specific situations.

Borrowers seeking to get assistance under the 504 Development Program are restricted by their average net income over the past three years (no more than $2.5 million annually, including affiliates) and net worth (no more than $7.5 million, including affiliates).

Businesses involved in real estate development, lending activities, gambling, and illegal activities are prohibited from receiving assistance from the loan guaranty program.

The government will monitor the business. Fears of "big brother" actually cause some small business owners to hesitate about the SBA guaranty program. Participation with the SBA includes no monitoring of the borrower's business activities, no extra government audits, and no interagency communications about the business operations among other federal agencies.

The SBA does not have the interest, personnel, or mandate to provide any extraordinary supervision of the business unless the borrower is in default of the loan. When the borrower is in default, the SBA's interest will be strictly focused on working with the lender to recover the loan.

Obtaining SBA assistance does not increase the borrower's chances of being audited by the IRS, Bureau of Labor, OSHA, EPA, Corps of Engineers, or any other government agency that regulates the operations of business and industry.

The lender does not care how good or bad the business is. This is totally false. Lenders participating with the SBA guaranty programs are responsible for making good loans. The SBA guaranty is intended to enhance a loan, not subsidize the lender to build a bad loan portfolio.

The unguaranteed portion of every loan will expose the lender to the full risk of the credit, and that portion is likely to increase in the next few years as funding for this program is restricted. Collecting bad loans can be very expensive in terms of time and money to the lender. And, if the lender does not maintain a good track record among companies it funds loans to, the SBA can restrict their participation in the program.

Do Affiliated Companies Affect the Application?

Affiliated companies affect the borrower's participation in the SBA loan guaranty programs by enlarging the parameters by which the lender has to be evaluated as eligible for participation. Affiliates are defined as any other business entity in which at least a 20 percent interest is owned by the borrower, or any owner of at least 20 percent of the borrower. The affiliated companies are considered collectively with the enterprise for which the borrower is seeking finance, for purposes of determining whether the subject company seeking financing is eligible under the program limitations.

That is, any and all business interests in which the borrower and any owners of the borrower, individually or collectively, own at least a 20 percent stake, are considered together with the entity seeking to borrow money. This composite is used to calculate the total sales, number of employees, net income, or net worth in determining the eligibility limitations for obtaining a loan guaranty.

The lender is required to confirm the borrower's eligibility if any affiliated companies exist. The borrower, therefore, should be prepared to provide the lender with financial information about the affiliated entities in order to allow assessment of eligibility. This financial documentation has to be provided to the SBA as well.

The Value of Relationship Banking

If the lender is a bank, be sensitive to the fact that the bank is in the business of providing many more services than commercial loans. In fact, banks have been actively expanding their list of services beyond the traditional services of cash management and handling currency to enter into other related fee-generating businesses, like investment securities and insurance.

Banks need deposits with which to make loans. It is not important where they get these deposits, or even whether they are time or demand deposits. Each day, banks need millions of dollars on deposit to meet their demands for cash to cover loans and withdrawals. Recognizing this aspect of the banking business, be prepared to be confronted with a request or requirement to utilize the bank's depository services if the business loan is extended.

Relationship banking can have many positive features, and it is important to know the dynamics involved so that you receive every advantage available. While the lending personnel are traditionally recognized as the bankers with significant influence in the business, there are many other persons who are worthwhile to know.

In measuring a banking relationship, there are many services that a business may utilize:

- ✧ *Demand deposit account (DDA)*—Many individuals and certainly every commercial business maintains a demand deposit account or checking account. These are funds that the depositor places into an account to avoid having to manage large or frequent sums of cash. These funds are withdrawn upon the depositor's "demand," a directive issued in the form of a written check or accessed with a debit card.
- ✧ *Time deposits (TD)*—These accounts are placed on deposit with a bank for a definite or indefinite amount of time. The bank pays the depositor interest on these funds, the amount of which varies according to how long the depositor agrees

to leave the funds in the account. There are a variety of time deposit accounts, including savings accounts and certificates of deposit, all of which have specific features and benefits.

◈ *Safe deposit boxes*—Banks provide safe deposit boxes within their vault for storage of a depositor's valuable assets or documents. For small businesses, think about a safe place to store property deeds, original patents, and computer backup storage media.

◈ *Merchant credit services*—Every retail business that accepts MasterCard, Visa, American Express, or Discover cards has to have a merchant account through which to clear these charges. These accounts are provided on a qualified basis, dependent on confirmation of the merchant's business operation and financial stability.

◈ *Credit*—The best-known service provided by banks is credit. There are more types of loans available than ever before, with banks using a variety of credit products to deliver funds to consumers for short-, intermediate-, and long-term reasons. Many banks make car loans, issue credit cards, and handle home loans.

The point of discussing these other services is to suggest that business borrowers should use their demand for these services as an attribute when requesting a commercial loan. If you can demonstrate to the lender that the accommodation of credit will also provide the bank with a substantive customer for other services, the lender may be persuaded to stretch in some ways to approve your loan request or grant more favorable terms. A combination of a few of these accounts can mean thousands of dollars in fee income to the bank, and can provide a new source of inexpensive deposits for them.

Considering all of the services used, personally and in business, you represent an impressive opportunity for the bank. Other shareholders, partners, and even senior managers can be included when you compile a list of potential business available to the bank.

The prospect of these other relationship accounts will not make a bad loan proposal good, but it can certainly enhance a less than perfect deal—and provide the lender with incentives to give you a chance. If you don't need this kind of assistance for loan approval, the relationship accounts may help improve the interest rate or other terms offered on the loan by the bank.

CHAPTER **9**

What to Do If the Lender Says No

Sometimes there just isn't a deal in the cards; today that may even be because the bank is incapable of making loans to anyone. Sometimes the lender errs due to poor listening skills or a misunderstanding. Why they use the word "no" is important to understand. Here you'll learn:

✧ How to interpret an application denial
✧ How to respond to an application denial
✧ How to move on to the next deal

How to Handle Rejection

Sometimes the lender says no—maybe even without conditions, exceptions, or encouragement; maybe even without a phone call or a letter. Regardless of how positive the discussions have been, how upbeat the loan officer is about your prospects, and how much the lender wants to say yes, your application is subject to denial.

Many lending personnel expose their distance from the decision-making process, or their inexperience, by continually encouraging you about the prospects of approval up through the last minute. But when the committee says no, the loan officer can find all sorts of things that are wrong with the proposed deal. This scenario goes back to the weaknesses in the loan approval process discussed earlier.

No is about one half of the possible replies available to the lender in responding to a loan request. You should listen carefully to the *no* to understand the different ways it may have been said. An astute borrower will listen carefully to the explanation spoken by the lender after the word "because."

The lender makes a decision based on business, not on personality. The lender is responsible for making a decision based on qualifying the loan request within the parameters that must be maintained.

Don't get mad, become defensive, be hurt, feel betrayed, or say anything that may irreparably damage future opportunities to obtain financing from this lender. Perhaps the loan officer has a difficult time being blunt; perhaps the loan officer is matter-of-fact about the unwillingness of the institution to provide the loan; or perhaps the loan officer feels uneasy about communicating the disappointing news.

No matter how well or how badly the lender delivers the answer to you, and regardless of how well or how badly you handle the news, it is important for you to keep a positive demeanor and be very cordial. You need the loan officer's assistance to understand the reasoning behind the lender's rejection. That assistance will not be forthcoming if you create an uncomfortable situation after being turned down.

How Did the Loan Officer Say No?

There are many ways in which a lender can say no. Listening to and analyzing the negative reply to the loan request is the next step in the loan application process. It is what the loan officer says that is important: the explanation, the details, and the analysis of your position. How does the lender say no?

"No, but . . . ," Perhaps the lender is providing you with ways to change the request in order to give the lender a way to say yes. Often, borrowers hear only the word "no" and miss the lender's request to hear the word "please."

"No, unless . . . ," Maybe the lender gave you a conditional no, which could be changed if you were to meet specified conditions or agree to more restrictive terms.

"I cannot say yes because . . . ," Sometimes the lender does not say no at all, but also does not say yes. Listening can sometimes tell you how to overcome the lender's specific reservations in order to get the final yes.

"Not yet . . . ," Maybe you've submitted the request too early. Is the lender not yet comfortable with the level of success of the business? Is it too early for substantive trends to justify your ambition to expand? Sometimes the lender is actually saying wait.

"No, because you . . . ," Maybe lenders turn down requests because of specific objections or reservations that they cannot overcome. Possibly

they have a concentration in a particular industry or have had a bad experience with it. Possibly they had previous dealings with you and weren't inclined to do it again. Identifying these problems will assist you in refocusing the loan request at a later date or submitting it to another lender.

"No, because we . . . ," Sometimes the restrictions of the institution will not allow a lender to say yes. Maybe the request is outside the lender's market area or greater than the lending limit. Maybe the lender is itself facing limitations on capital or a weakened financial condition. If the lender's answer to the loan request is no because of what they cannot or will not do, you can be encouraged that the request is valid. You can probably find another lender to agree with the request.

"Hell no . . . ," Sometimes a blunt no should cause you to reflect inward as to the validity of the proposal. Is it realistic that any lender will be able to extend the financing? Negative replies without explanations sometimes indicate fundamental weaknesses in the proposal. You can use a negative response constructively for redesigning the business plan.

There are as many variations of saying no as there are people and situations. It is not the answer you're seeking, but neither is it invaluable or irreversible. Listening to the loan rejection is the key to learning how to get the proposal approved.

What Is the Next Step?

There are many ways to respond to a loan denial. Selecting the correct response will be integral to improving the changes of getting approval the next time you present the proposal. Determining the next step requires that you fully understand how and why the lender turned the application down.

As mentioned earlier, it is imperative for you to carefully listen to the lender's explanation without allowing an emotional response to cloud understanding. Without putting the lender on the defensive, ask questions. Respectful inquiries and specific answers will benefit you in making the proposal succeed at a later date.

Several days later, you can call the lender to request an appointment for additional evaluation about why the loan was rejected. The purpose of this meeting is for you to learn by seeking answers from someone with a degree of expertise. These discussions are not intended to change the lender's mind about the proposed transaction, but rather to prepare you for the next lender.

Handling rejection:

✧ **Listen carefully to the lender's rejection.**

✧ **Determine whether there are errors in the lender's reasoning beyond a different of opinion.**

✧ **Don't get angry or take rejection personally—it's business.**

✧ **Ask questions and learn more about the weaknesses in the proposal.**

✧ **Address the weaknesses and try, try again.**

PART 3

In preparing for this interview, focus on business issues rather than personal reactions. By encouraging the lender to respond with directness, you can create an opportunity for instructive commentary.

From the lender's perspective, what factors about the business were not acceptable: the industry, location, products, employees, capitalization, track record, deal, or even management? What weaknesses need to be addressed in the business for the next loan proposal?

Was the negative reply due to the lender? Often, lenders steer away from particular loans because of a previous bad experience in the industry or because of the type of loan. Maybe the lender's loan policies, market area, or lending limits restrict participation in your request. Often, lenders do not think in terms of what can be done, but rather in terms of what cannot be done. The burden of asking the right question is usually left with the borrower, who must determine on what basis the loan officer will respond affirmatively.

Was the lender's rejection intended to be permanent, or can conditions or specific benchmarks change the response? Will the lender ever consider this financing? If so, exactly what changes or conditions are required? Where is the lender's level of comfort, and can you attain it? This information will give you more parameters in which to react and make future choices.

Maybe the lender is telling you to move on to the next lender. In this case, this lender can make recommendations about where else to apply. You can ask why the proposal may be acceptable somewhere else; the answer will help you know how to approach the next lender.

Responding to the Lender's Objections

Identifying the qualifications, exceptions, alterations, and finality of the lender's rejection helps you to determine why the lender said no. The following list includes some of the most common reasons for rejecting a loan request and some logical responses on your part:

Objection 1: The Business Is Undercapitalized

Lenders want you to have either contributed or earned a substantive portion of the net worth of the business. In comparing the total debt to the total equity, there should be some measurable part of the company's financing provided from a source other than the lender.

Response: You can take a number of measures to increase equity in the business:

✧ You can inject more money into the company from such sources as savings, a second mortgage on an owner's home, liquidation of other investments, and the cash surrender value of a life insurance policy.

✧ You can convert any subordinated debt or notes payable to the company to equity. Although this act may have consequences if and when the holders want to withdraw the money, it may be necessary to convince the lender of your first commitment to the success of the business.

✧ You can reduce any other liabilities of the company to a reasonable extent. Lowering the debt leverage can permit lenders to have a stronger position without other liabilities distracting from their ability to be repaid.

✧ If you don't have additional capital to contribute, maybe relatives, friends, employees, or suppliers would be willing to invest in the business. This additional capital could be structured to ensure their priority in redemption as soon as the business accumulated additional capital to satisfy the requirements of the lender.

Objection 2: The Business Has Not Earned Money Yet

Lenders expect that you can support the business strategy with a track record of business success. If the company has perpetually lost money, most lenders may reason that additional financing will compound those losses and you'll be unable to repay the borrowed funds.

Response: Your explanation of the financial history of the business (suggested earlier in the book) was not sufficient or was not reasonable. If the business has failed to profit, it is important to demonstrate why and to explain how you will correct the problem.

Sometimes your strategy to earn profits is as simple as acquiring more efficient assets to achieve profitability. Lenders can usually accept this strategy if you can prove that increases in productivity will indeed provide profits.

Sometimes, however, the strategy may be as vague as projecting additional expenditures on advertising and marketing. Lenders are less comfortable about financing this strategy since there are so many undefined and poorly understood variables that can cause failure.

You should provide candid and detailed documentation explaining the periods in which a profit was not earned. In comparing those loss periods to periods in which the business did earn profits, you can explain how the operations may have been different. Then explain how the loan proceeds will be used to position the enterprise in a manner that can return or deliver profits to the business.

Objection 3: The Proposed Loan Is Too Much Money

Lenders may try to lower the loan request by either reducing the marginal funds or trying to force you to spend less in a particular part of the proposal. Their intent is to control their exposure and perhaps get the loan balance down as a percentage of the collateral.

Response: Only you can decide if the business strategy can be achieved with a lower amount of funding. And, typically, only you will know if and how much extra financial padding was incorporated into the request, and can be lowered without affecting the business.

Your response has to be based on how much money is actually needed and how any expenditure can be reduced without having a negative impact on the business plans. Alternatively, offering to provide additional collateral may cause the lender to reconsider the restriction, since you've reduced the lender's perceived risk in the transaction.

Objection 4: The Business Strategy Is Not Sound

Loan officers will test your ideas against their career experience to evaluate whether the business has a reasonable chance of succeeding. If lenders have strong reservations about your prospects, they will not provide financing.

Response: Lenders are not always correct—and they are almost always conservative. Maybe you did not explain the business concept sufficiently to the lender, or maybe the loan officer has an incorrect or incomplete understanding of exactly what you plan to accomplish.

Review the business strategy carefully, making sure that it fully describes each detail of the concept. Support these ideas with the articles, surveys, marketing studies, and demographics that influenced, inspired, or convinced you to undertake this strategy.

Objection 5: The Business Is Too Risky

Lenders exclude some industries from their lending market because the real or perceived risks inherent in those businesses are beyond the acceptable parameters of the lender. These exclusions may apply only to the local lender, or they may be fairly common among most lenders, depending on the industry within which you operate.

Response: Perhaps you have not effectively communicated how some of the risks can be counterbalanced. Depending on the locale and nature of the industry, the lender that may not want to finance the business may be the only lender that can.

Therefore, you have to convince the lender that the risks can be eliminated or limited. For example, by accepting tighter terms or providing sufficient collateral, you can structure the transaction to protect the lender from exposure to costly servicing or potential loan losses.

Objection 6: There Is Not Enough Collateral

This objection is probably the one most often used by lenders to turn down a loan. The lender wants a minimum of 1:1 collateral coverage, based on a discounted valuation of that collateral. Usually lenders will use their leverage to encumber virtually every asset you have, even if those additional assets contribute little or no value as collateral to secure the loan.

The quantity and sufficiency of the collateral can overcome many objections, because lenders are usually only too glad to rent you your own money, even when that money may be tied up in other assets that can be encumbered for liquidation should the loan not be repaid.

Response: Your response should be based on an honest recognition of the true value of the collateral. How much would it be worth in liquidation? Lenders are inclined to sell off repossessed assets grossly under market, seeking merely to recover their loan balance rather than getting the full value of the assets.

You must learn about the market for selling assets similar to those offered as collateral. For example, a ten-year-old lathe that cost $5,000 has a discounted value for the lender. You should pay for an appraisal from a used equipment dealer or equipment auctioneer. The dealer can quickly assess what the equipment would bring in a timely sale or in an auction. This information is germane to determining the leverage the lender will give you on those assets.

Real estate assets also have to be valued based on appraisals. The lender will typically advance a standard amount of the market value, thereby providing a margin for the lender to cover the time and associated cost of selling the property.

If the lender has not valued the collateral adequately, you can provide additional information to prove the value. You can challenge the lender's assessments only when a different value can be documented. When asked to review their reasoning, lenders can at least recognize a compromise value based on the evidence you've produced.

If the assets are insufficient, offer to provide more collateral. Sometimes there are creative solutions to obtaining collateral value from assets that cannot be pledged. Review personal and business financial statements carefully, searching for a way to assign values to the lender.

In the absence of such collateral, you can seek assistance from relatives, friends, associates, or investors who might be willing to hypothecate personal assets to the lender in order to secure the loan. In effect, these third parties would be providing a limited guaranty for the loan, only to the extent of their ownership in the assets they would agree to use as collateral for the loan.

Objection 7: The Financial Projections Are Unreliable

Lenders will pay particular attention to the financial projections of the proposal to determine exactly how you intend to repay the loan. Based on contributing factors, the lender does not always agree with the conclusions about revenue production or the cost of operations. If the lender does not accept the projections, your ability to service the debt becomes questionable.

Response: Examine the projections carefully and ensure that the expectations have been adequately communicated. Reviewing the data or historical figures on which these projections have been based, you should ensure that this evidence is documented in the footnotes of the pro forma.

You may need to make modifications to correct an error discovered by the lender or to revise the calculations. When comparing the new numbers against the debt service to pay back the loan, you can determine if the deal is still feasible.

When you're confident with the numbers, present them again with a line-by-line discussion (as necessary) to convince the lender of the soundness of these expectations. Determining the basis of the lender's questions or doubts, you can attempt to validate those specific entries thoroughly.

Responding to any of these objections does not guarantee that the lender will change the decision, but it is the logical step to take after the loan has initially been rejected. Since you've invested considerable effort in educating this lender about the company, try to address these concerns before completely starting over with a new proposal to a new lender.

Keep Improving the Proposal

The burden to convince lenders to change the decision is on you. Lenders are responsible only for evaluating the information put before them. In fact, after a decision has been made, it can be more difficult to persuade someone to change it. But if the loan officer is candid about what influenced the decision, you may be able to challenge and overcome these objections. The loan could be approved quicker on reconsideration than if you started over with a new lender while not understanding why the first lender denied the loan.

While you are pursuing financing, it is important to continue updating the proposal with fresh information as it becomes available or as it is acquired. The company is completing a financial period every thirty days, and the financial information provided to the lender must be constantly updated to include the latest information.

If you come across pertinent information about the business, industry, or strategy to support the thesis of the proposal, the application should be updated with this information. Even if the proposal has already been submitted to the lender, the borrower should send the additional information for review.

Every sixty to ninety days (if the search for financing lasts for such a period), review the entire plan from beginning to end. You should edit the proposal for updated information, corrections, and consistency. During the review process, take advantage of any information or ideas obtained from a lender that turned down the request. By constantly polishing the proposal, you can improve the chances of success.

There Are Other Lenders

Borrowers often lose sight of the fact that there are literally thousands of lenders. Given the commodity nature of SBA lending, the borrower has access not only to the local banks but also to several nonbank lenders making SBA loans into any state.

Within these thousands of lenders, there are even more loan officers. Many of them will be less experienced in business than the borrower, and will be making decisions based on a limited career. Just because a lender reaches a certain conclusion does not mean another lender would reach the opposite decision. If you feel confident about the merits of the loan proposal, one lender's negative reply should not prevent you from presenting the plan to another lender.

PART 3

Different lenders have different loan appetites, different expertise, even different levels of acceptable risk. Keep searching until you find a lender that understands the business and feels comfortable with the management. These lenders are out there; they are sometimes just harder to find.

Sometimes You Won't Qualify

The final answer may be that your business does not qualify for the loan it seeks—not only with the lender that rejected the loan but with any lender. If the loan is turned down more than three times, there may be an inherent weakness preventing approval from any source. If this is the case, you may need assistance from someone who can objectively evaluate the situation and the financing. Whether turning to a business consultant, CPA, or lender, you should be able to rely on their direct experience and meaningful advice.

Sometimes there are other ways to accomplish your objectives than with a loan. Financing is not restricted to borrowing money but can include such diverse options as selling part of the business, franchising, or bartering. All of these are other ways to exchange value owned for value needed.

Sometimes you can reduce the loan by financing part of the transaction in another way. Although there are many possibilities, most of them may be more difficult, more expensive, and more time-consuming. But if you want the financing, you may have to take it in the manner in which it is available.

Maybe you've tried to obtain financing prematurely. Perhaps another six, twelve, or eighteen months would improve the chances of approval by demonstrating the validity of the business strategy or other measurements of financial success.

Recognize that time is a good investment and can be healthy for the business. It may not satisfy ambition, but it may allow you to obtain the financing from a position of strength. The established and stable record of a business decreases the lender's exposure, as well as the risk to the borrower.

Appendix

Web Resources

U.S. Small Business Administration (National Resource Websites)

www.sba.gov
www.sba.go/tools/resourcelibrary/publications/index.html
www.sba.gov/training/index.html
www.score.org/learning_center.html
www.sba.gov/tools/resourcelibrary/lawsandregulations/index.html
www.sba.gov/tools/forms/index.html
www.businessmatchmaking.com

Small Business Development Center (National Website)

www.sba.gov/aboutsba/sbaprograms/sbdc/index.html

General Business Assistance Websites

www.businessadviser.com
www.toolkit.com
www.businesstown.com
www.SBFI.org
www.AdviceOnLoan.com
www.CharlesGreenCo.com

SBA District Offices

http://www.sba.gov/localresources/index.html

Index